The Dissertation Strategy

ABD NO MORE!

Instructions and Samples to Develop a Quality Dissertation as Quickly and Painlessly as Possible

Jill Blackwell, PhD

Copyright © 2016

Except as provided by the Copy right Act, no part of this publication may be reproduced, stored in a retrieval system or transmitted in any form or by any means without the prior written permission of the publisher.

Table of Contents

Preface v

Section One: The Dissertation Proposal 1

Chapter 1. Your Desired Topic versus a Research worthy Topic 3
    Critical Analysis Form 4
    Just How Many Articles 7
    My Chair is Being Weird about My Project Idea 7

Chapter 2. Developing your Problem Statement 11
    General Problem Paragraph Template 13
    Specific Problem Paragraph Template 14
    Quantitative Study Problem Statement Samples 18
    Qualitative Study Problem Statement Samples 19

Chapter 3. The Method/Design for the Project 23
    Research Methods Made Easy 24
    The Qualitative Method and its Designs 25
    The Quantitative Method and its Designs 26
    Exercises to Master Methods/Designs 31

Chapter 4. Purpose Statement and Research Questions/hypotheses 37
    Purpose Statement Samples 37
    The Rest of the Problem Statement Instructions 39
    Research Questions/Hypotheses Samples 40
    Tying Everything Together for Alignment (problem, purpose, RQs) 42
    Sample Purpose Statements and Matching RQs 42

Chapter 5. The Rest of the Front Matter (finalizing Chapter 1 of the proposal) ... 47
    Theoretical Framework Section 48
    What Theoretical Extension Means 48
    Short Version Theoretical Framework Instructions/Samples 50
    Long Version Theoretical Framework Instructions/Samples 50
    Significance of the Study Section Instructions/Samples 53
    Introduction Section Instructions/Samples 55
    Background Section Instructions/Samples 60
    Summary of Chapter One Section Instructions/Sample 61

Chapter 6. The Literature Review Chapter (Chapter 2 of the proposal) 63
    The Timing of it All 65
    From Outline to Text 67
    Hot Spots (Writing and APA Style) and How to Avoid Them 68
    Samples 71

Chapter 7. The Method Chapter (Chapter 3 of the proposal)..................85
    Introduction to the Method Chapter Instructions..................................86
    Research Method and Design Section Instructions/Samples................86
    Operational Definition of Variables Section Instructions/Samples........87
    Population Section Instructions/Samples..87
    Sample Section Instructions/Samples..88
    Instruments Section Instructions/Samples..90
    Data Collection Section Instructions/Samples......................................92
    Data Analysis Section Instructions/Samples..93
    Assumptions and Limitations Section Instructions/Samples................94
    Ethical Considerations Section Instructions/Samples..........................95
    Summary of Method Chapter Section Instructions/Samples................95

Section Two: The Study and Dissertation Manuscript..........................97

Chapter 8. Conduct your Study (before and during)..............................99
    IRB Application Instructions..99
        Sample Participant Invitation Letter..100
        Sample Informed Consent Form..101
    How to Collect Qualitative Data Instructions....................................102
    How to Collect Quantitative Data Instructions..................................103

Chapter 9. Data Analysis and Reporting..105
    Quantitative Method Study Instructions..105
    Quantitative Results Section Samples..117
    Qualitative Method Study Instructions..139
    Quantitative Results Section Samples..139

Chapter 10. The Discussion Chapter..147
    Comparison to Existing Literature Instructions/Samples..................149
    Implication Paragraph Instructions/Samples....................................150
    Recommendations Section Instructions/Samples..............................153
    Conclusion Section Instructions/Samples..158

Chapter 11. The Defenses..163
    Slide Suggestions for Defenses..168
    Conclusion..173

Chapter 12. Abstract Samples..175

Chapter 13. Suggested Additional Resources if Needed......................177

References..179

PREFACE - HELLO ABD PERSON!

Well, you have made it this far! Quite an accomplishment I'd say! I hope you are as proud of yourself as I am of you!! You and I both know nothing about this journey has been easy, or even that rewarding yet. There have been frustrations, misunderstandings, lots of doubt, questions about your ability, and even lack of desire to finish this task. I don't know why it has to be this hard. I suppose if it wasn't then everyone would be embarking on this mission, but they are not. YOU ARE! You are special, important, and capable of seeing this goal of obtaining your doctorate degree to the end. I am here to assist with this last small step :) You can do this! I believe in you, understand your desire, and am certain about your capability to get to the finish line. I can visualize you there (at graduation) now. Can you see it? Try to conjure that image and hold it in your mind. Return to it as often as you can as it will be helpful with motivation, confidence, and belief in your ability - three very important things you will need to take with you on this important dissertation journey.

Not to bring you down, but only about 50% of students who begin a PhD program walk out with the degree. It is likely the ones who do not are in a terminal ABD state. I recently read great articles by Jill Yesko (2014) and Rebecca Schuman (2014) about the ABD dilemma. The articles noted the career consequences of a terminal ABD and the other about how to help with this devastating career situation. As I was reading these articles I thought, wow, what we really need is a book with concrete strategies on how to do each section AND to empower the students.

I hope you find the information in this book to be helpful in getting your project done. There are some stories and examples of negative chair comments. I am sharing these to let you know to not take things personally. Only some students get top notch chairs. Even top notch chairs may get frustrated, or have a bad day. Still, you (the student) should always be attended to with respect and courtesy. If not, please know any lack of respect shown to you is a reflection on them - and not you. If it gets too bad you can always request a chair change.

Something I found interesting in chairing/teaching and when working with dissertation clients was the existence of two camps of faculty (dissertation chairs and teachers who forgot how it was to not know something and those who didn't forget). Those who forgot often provide negative comments on work quality, chastise, and almost look for problems to point out. These are also the faculty who believe the dissertation process should be arduous and no one should get out in less than 10 years. That is simply not correct. It doesn't have to take a decade, or be painful to facilitate growth in students. I think what distinguishes me from some of my cohort (when teaching or chairing) is I make it a daily priority to assist - instead of judge. I fully recall feeling small and not *in the know*. I pride myself on facilitating knowledge transfer to others and not making them feel inadequate - to avoid interfering with their growth - as that would be doing great harm. This seems like a pretty obvious goal, but you would really be surprised by the number of people who are charged with training others who have forgotten.

We all were in your shoes (ABD) at one time - even your chair. Even the best researchers likely got chastised for grammar and poorly connected sentences. If your desire is to obtain your doctorate degree then you can do it. The only difference between you being ABD and me with my D (and your chair with their D), is that the rough dissertation point is behind me (and them) now. It will be behind you soon enough too. You won't forget though!

My advice to you if your chair/teacher is from the school of hard knocks is to do what you can to please them, use the samples/specific instructions in this book, DO NOT take anything (even their critical feedback) personally, and cultivate as thick a skin as you can muster. Maybe you can visualize them being a dissertation student (wearing their underwear sitting in the front row at your graduation). We are all products of our experiences. Perhaps their mentor was unusually challenging, or it took them 10 years to finish - and this is what they know. Maybe it is good you are going through this, so you can keep things in perspective when you work with others. Let's look at it that way!

Who am I? I have my PhD in Developmental Psychology. I went to grad school right after getting my Bachelor of Arts. I had a full ride scholarship! I was voted Outstanding Graduate Student by my faculty at DePaul University two of my three years at graduate school. I worked with the most interesting faculty on their fascinating projects and got to co-write a book chapter with the smartest woman I've ever met (Dr. Linda Camras). My grad school experience was good! My most prideful moment was overhearing one of my mentors (whom I respected immensely) tell my dissertation committee chair something about me in my first year. It is something I still think about today and I am sure led to my career choices and certainly led me to be writing this book. She said, "Jill has an advanced understanding of research methods and a unique ability to turn ideas into doable research, more than the other students, more than anyone I've seen." I didn't see this at the time. I knew my friends and classmates would come to me and ask about potential study designs. I recall my chair asking me to work with some undergrads on their senior thesis projects (in my first year of grad school – I was the only one to be asked to do this). He actually put me in charge of a few of the undergrad projects. I didn't really know what I was doing and was pretty nervous about it. There was one student I really helped design an excellent project, which was up for an award. I was asked to edit her final paper, but I was not confident in my ability to do this, and I asked my mentor to edit for her also. About a week after I gave the student my feedback she told me, "oh weird, all the comments you made were the exact same ones Dr. Michel made." This was another one of those life changing comments, as Dr. Michel was the most gifted researcher I knew. That year I was assigned full teaching responsibilities of an undergraduate

Research Methods class during my second year of grad school. I was the only grad student (without their MA) to be invited to do this. I still teach an advanced version of that very same class at DePaul University today! Back at the time I appreciated all of the support and recognition, but it didn't make me feel more confident or believe in my abilities. I wonder if that just comes with time and experience.

After I completed my grad school coursework and defended my Master's Thesis I took my "sweet" time to complete my dissertation project. I don't know why. It is difficult to explain. I couldn't have been a bigger go-getter in grad school. If someone would have told me it would take more than one year to defend my dissertation proposal, run the study, and prepare the write-up (doesn't that sound so easy) I would have told them they were out of their bleeping mind. Still, this is what happened - it took years! I sat and sat and sat around just not addressing what I needed to do. One day in the mail I received a picture of my favorite mentor sitting at her desk holding a huge sign that read, "FINISH." Something hit me. I promptly finished up my proposal, defended it, and carried out my challenging research with preschool students and their mothers. Once I sat down to do it, that part took almost no time at all. After I collected all the data and painstakingly coded it (hours and hours of children's facial expressions in an experimental and control task) I sat and sat again, for months and months. Then one day (I don't know what inspired me at this point - likely Divine intervention) I analyzed the data and wrote the results section and discussion section of the dissertation. It took only about a week to write both of the concluding chapters.

Later it struck me about how little time it really took to do the research and the writing. Most of the time spent "working" on my dissertation, was me just sitting around and not doing it. Once I decided to do it, it got done quite readily. I contemplated about the reasons for the delay for years and decided it must have to do with my lack of knowing what exactly to do. Don't get me wrong, my classes and mentors were all excellent and likely if I asked them for specifics they would have helped, but I didn't!! I think I thought I wasn't supposed to ask, maybe I should know how to do this (but that is not the truth). Maybe I just wanted to show up with some amazing document, so they would think I was a genius. Because I kept returning to this notion of the "whys" associated with this reality - I knew I wanted to help students. I thought I could help them to feel confident about their research abilities and give them the needed tools to develop quality projects as painlessly as possible.

While I was teaching at DePaul a friend told me about a great opportunity with a dissertation coaching company devoted to helping grad students complete their dissertations through dissertation coaching and consulting. I worked there for eight years! I helped hundreds of students get to the finish line! I helped students just starting out (to design their projects), in the middle, and at the end. One student I helped (a lot) won the Dissertation of the Year award at their university. It was a very rewarding experience.

Many mid-project students would contact the company because their chair was giving them a hard time, they had nowhere to turn, and they needed help. These students were my specialty. I swooped in with my developmental editing cape and fixed things. Students would write notes of thanks to me, so gratefully. I appreciated and remember all of these students! So many students identified me in their dissertation acknowledgements page as someone who was integral to project completion. I always thought, sheesh, I am just providing a little assistance here, but I knew - the assistance, because of this vulnerable, fragile, and high stakes (personally) time - was priceless. I also knew the students were appreciative of help with their documents and research, but most importantly I think they were most grateful for my positive and supportive attitude as well as my unwavering faith in their ability to complete their dissertation task - that was what seemed to me missing for most of the students who contacted our company.

Something I found unrewarding about dissertation consulting was reading the very negative, very unhelpful, and oftentimes *incorrect* dissertation chair comments. It was really more the rule than the exception that chairs were not being supportive. I found this different than my experience, so it was disconcerting. I always wondered if the students who needed assistance (the ones contacting the company I worked for) were the ones whose chairs were simply judging and evaluating (negatively) as opposed to teaching them how to conduct research. I vowed if I were a chair I would do it better. A wonderful chair position at an online grad school came to my attention, I applied and got it - I still work there. My mission was/is to teach students how to do research in a kind and respectful manner. I knew it was possible! In three years at my dissertation chair job I have helped 34 students obtain their PhD and I have about 20 more nearing the end of their projects. I just won an award for Outstanding Dissertation Chair 2016. I have publications with many of my graduated students (peer-reviewed journal articles based on their dissertation research - so their work was of good quality). I guess you would have to ask them if I was as nice about it as I intended to be- I hope I was!

Dissertation chairing is different than dissertation consulting. In consulting you fix things for students. In chairing you teach the students how to conduct a research project and how to write scientifically about the project. When you are the chair - you have to teach students how to fix things themselves. In order to achieve this difficult task of information transfer I developed specific instructions, templates, and samples to make the unique dissertation steps clear and accessible (some people refer to these items as feed forward - instead of feedback). Are the handouts effective? Currently I only have anecdotal information to offer you based on job performance, feedback from students, and feedback from other chairs and my student's dissertation committees. Compared to other chairs, I had about 50% more students graduate (than the average chair). I have received teaching awards. I have been asked to share the materials in this compendium with other chairs who also needed/wanted this type of information and for chair training purposes. One chair mentioned I should write a book to share this information...so here we are!

I am hopeful you purchased this book because you need concrete and specific instructions to complete your dissertation project. If there are other issues (e.g., you feel you are being severely mistreated by your chair, or you feel psychologically overwhelmed by the journey) and this book doesn't help, please seek other resources to take care of yourself. Now, let's get started on finishing this journey, so you can say YOU are ABD NO MORE!!

Acknowledgements

I am so very grateful to all of the doctoral students I had the honor to work with! Some of the included samples come from drafts between select students and me. Special acknowledgement and thank you to: Chris Beehner, DBA, Jessica Bennett, PhD, Allan Bourbina, PhD, Dora Cerge, EdD. Tom Lawless, PhD, Sheryl Matney, EdD, and Yvette Prior, PhD, Eric Puhlman, DBA, Jeannine Ray, PhD, Saif Rehman, PhD, Jeannette Sedor, PhD, Desiree Sylver-Foust, PhD, Phil Ulmer, PhD!!

Kindest regards,

Jill Blackwell, Dissertation Chair, Former Dissertation Consultant/Coach
jillpatterblackwell@gmail.com
NCU Outstanding Dissertation Chair 2016

SECTION ONE: THE PROPOSAL

CHAPTER 1: Your Desired Topic versus a Research Worthy Topic

If I had five dollars for every time a dissertation student came to me with their dissertation project idea and I had to tell them, "you just can't do a project based on something you think would be interesting for a dissertation, or based on something you noticed in your personal environment," I would be sipping drinks with tiny umbrellas on an island and not writing this book! What I am saying is - it is extremely common to get inspiration for your dissertation research idea by noticing something in your immediate environment. It is even great to identify a topic that is interesting to you, so you can stay motivated as you work on the project over time! BUT there is a deal breaking difference between a nice idea you are feeling passionate about and a *research worthy problem* as indicated by the current literature. If you select the wrong option you will likely add 12 (or more) frustrating months to your dissertation process.

Moreover, we know only about 50% of those who begin their dissertation work complete it. I am of the belief that latching on to a *desired topic* instead of a *research worthy* one may cause such attrition. I work with my students in all ways possible to bring their initial desired topic/project idea to fruition, but the topic has to be grounded in the literature, but more than that there has to be an expressed need for a particular project in some recent publications. Without that, it will just be too difficult for a student to defend their dissertation proposal (a dissertation proposal is a long document providing a persuasive argument about what research is needed - and why - in order to advance the literature).

In some cases we just can't get there, as there is no established need for research on the desired topic they selected, or there is no need for their particular project idea (no call for such information in the current literature). In those cases I don't let the students go chasing rabbits for more than a few weeks; I step in and try to mold the idea into a research worthy one. I always tell the students, "You can conduct any study you want without my or your schools' approval as soon as you get your doctorate degree. Hang on to that idea for your next project and break it out as soon as you graduate! Because - for this proposal - for dissertation research you need a project that will advance the current literature about a currently established problem (established by research - not only you)." Read on to learn how to find such a unicorn.

During grad school coursework you likely came across information in your classes (or just in real life) that seemed interesting. When I am assigned a student early on in the dissertation process I encourage them to keep a future research idea journal. When it is time to discuss a master's thesis or dissertation topic I ask what the student had in mind for the project. When they tell me, I say great, now please conduct a lit search of that topic (if you don't know how to do a lit search stop reading and make an appointment with your school librarian - in person if possible. By this point in your schooling someone should have made sure you knew about lit searches and shame on them for not!). With the results of the lit search I advise them to select the five most recent empirical journal articles (study write-ups) published in a peer reviewed journal (not someone else's dissertation) on the topic. I ask them to provide a critical analysis of each of the five articles using my Critical Analysis Form.

Critical Analysis Form

(1) APA style citation - You know what this is.

(2) Research method and design - Note the method (qualitative or quantitative). Also note the design (you will become more familiar with this information in Chapter Three of this book).

(3) Population and sample - Note the population (who the authors are generalizing to, which is different than the sample). The sample is comprised of the participants in the current study. People often get these two terms confused!

(4) Variables and instruments - Note the study variables and instruments used to assess them (in quantitative reports).

(5) Data collection strategy - Note how the researchers gathered their data, online questionnaire, in person questionnaire, qualitative interview, etc.

(6) Results - Note main findings.

(7) Author identified limitations - This information will be found in the article discussion section. In each and every study write up, researchers will include a *discussion section* where they discuss the study results. Note study weaknesses the authors pointed out as these sometimes can be used to justify additional research! This is the silver! I used to have this category on the form just say limitations, but students would really use the term loosely and say "oh the sample of 1,000 wasn't big enough," so now it is important for me to make sure they are recording what **the *study authors are noting as limitations/weaknesses*.** The added benefit of an "author identified" limitation is a citable source suggesting additional study is needed.

(8) Author identified proposed future studies - Here is the GOLD we are panning for! This information will also be found in the article discussion section. In each and every discussion section there is a paragraph about "future research" needed - to either clarify some problem that came up in the study, or about some new unknown the study uncovered, and there is an expressed call for a new study. This is where you will find the citable justification/rationale for your study! I cannot stress this enough - you will need these expressed calls for additional study to convince your chair, committee, and school that additional research is needed. Plus, it has to be cited. Without such calls for research (by experts) about what information is needed to advance a particular field or topic you will be hard pressed to get approval for your dissertation research idea.

I don't like having people do extra work, so the good news about critiquing articles with the Critical Analysis Form (CAF) is the information can be recycled for future use in the lit review. The lit review is a synthesized and critical review of published research (just what I am asking for in the CAF). In the lit review you provide study details (CAF items 2-5), note important results (CAF item 6), but the main focus in on CAF items 7 and 8, the problems with the literature (from gaps in understanding, equivocal nature of findings, disagreement between authors).

Be sure to save the article review write ups with each article, so you don't have to reread an article over and over (that is not a good use of time). Put the critical analysis form on top of it (if you print them out), or save it with the article on your computer and the main info will be condensed into this one excellent summary sheet. You can essentially copy and paste the valuable info when it is time to work on your lit review. Once you have pulled, read, and critiqued five articles, go find five more. You can use the initial search results, or you can get new ideas from the five articles you just read. Perhaps a source the researchers discussed will look interesting. When that occurs, flip to the reference section, get the citation, and obtain the new article. I suggest going five at a time as it seems manageable, and in no time you will have a decent understanding of the literature and a good idea of what research is still needed to solve a disagreement in the literature, or clarify something.

After you have read/critiqued at least five articles you may be thinking oh great, as it turns out, what research I was thinking is needed is needed. That is a good thought! Unfortunately, about 50% of you will be thinking the exact opposite though, and that is a tough day to have. Still, let's not give up hope on your original idea. Let's stick with the topic and review and critique some more articles. I will give you advice on what to do if it is turning out it doesn't seem like your study is needed to advance the literature later in this chapter. Please hang on and keep reading for now!

Just How Many Articles Are We Talking About

Students often ask how many articles they should review/critique. The answer depends on two things, the topic area and the scope of the project. Some topic areas are huge and there are many articles to review. Some areas are newer and there are fewer articles. I haven't decided which is more desirable. It is good to have many articles to get future research ideas, even if you have to read a few more. It is also good to have fewer articles to read and think about adding to that literature. Either way, it is a win-win, so all areas are good.

The scope of the project will also dictate how many articles are needed. In undergrad classes I give a specific number of needed articles for an assigned project reference section. When working with master's students I make suggestions, and for dissertation students I suggest a bit more (still with the topic area in mind). It is likely your chair has advised how many articles they want you to use to inform your project. If not, go ahead and ask them. Maybe your school dissertation manual makes a note about it.

When my students ask me this question I tell them you are done pulling articles when you have run an *exhaustive* search of the literature. I am sure they are thinking, "Well, I am really tired of finding more articles, is that what she means by exhausted?" No. An ***exhaustive search*** is accomplished when you are reading your five new article pulls from the literature and you are nodding as you read their introductions to their studies because you are familiar with all of the work they are citing! It is an exhilarating feeling - you will know it when it happens. Until that time, please keep pulling, reading, and critiquing five more articles.

My Chair is being Weird about My Project Idea

What if your chair is giving you a hard time about your project idea? To review, not all dissertation topic/project ideas are research worthy. It does not behoove you at all to latch on to a non-research worthy project idea, or try to convince your chair of its merit, or get mad at your chair for not recognizing your brilliance. Your chair is not trying to thwart your excellent ideas and/or hopefully not trying to have you just run a project they are interested in. Your chair is helping you identify a needed project that will add to the current literature (what is needed on this dissertation journey). Your chair wants you to graduate - maybe almost as much as you do! Still, you can likely garner support for your project idea as long as you can share two, three, or more citable calls for research. Send the article, with the Critical Analysis Form completed and jot down the citable calls for research to advance the literature - and in a nice way ask them to put that information in their pipe and smoke it :)

Remember the goal for this dissertation is to answer the current calls for research in your topic area. The goal is not to do the study you had your mind on for the last three weeks (or even possibly longer), that you are dying to know about, or that you think will be interesting. Do that study after you finish your dissertation. The dissertation will need to be based on the research being called for in the current literature on your topic - to advance the literature. In many cases this identified need for studies to advance the literature will match with your great idea for a study. Sometimes it won't. When it won't, try for a little while to make it work, but set a time limit for this and then move on when you have invested that set amount of time. Time is valuable in the dissertation journey (more time often translates to more money spent).

When you are not finding a match between your great idea and the need for research in your topic area you might still be able to get there. I call this technique convergence - it's sort of like flow :) Here is an email from a student at this exact stage (the uh oh, "I don't think my excellent study idea is really needed" stage) who was encountering exactly what I am talking about. She wrote, "I just had a session with a library specialist (at our school). We noticed that literature is limited on my specific topic. The librarian and I concluded that marriage and relationship coaching is an emerging field. With that said, should I modify my topic or can I still conduct a study for my dissertation on a field that is emerging and may not have a sufficient literature/studies?"

> Comment [JB]: You will learn how to differentiate between the general and specific problems for your problem statement in the very next chapter! If this makes sense now though, excellent!

Do you notice how calm, cool, and collected this note seems to be? I was so impressed by it. She also thanked me for my insight and gave her warm regards! Very unusual. This is what I wrote back: "So glad you worked with the librarian! In this case you could consider extending the coaching literature to this one area if there were calls to do that (as if some of the articles suggested such info was needed). For example, does the coaching literature in other areas (maybe with leaders or employees) suggest (by study authors in their future research directions) that further research should be carried out with other populations (maybe even clinical population)? If so, you could make the argument your group of married people is a different population, and such research will extend the coaching literature by answering a call for more information about its applicability to other settings/groups."

I continued on in my email, "Another strategy (maybe use a convergence of both strategies) is to go into the marriage/relationship literature and note the author identified calls for research - perhaps there is a call for research about the lack of information on different therapeutic approaches to help in this area. If that is the case, then you could suggest coaching might be viable with this group, but empirical evidence would be needed to support such a claim." I also wrote, "Sounds like your general problem could be something like marriage therapy is not completely working (or something like that). Then the bridge to the specific researchable problem (what research is being called for to advance the literature), which might be - traditional therapies don't work when two people are involved, and some experts suggested relationship building skills/coaching might be effective in marital therapy (if you can find a citation for it). Then logic on to say research has been called for to extend coaching efficacy literature to new populations (cite), and to evaluate the efficacy of alternative therapeutic strategies in marital relationships (cite), to inform clinicians working with this population (cite). In such an example your specific problem is the lack of understanding about coaching efficacy in marriage therapy, which is needed to inform clinicians working with this population. What do you think?"

My last sentence of the email to the student was, "OR you can find some of the most recent articles on your topic area and flip to their future research directions section (in their discussion section) and see what studies they are recommending to advance the literature. It is likely several of them are saying the same thing and you can just run one of those studies AND have citations for why that research is important." I am not going to tell you how it turned out, other than it did all work out!

I always remember my student's initial research ideas. After a dissertation defense (there is a lovely ring to those two words isn't there!) I ask the student if their next research project will be the one they initially wanted to run. Most of the time they chuckle and say, "oh no, that is not what the literature is calling for to solve this problem" (I do a happy dance in my head having graduated a true researcher), or they are inspired to run a study to address one of THEIR study limitations - research they called for in **their** discussion section! Only early on in the process have I heard a student mention how "different" this project is from their initial idea. In my head I know they are mad about it, but I also know I am doing them a big favor and may receive a thank you card about this very issue in the near future! Now that you have read study write ups from peer reviewed journals (at least five current articles), with a focus on the discussion sections - and future calls for research, you have a good idea about what information is needed to advance the literature. Now you are ready to prepare the most important section of your entire dissertation..... the problem statement. Onward!

CHAPTER 2: Developing your PROBLEM STATEMENT!

The problem statement is for sure the most important 300 words of your entire dissertation proposal. In these 300 words you must convey importance of your **topic/general problem**, salience of the general problem, and ramifications of this general problem. You also need to present the **specific problem (the problem with the literature)** that is interfering with solving the overarching general problem.

Students (and even dissertation committee members) seem to have a real problem understanding the difference between the **general problem** and **specific researchable problem**. Here is a way I explain this important difference to students and some committee members: You need to differentiate between the general problem and specific problem. The general problem is a salient societal problem (e.g., reading problems in children). The specific problem is derived from the general problem, but it is focused on the *problem with the research* that is interfering with the resolution of the general problem - and is what necessitates additional research - the justification for a dissertation (e.g., researchers disagree how to solve the reading problems in children) this provides the study justification - we need another study about it).

Because I explain this difference at least three times a week to PhD students as well as people with PhDs, I am going to go into a bit more detail about the distinction and offer you a template to use while developing your problem statement and also some samples. The template asks students to develop six focused/concise/cited sentences to present needed information about the **general problem** (three sentences) and needed information about the **specific researchable study problem** (three sentences) to provide the rationale and justification for the study. Whenever I share this template and information with other PhDs they are happy about it and tell me how helpful it has been for them and their students. I have yet to meet a researcher who had a problem with a problem statement of one of my students when presented in my proposed way. Bottom line, it works.

Most students like the template and samples too. The sample and template helps them defend their proposed study idea, it is effective, and people who read their dissertation proposal can clearly see the need for their proposed study in six sentences. When I work with students who are at the beginning stage of their dissertation I ask them to review/critique the five articles (as mentioned in the previous chapter), then I tell them - see if you can use that information to develop the six needed sentences for the problem statement. If they can, great! The hard part is over. If they cannot, I ask them to find five more articles to review/critique, and then take a stab at the six sentence problem statement once again.

In some instances a dissertation student may have two solid ideas for a dissertation and they can't decide which one is better. I tell them to develop the six problem statement sentences for both ideas and then decide. Each and every time this exercise has resulted in the student recognizing the superiority of one study idea (research problem) over the other.

The students who don't make progress with the template are ones who are really stuck on a non-research worthy proposed topic/study idea. These students cannot find support for either the existence/salience of the general problem in the literature. OR they cannot garner information about the specific problem (the problem with the literature) that suggests additional research is needed.

In the best case scenario - for students with a research worthy problem identified - it could take 15 minutes to prepare the needed six sentences for the problem statement. In the worst case scenario - I can sit around and wait for months for a student to come to the realization they have latched on to a non- research worthy topic (despite feedback about this issue). This plays out over weekly interactions about these six sentences. Me noting what is missing, what to look for to justify the problem, etc. Them saying they don't understand it, or they are still looking for sources. This challenging situation can be frustrating for me. I bet it is really frustrating for the students.

The problem statement, consisting of my suggested six sentences should be easy to develop (especially with the template and samples). When a student tells me about their study idea - I can rattle off the needed six sentences right off the top of my head because it is really just an excercise in logic. Still, I don't know if what I am saying is true according to the literature, and they will need to find the sources to make sure it is true and what exact research is needed. If it is not easy to develop the six sentences, the problem is most likely not with your logic skills, but with your identified topic/research idea, or you may not have reviewed enough literature to develop the needed six sentences. I tell my students to keep reading the current literature. If they hit 20 recent articles, but still cannot develop the needed six sentences for the problem statement, then it may be time to **dig in to the discussion sections of these 20 articles and see what research is really needed to advance the literature**. The study idea a student ends up with may be in line with their initial project idea, but it may not. What is most important though (for brining this dissertation to an eventual close) is to go with the problem identified in the literature - and develop a study to advance the literature. You can do your initial research project idea (that is not being called for by the literature) after you graduate with your PhD. Here is my problem statement template with my best wishes.

Dr. B's Problem Statement TEMPLATE: In your problem statement you will have approximately two paragraphs, six-seven sentences in total:

General problem paragraph. The first paragraph will present three sentences about the context of the **general problem** with citations. Begin the problem statement with the words, "The general problem is…..and finish it with a citation (the general problem is the context for the specific problem - remember the specific problem is the problem with the research). Sentence #2 should indicate the extent of this general problem with statistics and citations. Sentence #3 should indicate the ramifications of the general problem. This sentence should actually read, "The ramifications of xx (restate the general problem) are xx, xx, and xx. Be sure to use recent scholarly citations to support that others see this as a general problem, the stats or information demonstrating the salience of the general problem, and the consequences of the general problem. Plan about 150 words for this paragraph.

Specific problem paragraph. Next you will develop a paragraph about the specific problem that necessitates your proposed line of inquiry. The specific problem will emanate from the general problem, but will reflect two main ideas: (1) the problem with the current empirical literature; and (2) why additional research is needed (both with citations). Examples of problems with the existing research literature are disagreement in the field and the equivocal nature of results from different studies. ==Often you will find ideas about specific problems with the literature in the discussion sections== of empirical investigations under the **future research directions** section.

The specific problem paragraph will begin with Sentence #4 (of the problem statement) transitioning from the general problem to the specific problem. Sentence #5 will identify the controversy, lack of agreement, and lack of needed information (problem with the literature). Sentence #6 will present a sentence about WHY this information is needed (it will need to fulfill some practical application (e.g., inform stakeholders to develop mitigation strategies) that will also need to be cited. Sentence #7 should read "The specific problem prompting this research is..." where you present language that sums up the problem with the research in about four words, and why the information is needed (a four word summary of the practical info). This is the most important sentence of the problem statement because this one specific problem sentence will need to be aligned with the main purpose statement sentence, RQs, and methodology. Because it needs to be aligned, do not use a citation for this one concluding sentence about your identified specific problem. Once again, this is the most important sentence of the problem statement and MUST match with the purpose statement first sentence (where you will indicate your research approach and design) and the RQs and hypotheses for alignment. Plan about 150 words for this paragraph too.

Here is a brief sample, this is not accurate information, and it is just a sample so you can see the logical flow - the yellow highlighted areas are the mainstays that should be used in your problem statement.

General Problem Paragraph

Sentence 1: The general problem is military analysts are failing at detecting faulty equipment (cite).

Sentence 2: In the last year there has been a 90% increase in failures (cite).

Sentence 3: The ramifications of xx (state the general problem again - not detecting faulty equipment) include xx and xx (cite).

Specific Problem Paragraph

Sentence 4: There is a lack of agreement about effective solutions for not detecting faulty equipment (cite).

Sentence 5: Some researchers have suggested database solutions might mitigate this problem (cite); however, other researchers maintained other approaches are needed (cite).

Sentence 6: Information about effective solutions is needed to inform stakeholders responsible for training military analysts (cite).

> **Comment [JB]:** Remember: the specific problem is derived from the general problem, but it is focused on the problem with the research that is interfering with the resolution of the general problem - and is what necessitates additional research - the justification for a dissertation (e.g., researchers disagree how to solve the reading problems in children) this provides the study justification - we need another study about it).
>
> Such calls for research are found in the discussion sections of empirical studies under future research directions).

Sentence 7: The specific problem that prompts this research is a lack of agreement about solution efficacy, which is needed before information can be developed to support and train military experts about detecting faulty equipment.

> Comment [JB]: Restate from sentence four about the problem with the literature
>
> Comment [JB]: Restate from Sentence #6 about the practical need for the information
>
> Comment [JB]: Use more than one article and locate differences in author identified implications to demonstrate the problem with the literature.
>
> Comment [JB]: Use the future research directions section to find support for what exact research is needed next in the research process.

Seems straightforward and easy right?! Problem statement development is really an exercise in logic. This logic exercise requires an understanding of the needed research to extend the literature on a particular topic, which can be found in the discussion sections of peer reviewed journal articles.

Problem statement Sentence #4 nuances. As you can see, Sentence #4 is really about why we are having problems solving the general problem. It is a bridge between the general problem paragraph and what additional research is being calling for. Once a research project is completed the author develops ideas about their results that can be used to inform their originally identified general problem. Typically this information will appear in the implications section (of their discussion section).

For problem statement Sentence #4 - you might have two different articles that are both suggesting different implications for their results (different ways to solve their identified general problem). In that case, use a bit of induction to combine the specifics into a new problem with the literature for you to solve. If researcher A says this is important to solve the general problem and researcher B says this is important to solve the general problem - that looks to me like a disagreement about how to solve a problem (an equivocal state in the literature) and MORE RESEARCH IS NEEDED!! There is your justification with two citations!

Problem statement Sentence #5 nuances. In some cases you will get lucky and there will be a black and white call for a specific project that you were interested in doing right in that future research directions section of the discussion section of the empirical article. If that is the case, your Sentence #5 could read: research has been called for to clarify X (cite). You could hopefully easily find a citation about why that information is needed right in that same paragraph of the article to inform your Sentence #6, such as "This information is needed to inform the stakeholders (cite)."

Still, it may not be as black and white as that and you may not find specific calls for research that you wanted to do (have I not convinced you though - that is the best way to go :). What if five researchers from the different articles are all calling for different particular studies to clarify something? That is still okay, you could develop your Sentence #5 to read: "Some researchers have called for additional research about the efficacy of treatment x (cite) especially in a sample of individuals with PTSD (cite) in order to inform the literature." See how we combined the two calls for research into one doable project idea.

Just one more thing to consider - I promise. In the next chapter you will learn about the two research methods you have to choose from for your dissertation research. I mentioned your specific problem statement will need to be **aligned** with your method (and other things, but let's just worry about the method for now). "Yes" you just answered - good, you remembered - it was just earlier in this very chapter. Well, without giving away too much information about methods before the next chapter, but also without asking you to flip back here after you read that chapter, your Sentences #5 and #7 should reflect the type of method you will propose.

So, if the research is suggesting that cause and effect information is needed, or information is needed about a relationship between existing variables - you will need to conduct a quantitative study. If the research (and your Sentences #5 and #7 are suggesting what we really need is to consider some group of people's in-depth perceptions about something then you will propose a qualitative method (most likely a case study in that example).

What I am saying is there is a whole chapter on what method/design to select next, but really your proposed research should follow what information is needed - as you will indicate in

Sentences #5 and #7 of this problem statement. At any rate, the two areas will need to match. If you indicate perceptions are needed in your problem statement, you shouldn't propose a quantitative study to determine the efficacy of Treatment X as your problem and method would be out of alignment. You will read more on this in the next chapter. Here are sample problem statements for both qualitative and quantitative methods (see if you can note the differences).

QUANTITATIVE Study Samples

   Problem statement sample #1. The general problem is the inability to identify what leads individuals diagnosed with a serious mental illness (SMI) to become violent (Walsh & Yun, 2013). Researchers noted those diagnosed with psychotic SMI disorders show the highest risk for violence at an increase of 49% to 68% (Nederlof, Muris, & Hovens, 2013). The ramifications of not being able to identify the combination of risk factors that leads to violent behavior among those with SMI, inhibits an accurate clinical ability to predict risk of violence, which has led to deaths of both the innocent and those suffering from SMI (Metzel & MacLeish, 2015).

   Attempts at predicting violent behavior in the SMI population have been made; however, researchers disagree about which factors create the largest risk of violent behavior (Lamsma & Harte, 2015; Metzel & MacLeish, 2013; Walsh & Yun, 2013). Researchers identified positive symptoms of psychosis that could lead to violent behavior, specifically those individuals that present as paranoid or hostile (Walsh & Yun, 2013). However, other researchers noted symptoms of mental illness, which affect aggressive behavior in varying degrees, but were not responsible for all violent or criminal behavior (Peterson et al., 2015). Still other researchers suggested the possibility of a violent subgroup within the SMI population (Lamsma & Harte, 2015). The equivocal nature of the literature on risk factors for violence in the SMI population is interfering with assessment and treatment among the SMI population (Lamsma & Harte, 2015; Jakhar, 2015;

> **Comment [JB]:** State the general problem and cite
>
> **Comment [JB]:** A sentence about the salience of the general problem
>
> **Comment [JB]:** The ramifications of the general problem.
>
> **Comment [JB]:** This is the problem with the literature
>
> **Comment [JB]:** This is why the information is needed - the practical application.

Peterson, 2014; Simpson, 2015). The specific problem that prompts this research is the lack of agreement about risk factors for violence in the SMI population, which is needed to inform clinicians serving this population.

Problem statement sample #2. The general problem is high numbers of employee turnover in the accommodation and food service industry (Kim, 2012). The 2012 voluntary turnover rate for employees in this industry was 39.7%, more than double the overall U.S. turnover rate of 18.8% (U.S. Department of Labor, 2013c). The ramifications of employee turnover are additional direct costs of recruitment and selection (Jacobs, 2011), and the indirect costs of reduced productivity (Park & Shaw, 2013), service disruption (Hauskenecht & Trevor, 2011), reduced revenue (Shaw, 2011), and reduced customer satisfaction (Dentert et al., 2007).

Researchers demonstrated workplace spirituality and turnover intention to be negatively correlated in several industries, with increased levels of workplace spirituality resulting in reduced employee turnover (Crawford et al., 2009; Hong, 2012). However, research conducted in other industries cannot be generalized to the food service industry, because no other industry is engaged in the simultaneous production of a customized product and the delivery of an individualized service to the extent of the food service industry (Park & Shaw, 2013). Moreover, experimental research is needed to determine if interventions to increase workplace spirituality influence employee turnover intention (Geh & Tan, 2009; Tevichapong et al., 2010). The specific problem is a lack of experimental research about the efficacy of interventions to increase workplace spirituality to influence employee turnover in the food industry, which is needed to inform stakeholders charged with developing strategies to reduce employee turnover in the food service industry.

QUALITATIVE Study Samples

Problem statement sample #3. SROs have been used in schools since the 1990's with the primary objective of preventing violence (Weiler & Cray, 2011), and although the rate of violent crime has statistically been decreasing since the 1990s (Jennings et al., 2011), the general problem is violent crime is still occurring (Robers, Zhang, & Truman, 2012). In the 2010 school year, 359,000 students were victims of violent crimes within schools (Robers et al., 2012).

Researchers suggested one reason for the continued violence may be because SROs do not incorporate the elements necessary into their RRPs for their schools in order to respond to acts of violence (Stone & Spencer, 2010). Although some states have enacted legislation mandating the development of RRPs that target specific areas, it is critical that all schools adopt a plan that addresses prevention, protection, mitigation, response, and recovery (Department of Education 2013). However, researchers are uninformed about what elements SROs have included in their RRPs and how these elements influence the RRPs during the development process (Cornell, 2011). In addition, researchers are unknowledgeable about interagency communication and collaboration between SROs and stakeholders during the RRP development process (Collins, 2007). Information about RRP development is important to ascertain as it may impact program funding decisions (Raymond, 2010) and research about communication and collaboration among agencies that extends to roles, responsibilities, and expectations of those involved is needed before strategies to develop future RRP guidelines can be promulgated (Daniels et al., 2011). The specific problem is strategies to foster effective RRPs cannot be promulgated until SROs' perceptions about RRP development, the elements that influence RRP development, and interagency communication and collaboration in the development of RRPs are expanded.

Problem statement sample #4 qualitative study. The general problem is conventional teaching methods no longer trigger students' motivation to learn (Aziz-Ur-Rehman et al., 2012) especially with the influx and influence of technology usage in their daily lives (Cubukcuoglu, 2013). In 2004, the National Research Council demonstrated that approximately 40% of high school students are uninterested in school, exhibit little effort towards finishing classwork, and are detached from learning (Center on Education Policy, 2012). The ramification of unmotivated students not only hinder learning, but can discourage teachers from creating a student-centered classroom that motivates students to learn (cite). Additional consequences of unmotivated students include low academic success, disruption of the learning environment, and higher dropout rates (Center on Education Policy, 2012).

Researchers have shown technology use by teachers can increase student interest and enhance teaching (Lin & Jou, 2013); however, there are problems with teacher utilization that require additional study (Gilakjani & Lai-Mei, 2012). Perception is an essential factor in how teachers embrace technology (Cubukcuoglu, 2013); however teacher's perceptions about the reasons for using or not using technology in their pedagogic practices is currently unknown (Gilakjani & Lai-Mei, 2012). This is problematic as a failure to identify and address teachers' perception of combining technology with their existing pedagogy to enhance teaching which could interfere with the success of technology integration efforts and deserves further attention (Cox, 2013). The specific problem prompting the need for this research is before professional development and training can be organized to promote technology integration in the classroom, information on teachers' attitudes and perception of technology and what makes them want or need to use technology to enhance teaching and learning is needed.

CHAPTER 3: The Method/Design for the Project

This chapter is all about the two research methods you have to choose from and the five designs most commonly used in dissertation research. It is important to discuss the method/design at this juncture (even before it is time to consider developing your method chapter for the proposal) as you will need to know the name of the method and the name of your design in order to develop your study purpose statement. Interestingly, students spend a lot of time hemming and hawing about which method/design they want to use. In reality, **the method/design will be determined by the missing literature and what you identified as your specific problem** (so it is not really your choice of which method you prefer to use). Sometimes people use the terms method and design synonymously, but it is better to use the term **research method** to refer to the type of research method (there are just two "methods" to choose from - qualitative or quantitative) and to use the term **research design** to refer to the "design" under the particular method (there are about three popular qualitative designs and three popular quantitative designs).

I teach method/design information to undergrad psychology students in an advanced research methods class and I am always surprised when only about half of the students each quarter understand this information right away. I guess I shouldn't be surprised anymore! I can help most of them to understand it over the rest of the quarter, but there are always about two students (out of 40) each time who mistakenly label their final project - a true experiment design - as a correlational design. When this happens I patiently explain the difference again, but inside my head I am screaming! When I worked at my dissertation consulting job and my dissertation chair job, few to none of my clients/students were aware of the differences between the methods/designs, so don't feel bad and just read on!

Research Method

Again, there are only two research methods and each has different designs that represent the methods. The decision about which research method should be used is dictated by what is already known about the topic and what information is needed (what type of information has been called for by other researchers to add to the literature). Students often want to select the method based on which one they feel more comfortable with, but the decision should be made based on what information is needed to extend the empirical literature. Besides, both methods have parts about them that are easy and challenging - it is not the case that one method is easier to carry out than the other.

A qualitative method might be less challenging in the beginning (no need to identify specific variables, instruments, or hypotheses; but data analysis and interpretation can be quite challenging). In contrast, a lot of thought goes into the early stages of quantitative method studies, but data analysis and interpretation is much more straightforward. At any rate, it is best to let the research method decision be dictated by what type of information is needed to extend the empirical literature about your topic. There is also a third research method, a mixed method where both qualitative and quantitative methods are combined. I always discourage my dissertation students from this research method, unless there is a real reason to do it - **remember as dictated by the literature**. It is often quite an undertaking to master both method components and would likely add much time and pain to the dissertation process. When I ask a student to persuade me why a mixed method is needed, I hope to hear they have scoured the literature and this is the next step in the research process. This has yet to be the case - even once, so I feel comfortable encouraging one method or another for your dissertation. There is lots of time for your future research, you want to get your dissertation done and you want it to be a quality piece. It is often outside of the skill set of first time researchers to pull off a quality mixed methods study.

The Qualitative Method and its Designs

Qualitative research is conducted in early stages of topic exploration - when there is not a lot is known about a topic, or when in-depth information about people's perceptions are needed (use a case study design), or when rich, in-depth information is needed about people's experiences with a unique phenomena (use a phenomenology design). Under a **qualitative research method paradigm** there are three popular *designs* to choose from (e.g., case study design, phenomenology design, and grounded theory design). **The design decision should also be dictated by what information is needed to extend the literature in your topic area**.

The most popular qualitative research designs are **case study design** (to garner information about perceptions) and **phenomenology** (to garner information about people's experiences with unique phenomena). An example **case study design question is**: what are people's **perceptions** about mindfulness meditation? An example **phenomenology design research question is:** What are the **experiences** of practitioners of mindful meditation? By far, case studies are the most popular. In my experience (and with my understanding of beginning research student's ability to conduct qualitative interviews) the depth of the interview needed to get adequate data for a phenomenological study is very difficult unless the student has extremely advanced research and interviewing skills. The second deal breaker for this design in dissertation research is the need to justify the uniqueness of a phenomenon and to convince the reader that research has been called for to describe such unique experiences. Most often there are calls for perceptions about something (which would justify a case study) rather than rich and detailed information about an experience with unique phenomena.

In qualitative research there are no specified variables, or predicted relationships among variables. There are no hypotheses to generate only research questions. Qualitative research can generally not be used to answer questions about causality, correlations, or differences between variables.

The case study design has two nuances you need to address. The first is to decide whether you will use a **single case**, or a **multiple case** design. In a nutshell, a single case will be easier and just as informative as a multiple case. A multiple case may have better generalizability, but it will be much more challenging and likely time consuming. There is a little more to it than this example, but you can think about it this way - in a single case you will collect your qualitative data from one school or district that is similar. In a multiple case you collect your qualitative data from more than one distinct district to get a different understanding of perceptions in different areas.

The next decision is whether you will use an embedded case, or a holistic case. In a holistic case you have just one unit of analysis (e.g., faculty members), but in an embedded case you have subunits of analysis. Let's say your unit of analysis was people, who work in a school, and your two subunits were (a) faculty members and (b) students, and you were going to collect data from both subunits and even compare responses to similar interview questions - that will make it **embedded as opposed to holistic** (in holistic you only focused on the one group - students). You can even generate a research question about this comparison of perceptions (e.g., how do faculty member **perceptions** about mindfulness meditation differ from student perceptions about mindfulness meditation).

The Quantitative Method and its Designs

Quantitative research is conducted when a researcher wants to determine or predict (instead of just explore) something. Under the **quantitative research method paradigm** there are three popular designs to choose from (e.g., true experiment design, causal-comparative design, or correlational design). Each of these designs only allows you to answer a specific type of question, so it is easy to determine which quantitative design to use, once you figure out what information is needed to extend the literature.

Generally speaking you can find such calls for research from other researchers towards the end of their empirical and often peer-reviewed journal articles. In the **discussion** section (there is usually a heading for this discussion section) researchers suggest what future research is needed based on the limitations/weaknesses of their study. Such citable calls for research can be used to defend the need for your additional proposed research.

In a **true experiment design**- questions of **causality** can be addressed via exploration of a manipulated independent variable (IV) on a dependent variable (DV), such as: What are the effects of yoga (IV) on stress levels (DV) in college students. The IV is what you vary and the DV is what you measure. You will determine what the manipulation will be (you will refer to this as the independent variable) and you will determine the levels of the independent variable (I will have two levels of the IV of yoga - one level is 30 minutes of yoga program A and one level is no yoga). I could also choose to have three levels of my IV (30 minutes of yoga, 30 minutes of the same yoga routine in a hot room, and no yoga). The decision of what the manipulation will be and how many levels to include will often depend on (guess what I am going to say here) yes, the literature and what information is needed to extend the literature and/or answer unanswered questions.

You could also choose to have more than one IV. If this is the case you would refer to your design as a factorial true experiment (the terms factors and IVs can be used synonymously) and you could assess main effects of each IV on the DV as well as an interaction of the IVs on the DV. You could also choose to have more than one DV - again if the literature suggests another variable should be measured.

In a **causal comparative design** - questions of **differences** can be addressed via exploration of a non-manipulated independent variable on a dependent variable, such as: Do smokers and non-smokers (IV is smoking status) differ in lung cancer rates (DV)? There is still an IV with levels, but you are not manipulating the IV. Instead you are finding out where a person sits on some inherent difference (do they smoke or not) and they are essentially placing themselves into the IV level. Causal comparative designs that make use of "selected" IVs (inherent to the individual) to compare levels of non-manipulated IVs are sometimes referred to as quasi-experimental designs because the researcher only has partial control of the IVs (you did pick them - didn't you :). Sometimes chairs like to refer to such designs as "ex post facto" (because we are measuring effects after the fact - of the IV difference), but to be most accurate you can argue with your chair until you get them to use the correct name - causal comparative, or even differential, or just let them have their way.

Similar to the true experiment, you can have more than one IV or DV in a causal comparative design. If you have 2 IVs (factors) you add a new qualifier to your design name - factorial. You could refer to this as a two factor, or factorial causal comparative design. The purpose of having more than one factor is to see how each IV impacts the DV separately, but also how they work together to impact the DV (their interaction). Factorial designs provide a more complete picture of a variables' impact on a dependent variable. In a factorial design every level of every IV appears in combination with every level of every other independent variable.

We can describe such designs (with more than one factor/IV) with an equation, whereby each IV gets a place in the equation ____ X ____. I know from looking at the previous sentence that there are 2 IVs (one for each place before and after the X). The number that goes ON the line is the number of levels associated with each IV. So, if my first IV had 2 levels, and my second IV had 2 levels, I would have a 2 x 2 either true experiment or causal comparative factorial design. If you see a 2 x 3 describing research, you know there are 2 IVs, one IV with 2 levels and the other IV with 3 levels. What if you had three IVs, one IV had two levels, one had six levels, and one has 3 levels? Your equation would look like this - 2 X 6 X 3. Did you guess that? If you multiply the equation out - you will know how many conditions you have - in a 2 X 2 you would have four conditions, and with a 2 X 3 you would have six conditions. As you should strive to have representations in all of your conditions, as a chair I only allow my students to have two IVs, with no more than two levels each. That's four conditions to fill! That is a lot for a student working on their dissertation! The only thing you need to know about more than one DV at this time is that it is okay to have two DVs (you shouldn't have more than two though - unless absolutely needed **as indicated by the literature**). If you have one DV then you use an analysis of variance (ANOVA) to analyze your data (no matter how many IVs you have), but if you have more than one DV then you use a multiple analysis of variance (MANOVA) to analyze your data (no matter how many IVs you have), more information on this later.

This causal comparative design comes in very handy because **some variables are impossible to manipulate** (e.g., diabetes status - yes or no) - you can't make people have a certain disease. It would also not be ethical to manipulate other variables (e.g., stress levels of a person). Because of the nature of such variables often times a true experiment is just not possible. Still, you could conduct a causal comparative design and compare two groups of people, smokers and non smokers (non manipulated IV) and measure their heart disease symptoms (in the same way) to determine if there are significant differences in number of disease symptoms between the two groups, but because the IV was not manipulated you cannot interpret this difference to be "causal" (the symptoms may be due to a third variable you didn't select). Still, you will get important information to share.

In a **correlational design** - questions about the **relationship between two or more numeric** dependent variables can be addressed, such as: Does life change unit score (DV) correlate with number of illnesses in a year (DV)? There are really no independent variables that you will "vary." You might really want to conduct a true experiment; however, many of the variables of interest to researchers cannot be manipulated due to the ethical reasons covered above. To work around this situation you could conduct a correlational study where you assess the relationship between number of cigarettes smoked (DV) and the extent of heart disease symptoms (DV). Still, even if there was a significant correlation you wouldn't be able to imply that smoking "causes" heart disease.

Some students want to use regression, moderation, mediation, or modeling analyses (more info on analyses in the results chapter, but...). In these cases, you still have a correlational design and something close to an independent variable, but you can't call it an independent variable, you refer to it as a predictor variable. Moreover, the measured variables are not really "dependent" on another, so you don't use the term dependent variable either, instead you use criterion to refer to this measured variable with your correlational design with regression. In this case if you have more than one predictor variable and only one criterion variable you would use multiple regression. If you had one predictor variable and more than one criterion variable you would use multivariate regression to analyze your data.

The most important correlational design issue is **correlation does not equal causation.** As indicated above, the only way for researchers to suggest a causal connection between two variables is to manipulate one of them (IV) and measure a dependent variable. Even if you are using regression and have predictor variables, you are still not close to the high internal validity level afforded by a true experiment. Researchers have to be careful not to make causal conclusions when it is not appropriate. True experiments can be used when you manipulate a treatment for smokers (half of your participants get the cessation treatment and the other half don't). Then causal conclusions can be made about the treatment in topic areas where individual differences exist, but cannot be manipulated - and you can still run a true experiment.

Do you see how each quantitative design can only be used to answer one type of particular question? Remember, the type of information needed to extend the research in your topic area really does dictate the design (and method), so there is no need to worry about which design/method to "pick."

Exercises

To help you conceptualize your research idea in different ways, try developing four potential studies about the same topic with three different designs in your topic area. Develop a:

- quantitative (method) true experiment (design) study
- quantitative (method) causal comparative (design) study
- quantitative (method) correlational (design) study
- qualitative (method) case study (design) study

Then answer the following questions for each study. This exercise won't take long, but it will be extremely helpful in understanding the two different methods and designs under each method! Also, if you answer these questions (for your selected design) and take the answers to your dissertation chair as is, she will think you are a ROCKSTAR! Not only do you understand research methods/designs, but you have done the hard work of conceptualizing a project to answer a call for research. OR, what if you took all four samples designs flushed out - questions answered- to your chair and asked for their opinion. They would fall off of their *chair* and move you to the head of the class!

Quantitative (method) true experiment (design)

1. What is the main purpose of your study? (Remember in a true experiment you can determine cause and effect by manipulating an independent variable (giving one group a treatment and one group no treatment).

2. What research question are you interested in investigating? (In a true experiment your research question will be about -how an IV effects a DV - name them both in the hypotheses and the IV levels - for example: How does food modification program impact cholesterol score?).

3. What are your specific hypotheses? (In a true experiment your hypothesis will be about -how an IV affects a DV - name them both in the hypotheses and the IV levels - for example: Participants receiving a food modification program will have lower cholesterol scores than participants who do not receive a food modification program).

4. How will you operationalize your independent variable (IV)? Describe their levels. (Levels of an IV are the different applications. In the above example food modification is the IV - you could have two levels of this IV - treatment or no treatment. The levels would be a treatment group who received the food modification; and the control group who did not. If you wanted three levels of this IV you could have the control group as one level, a two week treatment group as a second level, and a four moth treatment group as the third level).

5. How will you operationalize your dependent variable (DV)? How will it be measured (name the instrument)? In the above example cholesterol score is the DV. You can decide how to measure it. You could do so subjectively by asking them their score, or objectively by taking blood an assessing it for cholesterol.

Quantitative (method) causal comparative experiment (design)

1. What is the main purpose of your study? (Remember in a causal comparative experiment you **cannot** determine cause and effect, **but** you can evaluate differences between preexisting groups (men/women) to see if one group is significantly higher or lower on your DV of interest, and infer such group membership differences may impact the DV.

2. What research question are you interested in investigating? (In a causal comparative experiment your research question will be about DV differences as a function of different levels (groups) of your IV. Name the DV and the IV levels - for example: Are there gender and rank differences of PTSD symptom rates in combat veterans? Note how there are two variables/factors here. You will need a research question and hypotheses for each one. You will also need an interaction hypothesis for both IVs on the DV.

3. What are your specific hypotheses? (In a causal comparative experiment your hypothesis will be about the IV level (group) differences on the DV. Name both IV levels and the DV hypotheses. From the above example with two factors/variables: (1) Female combat veterans will have significantly higher PTSD symptoms rates than male combat veterans. (2) High ranking combat veterans will have significantly higher PTSD symptom rates than low ranking combat veterans. (3) There will be an interaction between gender and rank on PTSD symptom rates.

4. How will you operationalize your independent variable (IV)? Describe their levels/group. (Gender is the IV, and male/female are the two levels). If rank is the IV you could have two or three levels (Private and Sergeant) and to operationalize them you name them and indicate the level/group membership criteria about just that variable).

5. How will you operationalize your dependent variable (DV)? How will it be measured (name the instrument)? In the above example PTSD symptom rate is the DV. You can decide how to measure it, but it will likely be with an already published PTSD assessment.

_____

Quantitative (method) correlational (design)

1. What is the main purpose of your study? (Remember in a correlational design you can determine the strength and direction of a relationship between two or more numeric type variables).

2. What research question are you interested in investigating? (In a correlational design your research question will be about the relationship between the variables - for example: what is the relationship between number of illness per year and number of times hand washing in a day?)

3. What are your specific hypotheses? (In a correlational design your hypothesis will be about the relationship between the variables - for example: teachers who wash their hands more times in a day will have fewer illnesses in a year).

4. How will you operationalize your DVs? How will it be measured/name the instrument? (remember there are no independent variables in a correlation design). You could measure the number of times they hand wash by using a self-report questionnaire. Also on this questionnaire could be a question about the number of illnesses they had during the year. For other variables you can use longer instruments with more than one question.

Qualitative (method) case study (design)

1. What is the main purpose of your study? (Remember in a qualitative case study you can "explore perceptions" from some small group of people.

2. What research questions are you interested in investigating? (There are no hypotheses with this design). For example: (1) what are pediatrician's perceptions about treatments for anxiety in children? (2) How do pediatricians perceive the use of meditation for children with

anxiety? (3) According to pediatricians what information about alternative treatments is desired?

3. Who will your subjects be?

4. Where will you interview them?

5. What are some potential interview questions?

CHAPTER 4: The Purpose Statement and Research Questions/Hypotheses

Okay! So you have a wonderful research worthy topic/idea! You have a problem statement! You have a good understanding of methods/designs. What it next? It is time to develop your purpose statement.

Purpose Statements

There are just a few rules to be aware of with respect to the purpose statement. If the problem statement is the most important 300 words of your dissertation document, then the main purpose statement sentence (the first sentence of your purpose statement) is the most important sentence of the document. Whenever you reiterate the purpose and you will at least one time in each chapter of your dissertation - be sure to use the word **purpose** (not objective, or goal) and be sure to phrase the purpose sentence in the exact same way each time. This is the only sentence that can be reused, and it MUST be reused, so you don't confuse your reader.

The main purpose sentence. Here are the components of this important sentence. You will always begin the purpose statement with a sentence that looks like this... The purpose of this XX study.... You will replace the XXs with the method type (remember qualitative or quantitative) and the design type. You will follow with the few words from the problem statement - specific problem paragraph, specific problem sentence.

Let's say the first part of your specific problem statement sentence read, - "The specific problem is lack of agreement about the efficacy of stress management interventions targeting organizational stress have not been evaluated...." - then your purpose would be the exact flip side of this with just the method and design noted..... "The purpose of the current quantitative true experiment study is to determine the efficacy of stress management interventions targeting organizational stress." **There is no guesswork, there is no need to negotiate or get creative. In black and white you will just report the method and design and the few words from the**

specific problem sentence to tell the reader that you are going to fix the problem with the literature by doing exactly what is called for. Also please note how one is for sure a "problem" and one is for sure a "purpose." If I had a penny for the times students have presented these two things in the exact opposite manner I would be on my second vacation right now!

Alignment. Remember our discussion about alignment. The sections that need to be aligned are the specific problem sentence (the problem with the research that necessitates further research), the main purpose statement sentence, the method/design choice, and the research questions/hypotheses. Some students develop a great specific problem sentence and then come up with a completely different purpose sentence. I can go back and forth with this student several times. I will try to show them the difference by highlighting both sentences and asking them if they seem to be addressing the flip sides of the same issue. When that doesn't work I will take both highlighted sections and show them the two options, if you want your purpose to be xx, then your specific problem has to be xx (the matching flip side); if you want your specific problem statement to be xx then your matching purpose sentence needs to be xx. Even when I spell it out, some students still have a real difficulty understanding this concept of alignment. I don't know why that is. I think it might have to do with concerns about repeating themselves, but that is the dissertation. Over time and with patience on my part and diligence and flexibility on the student's part we get the two sections aligned. Because it is difficult, here are some more examples of matching specific problem sentences and purpose sentences. Test yourself and see if you can come up with the matching problem sentence before you read what I came up with.

Alignment sample #1. The specific problem that prompts this research is the lack of agreement about risk factors for violence in the SMI population, which is needed to inform clinicians serving this population.

The purpose of this quantitative causal comparative study is to determine risk factors for violence in an SMI population.

Alignment sample #2. The specific problem is a lack of experimental research about the efficacy of interventions to increase workplace spirituality to influence employee turnover in the food industry, which is needed to inform stakeholders charged with developing strategies to reduce employee turnover in the food service industry.

The purpose of this quantitative true experiment is to determine the efficacy of interventions to increase workplace spirituality on employee turnover in the food industry.

Alignment sample #3. The specific problem is SRO perceptions about RRP development are unknown and needed to inform strategies to foster effective RRPs.

The purpose of this qualitative, holistic, and single case study is to explore SRO perceptions about RRP development.

Alignment sample #4. The specific problem that prompts this research is information on teacher and student perceptions of technology to enhance learning is needed, in order to inform professional development and training on technology integration in the classroom.

The purpose of this qualitative, embedded, and single case study is to explore teacher and student perceptions of technology to enhance learning.

Comment [JB]: Can you see how each member of the pair is the flipside of the other? If so, you are more than half way there! This is alignment! The RQ section is the last one to keep aligned with these two.

The Rest of the Purpose Statement

What to include in the rest of the purpose statement is usually up to your degree granting institution, but it is usually concise, one paragraph, and extremely straightforward. Most schools have guidelines for this section in terms of length and specifics to include.

What is most common (and if you are in doubt - start with this strategy and then make modifications based on your chairs' feedback) is to open with the main purpose sentence. Then follow with one sentence about why that method and design is most appropriate for the topic. Then follow with one sentence about the study population. Then follow with one sentence about the study sample. Then one sentence about the study variables, then one about data collection, and then one about data analysis. I have some sample purpose statements (both qualitative and quantitative) below.

Research Questions/Hypotheses

Students get nervous about selecting the proper RQ and hypotheses, but there is really no need for such angst. **Depending on your method/design, the RQs and hypotheses are already determined for you, so it is really a matter of just getting it right.** Research questions and hypotheses for quantitative methods look different than those for qualitative methods (also there are no hypotheses for a qualitative study, just research questions). The design makes a difference too. Here are the rules:

1. For a **true experiment** your RQ is about the effect of one variable on another.
   - How does Treatment X reduce PTSD symptoms in combat veterans?
   - H_0. Combat veteran participants receiving Treatment X will have similar PTSD symptom scores as combat veteran participants receiving no treatment.
   - H_1. Combat veteran participants receiving Treatment X will have significantly fewer PTSD symptoms than participants receiving no treatment.

2. For a **causal comparative design** your RQ is about differences between levels of a selected independent variable on a dependent variable.
   - How do managers and employees differ in amount of stress work stress symptoms?
   - H_0. There will be no significant differences between managers and employees on

amount of work stress symptoms.

- H1. There will be a significant difference between managers and employees on amount of work stress symptoms.

3. For a **correlational design** your RQ is about how two or more quantitative dependent variables relate. [Comment JB: Remember: correlational designs fall under the quantitative method]

    - How does the number of stress symptoms in a given month correlate with number of migraine headaches in the same month in trauma nurses?

    - Ho. There will be no correlation between number of stress symptoms and number of migraine headaches in the same month in trauma nurses.

    - H1. There will be a significant positive correlation between number of stress symptoms and number of migraine headaches in the same month in trauma nurses.

4. For a **case study design** your RQ is about perceptions. [Comment JB: Remember: case study designs fall under the qualitative method]

    - How do teachers of foreign languages perceive current instructional methods?

5. For a **phenomenology design** your RQ is about lived experiences. [Comment JB: Remember: phenomenological designs fall under the qualitative method]

    - What are the lived experiences of police officers caught in the line of fire?

Tying Everything Together for Alignment (problem, purpose, RQs)

Well, we got here and it really wasn't that hard, was it! Once you have the problem statement, purpose statement, and RQs sections developed and they are nicely aligned - you can take this great **mini proposal** to your chair for feedback. If a student came to me with such information developed I would fall off my chair (again with this), praise them profusely, and then let them run this excellent project plan! If you follow this guidance and you have a different experience with your chair - please email me!

Sample Purpose Statements and Matching RQs/Hypotheses

Purpose statement sample # 1 - qualitative method/case study design (Prior, 2015). The purpose of this qualitative, multiple-case, holistic study is to explore the physical and psychological needs of employees in the hospitality industry. A multiple, holistic case study was selected for this research because it will allow for the identification of the needs of employees within different restaurant settings. A multiple case study can be more robust and have stronger external validity than a single case because it allows the researcher to examine several settings in order to identify similarities and differences between cases (Baxter & Jack, 2008). A single case is chosen for cases with unusual or unique settings, which is not the case in this study as the restaurant settings will be typical organizations on the east coast of the United States. A holistic case study was chosen because there is a single unit of analysis for each case, employee needs. No subunits were identified and so the holistic design was selected, however, as data unfolds during the study the unit of analysis may need to be reexamined to match the discovery of any new information (Simons & Mawn, 2012; Yin, 2009). The study population is employees from the hospitality industry on the East Coast of the United States. The sample will include 15 employees from the hospitality industry who will be selected via purposive criterion sampling. The sample size of 15 was determined by considering the single point of contact with each participant and the anticipated 90-minute length of the interview (Marshall, Cardon, Poddar, & Fontenot, 2013). Similar qualitative studies have used comparable sizes; for example, Pechlaner and Volgger (2012) reached saturation with 15 interviews and Komppula (2014) attained saturation in 9 interviews. Data collection will include face-to-face interviews using a pilot tested semi-structured interview guide with open-ended questions about the physical and psychological needs of employees in the hospitality industry. Data collected from the qualitative interviews will be transcribed then coded and analyzed with Dedoose software and themes will be clustered according to the variety of needs that employees have at work (Sinkovics & Alfoldi, 2012).

Research Questions
RQ1. What are the physical, extrinsic needs of employees in the hospitality industry?
RQ2. What are the psychological, intrinsic needs of employees in the hospitality industry?
RQ3. Are there differences in extrinsic and intrinsic motivational needs of employees in the hospitality industry across different settings?

> **Comment [JB]:** This RQ addresses the multiple case component of the case study design - the different data collection settings

---

Purpose statement sample #1 - qualitative method/case study design. The purpose of this proposed qualitative, single, embedded case study is to explore the perceptions of learners and faculty members about currently used teaching methods and how to improve them in post-secondary mathematics online courses in order to impact both practice and theory. A case study design within the qualitative approach was deemed most appropriate for this topic, as the needed information, to understand the perceptions of the learners and faculty members in post-secondary mathematics online courses, is a relatively new phenomenon (Yin, 2014). An embedded case was chosen to allow for a comparison of different units of analysis, both faculty and learners. A sample size of 6 to 10 learner participants will be selected from learners who were enrolled within the last three years in one or more post-secondary online mathematics courses in the United States from at least two different institutions. These learners may or may not have successfully completed the mathematics courses. A sample size of 6 to 10 faculty participants will be selected from learners who were enrolled within the last three years in one or more post-secondary online mathematics courses in the United States from at least two different institutions. Both faculty and learner participants will participate in face-to-face semi-structured interviews with the researcher.

The interviews will be facilitated by a field tested; researcher-developed 10 question interview guide created to ascertain information about currently used teaching methods and how to improve them. Data from the learner and faculty participants will be transcribed, coded, put into categories, compared, and synthesized into common themes (Yin, 2014). Microsoft Word will be used to transcribe the interviews. After the data have been analyzed and a draft of the study has been completed, each participant will be able to proofread his or her section of the research--member checking--to verify the accuracy of the analysis without researcher bias (Andrews, 2012; Stake, 2010).

Q1. What are the perceptions of learners about currently used teaching methods in post-secondary online mathematics courses?

Q2. What are the perceptions of faculty about currently used teaching methods in post-secondary online mathematics courses?

Q3. What are the perceptions of learners about how to improve post-secondary online mathematics courses?

Q4. What are the perceptions of faculty about how to improve them in post-secondary online mathematics courses?

Q5. How do faculty member and learner perceptions about post-secondary online mathematics courses compare?

> **Comment [JB]:** This RQ reflects the embedded subunit (learners and faculty) comparison component

---

Purpose statement sample #3 - quantitative method/true experiment design (Beehner, 2015). The purpose of this quantitative experimental two group pretest-posttest study is to determine whether the implementation of a workplace spirituality program impacted turnover intention in multiple food service organizations. The population will be employees of food service industry organizations in the state of Florida. The sample will consist of a minimum of 52 food service employees, with a minimum of 26 employees in the control group, and 26 employees in the experimental group, as determined by a priori sample calculator. The independent variable for this study is a workplace spirituality intervention modified for use in the food service industry. The independent variable has two levels and participants were randomly assigned to receive the workplace spirituality intervention, or no intervention. The dependent variable is turnover intention (measured by the Work Environment Scale). Data analysis will consist of a between groups analysis of variance (ANOVA) to compare turnover intention change scores as a function of participation or non-participation in the intervention (Vogt, 2007), and a nested or hierarchical analysis of variance (ANOVA) to compare turnover intention change scores of subgroups within each group, as a function of participation or non-participation in the intervention.

Q1. To what extent, if any, does the implementation of a workplace spirituality intervention program impact turnover intention among employees in food service organizations?

Q2. To what extent, if any, does the implementation of a workplace spirituality intervention program in different restaurant locations impact turnover intention differently among employees in food service organizations?

$H1_0$. The implementation of a workplace spirituality intervention program (modified version of the Spirituality and Healthcare Workshop) does not impact turnover intention, as measured by scores on the Work Environment Scores survey of subgroups within each group, among employees in food service organizations.

$H1_a$. The implementation of a workplace spirituality intervention program (modified version of the Spirituality and Healthcare Workshop) significantly impacts turnover intention, as measured by scores on the Work Environment Scores survey of subgroups within each group, among employees in food service organizations.

H2$_0$. The implementation of a workplace spirituality intervention program (modified version of the Spirituality and Healthcare Workshop) in different restaurant locations does not impact turnover intention differently, as measured by scores on the Work Environment Scores survey between the subgroups of restaurant locations, among employees in food service organizations in.

H2$_a$. The implementation of a workplace spirituality intervention program (modified version of the Spirituality and Healthcare Workshop) in different restaurant locations does impact turnover intention differently, as measured by scores on the Work Environment Scores survey between the subgroups of restaurant locations, among employees in food service organizations.

Purpose statement sample #4 - quantitative method/causal comparative design (Puhlman, 2016). The purpose of this quantitative causal comparative (ex post facto), nonequivalent group study design is to investigate the impact of a LMASS strategy on customer satisfaction in the health insurance industry. The geographical location for this study is the state of Tennessee. Archived customer satisfaction data will be used to compare customer satisfaction prior to and following LMASS implementation at Health Insurer A. Health Insurer A is a LIHI and leaders of Health Insurer A contracted as a managed care organization (MCO) provider with the Bureau of TennCare to manage a segment of the Medicaid population receiving Tennessee Medicaid benefits. The independent variable is leaderships' application of a LMASS program at Health Insurer A where the independent variable has two levels: (a) prior to LMASS implementation taking place in 2010 and (b) following LMASS implementation in 2012. The level two period includes a one-year learning curve. LMASS at Health Insurer A entails a top-down, bottom up approach where executive leadership listed LMASS as a major component of corporate strategy and created a department where staff is dedicated to lead the organization in LMASS efforts (Health Insurer A, Personal Communication, 2013). The dependent variable is archived customer satisfaction data from both year sets in which a comparison of customer satisfaction prior to and following the LMASS strategy will occur to determine if a change in customer satisfaction occurred. Customer satisfaction data exists within the Consumer Assessment of Healthcare Providers and Systems (CAHPS) Health Plan Survey, and leadership of the US Agency for Healthcare Research and Quality can provide data access to the researcher (HHS, 2011). CAHPS is a program of the U.S. Agency for Healthcare Research and Quality (HHS, 2011), and the CAHPS Health Plan Survey is a standardized quantitative metric from Healthcare Effectiveness Data and Information Set® (HEDIS®) and CAHPS (Healthcare Effectiveness Data and Information Set, 2011). A common method for comparing data from two or more groups is an analysis of variance (ANOVA; Huitema, 2011). Accordingly, a one-way univariate ANOVA will be conducted to evaluate customer satisfaction data from 2010 (prior to LMASS implementation) and 2012 (following the LMASS implementation).

Q1. Will customers who received services from Health Insurer A after LMASS implementation have significantly higher overall customer satisfaction than customers receiving services from Health Insurer A prior to implementation of LMASS.

H1$_0$. Customers who received services from Health Insurer A after implementing LMASS will not have significantly higher overall customer satisfaction than customers receiving services from Health Insurer A prior to implementation of LMASS.

H1$_a$. Customers who received services from Health Insurer A after implementing LMASS will have significantly higher overall customer satisfaction, as indicated by CAHPS, than customers receiving services from Health Insurer A prior to implementation of LMASS.

Purpose statement sample #5 - quantitative method/correlational design (Sylver-Foust, 2015). The purpose of this quantitative non-experimental predictive correlational study is to explore how the dimensions of collegiality, facilitative leadership, and distributed power of the CLS predict employee satisfaction and organizational commitment within federal agencies. The population of the study is approximately 315,000 federal government employees throughout the US. The sample of the study will be 107 participants, as deemed necessary by a priori G*Power analysis to achieve statistical power of .05. The study participants will include full-time federal government employees between the ages of 18 and 65 throughout the US. The predictor variables collegiality, facilitative leadership, and distributed power of the CLS will be measured with already existing instruments. Collegiality will be measured with the Collegiality Scale (CS) developed by Hoy, Smith, and Sweetland's (2003), which provides statistical data about employees' perception of leaders' portrayal of collegiality; as well as employees' perceptions of colleagues' collegiality. Facilitative leadership will be measured with the Facilitative Leadership Scale (FLS) developed by Hirst, Mann, Bain, Pirola-Merlo, and Richver (2004), which yields statistical data about leaders' behaviors in facilitating and promoting collegiality within the workplace. Distributed power will be measured with the Distributed Power Scale (DPS) developed by Slattery and Goodman (2009), and represents employees' perception of distributed power within the organization. To gather statistical data about employee satisfaction, participants will complete the employee satisfaction scale (ESS) developed by Andrews and Withey (1976). Participants will also complete the organizational commitment scale (OCS) developed by Marsden, Kalleberg, and Cook (1993) to gather and examine information regarding the degree of employees' commitment to their organization. Descriptive analyses will include calculation of variable means, standard deviations, and graphs for each of the study variables. Inferential analyses will include multiple regression analysis to determine the predictive relationship of the CLS dimensions collegiality, facilitative leadership, and distributed power (predictor variables) on employee satisfaction and organizational commitment (criterion variables).

Q1. To what extent, if any, does collegiality, facilitative leadership, and distributed power of the CLS predict employee satisfaction in the federal government?

Q2. To what extent, if any, does collegiality, facilitative leadership, and distributed power of the CLS predict organizational commitment in the federal government?

$H1_0$. Collegiality, facilitative leadership, and distributed power of the CLS predict employee satisfaction in the federal government.

$H1_a$. Collegiality, facilitative leadership, and distributed power of the CLS do not predict employee satisfaction in the federal government.

$H2_0$. Collegiality, facilitative leadership, and distributed power of the CLS predict organizational commitment in the federal government.

$H2_a$. Collegiality, facilitative leadership, and distributed power of the CLS do not predict organizational commitment in the federal government.

CHAPTER 5: The Rest of the Front Matter

As I mentioned in the middle of the last chapter you can take your mini proposal idea (problem statement, purpose statement, and research question) to your chair for some initial feedback, even before you develop the rest of the first chapter of your dissertation proposal. Once your chair provides "buy in" to the mini proposal you can develop the rest of the sections for Chapter One (what I refer to as front matter - everything before the lit review) of the dissertation proposal.

There is variability in sections required for Chapter One of your dissertation proposal and dissertation manuscript. Students from some schools need an introduction, some need a significance section, some need a background, some are not allowed to have a background section, some need have a chapter summary, and some don't. Some need to discuss their theoretical framework in Chapter One of the dissertation, some are required to cover the theoretical framework in Chapter Two (the lit review), and some aren't required to cover a theoretical framework.

We know with certainly you will need the sections we covered so far (problem statement, purpose statement, section on research questions) in the first chapter of your dissertation. I will provide information and examples of other possible sections you will need to include in your Chapter One, but do check with your school's proposal/manuscript instructions, so you are not creating extra work for yourself, or missing an important section when you turn it in.

Chairs and committee members can find several things irritating. One is a missing dissertation proposal section (as indicated as required by the school template). The other biggie is when the sections are out of order (from the order indicated in the template). I think we think those two things are such easy things to verify, if these obvious things are not taken care of - then we just assume there are significant issues. I know some chairs who immediately stop reviewing a student's project when they encounter a missing section, extra section, or out order section. SO, the bottom line is, don't veer (at all) from the school proposal/manuscript template.

Theoretical Framework

At my current place of employment students getting a PhD must advance a theory, but students getting an applied doctorate degree (DBA, EdD) do not need to advance a theory - they just need to indentify one to inform their study (more like a conceptual framework). Do you see the difference; it is subtle, but important. Life would be much easier if you could just use a theory to "inform" your study. Attribution theory can be used a theory to **inform** a study about situational and personality characteristics of loved ones versus coworkers. But, if you need to **extend** a theory like attribution theory you will need to come up with an identified problem with the theory that requires an extension, or some clarification to justify additional research to advance/add to a theory. Is this making sense? Let's think about it a different way.

What Theory Extension Means

For many PhD students they need to EXTEND a theory (not only just use it to inform your research ideas as in the case of the applied dissertation). Most students' first attempt at describing why a theory needs to be extended focuses instead on practical ramifications of the study not being conducted. That is good information for certain parts of your dissertation (YOUR PROBLEM STATEMENT), but that type of information does not necessarily relate to a theoretical extension. Remember there is a difference between a theoretical problem and a practical problem. You write about your practical problem as the specific study problem, but you write about this second problem (the theoretical one) separately. Your research will inform both, but likely it will have more practical applications, that is why it is the specific problem that reflects the purpose of your study.

There can be a "gap" in the empirical evidence, but that is not a theoretical gap per se. Identify what is wrong with your selected theory that requires additional research. For example, a practical gap is to inform people using the programs, but a theoretical gap has to be a problem with the theory (e.g., not extended to certain groups, disagreement about aspects of the theory among researchers, etc).

Theories can need to be **extended** because (1) they don't cover a certain population/group, and you need to extend it to a new population to identify the boundary conditions of the theory. (2) Another reason for theory extension is a disagreement in how researchers view the theory. Some researchers say it can be applied all the time, others say it can only be applied in times of stress (altruism/helping theory - is it in place all the time, or only when there is little cost to the helper). (3) A third reason for theory extension is there are competing theories and more research is needed to determine which one may be better (do opposites attract, or do similarities attract).

What is important when finding a theory to extend is to locate some current research to point out the problems with a particular theory. **This type of information can often be found in textbooks and other books (even more so than in empirical article) as such books often explain more than one theory and point out advances and disadvantages of current understanding of the theory.** You can cite the textbook author if they suggested additional research was needed to clarify a theoretical "problem."

Much like with the problem statement you will need to note the problem with current understanding of a particular theory in order to justify the need for more research. Similar to the problem statement (and the practical problem prompting the need for your study), you can't just tell the reader what theory you think needs to be extended, other experts have to agree with you and have to had called for such an extension. Some students need to develop an entire theoretical framework section, others need to just cover the problem with the theory that suggests additional research is needed to extend the theory somewhere in Chapter One. I have included examples of both forms for you. Please try to figure out what is needed. If your template and your chair don't asked for a theoretical framework discussion in Chapter One or in Chapter Two - then by all means consider yourself a little lotto winner and skip the rest of this section... lucky!!

==NOTE: You will not have a research question about your theory per se, but the answers to your RQs will inform/extend the theory! Think about it this way after you develop each RQ you could ask yourself: If I reject this null hypothesis - how will that extend the theory. If I do not reject the null hypothesis - how will that extend the theory. I have a sample of looking at it this way.==

==A student was doing a study on the effects of social support and resilience levels (high and low - for both independent variables) on PTSD symptom number. He selected conditioning theory to extend. He told me..... If I don't reject the null (no difference in PTSD symptoms as a function of social support or resilience level then the theory then that would not provide empirical support for the addition of such variables into Pavlov's conditioning theory. However, if there are significant differences then social support and resilience will work to lessened the fear and associated response involved with an unconditioned stimulus of the combat veterans.==

Short Version Theoretical Framework Section

Here is a short version theoretical framework sample. The point of the short version is to communicate a theory extension is needed based on some citable problem with our current understanding (or even use of) the theory. Similar to the problem statement I have a template. The recipe is: **Sentence #1** - name the theory (cite). **Sentence #2** - describe the theory (cite). **Sentence #3** - note the identified theoretical problem (cite) and what research is needed to extend the theory (solve this identified theoretical problem) and cite that too.

Theoretical framework sample #1. This research will extend the general aggression model (GAM). GAM is a framework that combines mini-theories of aggression into one theoretical framework (Dewall, Anderson, & Bushman, 2011). GAM has been used to explain the relationship between aggression and violence and provides insights about how to reduce aggression (Dewall et al., 2011; Jakhar, 2015; Walters, 2014). However, some researchers argued the superiority of the diathesis-stress model in explaining aggression through a biological and stress response (Ferguson, 2012; Malone, 2012) and research is needed to determine which theory is more appropriate with certain populations. Research has also been called for to determine application of GAM in different populations (DeWall et al., 2011).

Theoretical framework sample #2 (Ulmer, 2016). This research will extend appreciative inquiry (AI) theory. AI is used in higher education, but information is needed to determine the appropriateness of an AI extension to K-12 education (Preskill & Catsambas, 2006; Welsh & Metcalf, 2003). Additionally, clarification of AI in the form of contributing variables has been called for and information is needed about whether or not teacher attitudes toward the accreditation process and professional development are important in AI (Thibodeau, 2011).

Long Version Theoretical Framework Section

You can tell if you need a long version theoretical framework section by noting if there is a heading for such a section in your template, and then what type of heading it is. If your template gives guidelines for pages for a particular section that would be a nice indicator as well. If not, you can always start with the short version and then move to a longer version if additional information is requested. In the long version the whole first paragraph is spent describing the theory. The second paragraph is about how the theory is used in research and current research about the theory. The third paragraph is about the theoretical problem and the citations indicating what additional research is needed to solve the theoretical problem.

Theoretical framework sample #3 (Bennett, 2016). Research is needed to extend social justice theory (SJT). SJT was created and developed in the 1970's, mainly by philosopher John Rawls (Bankston, 2010). According to Bankston (2010), SJT is based on two principles. The first principle is a "…matter of redistributing goods and resources to improve the situations of the disadvantaged" and the second principle focuses on the fact that the disadvantaged have the right to these goods and resources, to align them better with the rest of society (Bankson, 2010, p. 165). SJT theory is used to determine how political and economic principles and events shape society, and how to best utilize resources for society in general regardless of status (Bankston, 2010).

The theoretical problem is the majority of planning and execution of health policy is in response to an event occurring, therefore these policies are limited in scope and do not fully address the needs of populations (Venkatapurman & Marmot, 2011). Further information is needed to address the philosophy of health determinants and social justice (Venkatapurman & Marmot, 2011) and expand SJT (List, 2011). According to List (2011), the needed approach to securing better health care for the underserved communities is through the social justice framework and providing incentives for physicians to treat the disadvantaged populations. Health policies, such as the HITECH Act, are based upon the political beliefs that "…they distribute significant and diverse benefits and burdens across individuals and groups" (Venkatapurman & Marmot, 2011, p. 85). This focus can lead to ethical considerations on how to best justify the use of limited resources within society (Venkatapurman & Marmot, 2011). The philosophical focus of SJT does not fully address the situations of rural people and their health determinants, regardless of the discussions taking place (Khoo, 2013). Information about EMR implementation in rural physicians will add to SJT and extend it to a new population.

Theoretical framework sample #4 (Sylver-Foust, 2015). The theoretical framework expanded in the current research is collegial leadership theory (CLT). CLT was developed from behavioral science research (Davis, 1968); rooted in educational research (Brundrett, 1998); and is part of the social behavior theory, which is used to explain the CLS social constructs related to organizational culture, friendliness, and social connection (Hatfield, 2006). The concept of the CLS was developed as part of the educational development theory (Bush, 2000); is the leading paradigm relating to the management of academic institutions (Brundrett, 1998); and is a leadership and power relationship model (Davis, 1968; Jarvis, 2012).

Researchers have recently examined the CLT to investigate the CLS as part of organizational effectiveness (Akert & Martin, 2012). While investigating organizational effectiveness of the CLS within academia, researchers concluded the implementation of the CLS has a positive and significant influence on: employee interaction, sharing of resources, and collaborative behaviors (Freedman, 2012); professional development, the establishment of common goals, and the alignment of expectations (Hoy et al., 2003; Shah & Abualrob, 2012); employee productivity and effectiveness (Likert, 1977; Shrifian, 2011); employees' motivation, customer satisfaction (Adhikari, 2010); and organizational commitment (Balsmeyer, Haubrich, & Quinn, 1996).

Akert and Martin (2012) employed a quantitative approach to examine the CLT to gain an understanding of the various impacts of distributed power of the CLS by surveying teachers and principals. The distribution of power was determined to be a key aspect of organizational success (Akert & Martin, 2012). Researchers suggested for organizations to be successful, collegially, distributed power, and facilitative leadership of the CLS must be employed (Akert & Martin, 2012; Howze, 2003). However, more research is needed in settings outside of education to determine if such findings will generalize across employment disciplines (Giffords, 2009). Specifically, information about collegiate leadership behaviors is needed in federal agencies (White, Carvalho, & Riordanc, 2011) and would extend the CLT to a new population. Moreover, because most research about the CLS has been conducted in academia, generalizing the findings from previous research outside of academia and to the federal government may not be appropriate due to the differences in organizational structures, stakeholders, missions, and cultures (Giffords, 2009); therefore, additional research is needed. The proposed study will extend the CLT outside of academia into federal agencies and will extend the theory to address the relationship between the CLS and work variables, including, employee satisfaction and organizational commitment, as suggested by (Hatfield, 2006).

A final note about theoretical frameworks. A common misconception about theoretical frameworks (often made by committee members) is that there should be a research question about the theoretical framework. That is indeed incorrect. There should be a research question that will allow the student to use the answer to that research question to extend the theory, but there will not be a specific research question about a theory. Let's look at Sample #4 right above. The theoretical extension information needed is.... can CTL extend outside of academia. You would NOT have a research question asking... RQ. Does CLT extend outside of academia? That is not appropriate. Instead, what you would have was a RQ that was aligned with your method (discussed in the previous chapter), most likely something such as.... RQ. To what extent, if any, do collegiality, facilitative leadership, and distributed power of the CLS predict employee satisfaction in employees of the federal government? This RQ is aligned with the study purpose/specific problem/and study variables. When you address this RQ via your implications you can address how the answer to this RQ impacts the theory of CLT. You can even have a special section in the discussion section about how the findings impact the theoretical framework. What you cannot have is a specific RQ about the theory because then your RQ would not be aligned with your specific problem and purpose (which likely focus more on a practical application) and/or your study variables that are not theoretical.

If someone asks you to include a RQ about your theoretical framework extension you could try to explain what I just did if you feel strongly about it. If not, you could add one in and most likely someone else along the way in the review cycle will have you remove it. When I worked as a Dissertation Consultant I always told students - your chair/committee is always right. If they want it, let's do it - even if it was incorrect. That is something that bothered me about that job! As a Dissertation Chair I make sure I am correct before I request information, or disagree about something I think I know. I know all Dissertation Chairs do NOT make that a priority and I really wish they did!

Significance of the Study Section

If you need a significance of the study section be clear and concise. It will be best to have about two or three paragraphs where you make the case for why the research is important - how it contributes to the literature problem (why more research is needed and what will it clarify). You can also note cautiously how your study can inform practice. If you are required to extend a theory, address how it can inform the theoretical problem. Do not discuss possible outcomes of the analyses (in the proposal) and what it will mean if the hypothesis is supported, but you can revisit this section when you move from your proposal to the manuscript and be more definitive about how your study can contribute to the literature.

Don't play up the significance of the study. I have never ever seen a committee member (or other chair) encourage a student to be bolder with their ideas about why their study is significant. In each and every example of corrections needed for this section the comments are, "please rein this in, your study will not do it," or "it is highly unlikely this 10 person study will solve this theoretical problem, please be more realistic." So promise, with a qualitative study with 10 participants you should not write your study is significant because you will solve world problems or it will give clinicians what they need to treat PTSD. Those are obvious exaggerations, but still try to keep things in perspective. If you are obtaining perceptions about what would be helpful for clinicians treating PTSD write something such as the results might inform future practice by clarifying one particular component. Here are some samples of significance sections.

Significance sample #1 - for the proposal (Sylver-Foust, 2015). This study is practically significant because ineffective leadership within the federal government equates to billions of dollars in avoidable costs associated with employee inefficiencies, duplication of efforts, and increased recruitment and development as a result of employee turnover (GAO, 2012). The results of the study may benefit future researchers, as well as federal government employees and leaders by providing clarification about variables hypothesized to be salient. As employees' perceptions and behaviors are highly affected by the behavior of organizational leaders (Sabir, Sohail, & Khan, 2011; Secretan, 2005); leaders' behaviors must be addressed in strategies for improving employee satisfaction and organizational commitment (PPC, 2013). Moreover, a study focusing on the CLS in a federal culture may lead to strategies to augment effective leadership, which may in turn increase federal employee satisfaction ratings (PPC, 2013).

This study is also theoretically significant. The investigation of the study variables will enhance the theoretical literature on the CLT within non-academic organizations as called for (Singh, 2013). This study may provide information that can be used to enhance federal government leaders' understanding of the impact of promoting the adoption of CLT, or aspects of the CLT, on employee satisfaction and organizational commitment as needed (Giffords, 2009; Singh, 2013).

Comment [JB]: See, small, but important

Comment [JB]: May lead to .....

Significance sample #2 - updated after the data was analyzed for the final manuscript (Cerge, 2014). The study was practically significant as the results of the investigation provided needed information about whether or not robot teachers can be used as a valuable tool to improve academics and increase science motivation in at-risk ninth graders (Chen et al., 2010; Cummins et al., 2008; Ludi, 2011; Negron et al., 2011). This information was important to ascertain as repeated failure at this level often leads to an increase in frustration, a decrease in motivation, and eventual school dropout (Neild et al., 2008), and strategies to support such learners (to increase motivation) was called for.

The results of the results the study may ultimately impact academic achievement in a settings with teacher shortages. Because there is a shortage of teachers in the Virgin Islands (Morrison, 2007), the current study findings may provide support for other researchers who suggested robotic teachers may be utilized in the areas of basic math and reading to assist at-risk learners who are in high school and are in danger of failing (Swanson & Spencer, 2011). While robots will never replace the human teacher, the current findings are significant as in the future they may inform stakeholders charged with facilitating instruction by clarifying needed information about robot efficacy in teaching (Chen & Chang, 2010; Han et al., 2009). The study filled an identified gap in the literature and call for information on the value of robotic instructors at the high school level in the areas of science motivation and science achievement (Hashimoto et al., 2013; Park et al., 2011). While the results from the current study will not lead to the eradication of certain human teaching methods, the study findings may provide information for educators that could possibly support student motivation and science success in ninth grade at-risk classrooms.

Introduction Section

The introduction section most likely presents before the study problem and study purpose sections. Indeed, it is usually the very beginning section of the dissertation. Students are often stressed about how to begin this important section of the document and wonder how broad they should be what the opening sentence should be, and how much specific information is needed, etc. The school I work for has a strict 2-page limit for the study introduction section. You should check to see if your school has a page restriction, and/or the introduction section guidelines.

Even when there is not a hard limit it is best to keep this section short and concise as well. You don't want your reader 10 pages into the document not really knowing what it is about. I instruct my students to use the two pages to expand on the general problem from the problem statement in one page (remember you only had three sentences to discuss it in the problem statement and you likely wanted to say a bit more about it). Include such an expansion in this introduction section, so the salience of the general problem really stands out. Then spend the second page of the introduction describing the problem with the literature that suggests the need for additional research. If this introduction section presents right before the problem statement it is the perfect transition to the concise problem statement. Almost all sentences are cited in the introduction. Avoid creative writing, colloquialisms, and anthropomorphic writing.

Here are some notes about paragraph organization and grammar in general. Paragraphs should only be about one main idea (this is very important in technical/academic/scholarly writing - the style for the dissertation). Make sure each paragraph has a topic sentence that reflects each and every sentence in the paragraph. The topic sentence may or not be cited, but the rest of the sentences in the paragraph should be cited. Within each paragraph the sentences are presented with general ideas appearing first and then moving to the specific. Be sure to cover what information is needed (cite the authors who called for the research and indicate specifically what research they called for) to fix the literature problem (you know, the specific problem). You can also note the practical applications of the information with citations.

You will begin to recognize some of the information from past samples in this book. It might strike you that it seems like the students are repeating themselves. It is the case that you have to refer to things (especially to general problem, specific problem, variables, and purpose) consistently and similarly throughout the document. It is almost a case of presenting very similar information (about the need for the study to defend your proposal) similarly, but with a twist for whatever section is needed for the dissertation. You cannot copy and paste from section, you will need to say similar things, but in a new (but not too creative) manner. Remember the only sentence/info that can be copied and pasted (and needs to be) is the main purpose statement sentence and the RQ. The main purpose statement sentence and the RQs have to be 100% consistent throughout. Here are some sample introduction sections. I included several so you can get the feel for how to sum up your topic concisely, provide definitions when essential, and still present the research problem (the problem with the literature prompting the need for additional

research - your rationale) all within 2 pages.

Introduction sample #1 (Beehner, 2015). The topics of employee turnover and turnover intention have been investigated for more than 50 years (Holtom, Mitchell, Lee, & Eberly, 2008); however, employee turnover remains an important issue and challenge for contemporary organizations (Hassan, Hassan, Din Khan, & Naseem, 2011). Employee turnover is defined as the ratio of the number of employees replaced during a specific timeframe in an organization or industry to the average number of employees in that organization or industry (Iqbal, Kokash, & Al-Oun, 2011). Turnover intention is defined as the behavioral attitude of a person desiring to withdraw from an organization (Aydogdu & Asikgil, 2011), and shown to be an effective predictor of actual turnover (Vardaman, 2012).

Employee turnover is a significant problem in the accommodation and food service industry. In 2012 the voluntary turnover rate for employees in this industry was 39.7%, more than double the overall turnover rate of 18.8% in the United States (U.S. Department of Labor, 2013c). The accommodation and food services industry comprises organizations engaged in providing lodging to customers, and in the preparation of beverages, meals, and snacks for immediate consumption (U.S. Department of Labor, 2013b). The voluntary turnover rate for the food service industry segment was estimated to be 80% in 2012 (Quick Service Restaurant, 2012). Employee turnover adversely impacts organizations, in terms of the direct costs of recruitment and selection (Jacobs, 2011), and the indirect costs of reduced productivity (Hausknecht & Trevor, 2011; Shaw, 2011; Tracey & Hinkin, 2008), service disruption (Hausknecht & Trevor, 2011), and reduced revenue (Shaw, 2011; Tracey & Hinkin, 2008).

Workplace spirituality is a variable gaining prominence in the investigation of the antecedents of turnover intention (Giacalone & Jurkiewicz, 2010). In order to reduce employee turnover, researchers examined relationships between modifiable factors and turnover intention (Radzi et al., 2009), including workplace spirituality (Hong, 2012). Researchers demonstrated workplace spirituality and turnover intention to be negatively correlated, with increased levels of workplace spirituality resulting in reduced employee turnover (Crawford, Hubbard, Lonis-Shumate, & O'Neill, 2009; Hong, 2012). However, the focus of research on the relationship between workplace spirituality and turnover intention was with limited industries and geographic areas (Crawford et al., 2009; Hong, 2012). Moreover, experimental research is needed to determine the impact of workplace spirituality interventions on employee attitudes including turnover intention (Geh & Tan, 2009; Tevichapong, Davis, & Guillaume, 2010). Information concerning the antecedents of turnover intention is also needed to provide stakeholders with sufficient information necessary for the development of employee turnover strategies in the food service industry (Kim & Jogaratnam, 2010; Tracey & Hinkin, 2008).

> **Comment [JB]:** In the proposal verbs like this will be in future tense. When you go back and update the proposal after your research is conducted (for the dissertation defense) you will change this verb to past tense

Introduction sample #2 (Matney, 2015). The Developmental Disabilities Assistance and Bill of Rights Act include a national goal and principles that support providing people with intellectual and developmental disabilities (DD Act, 2000). Councils on Developmental Disabilities (DD councils) were created to address important issues for people with developmental disabilities and their families through advocacy, capacity building and systems change (DD Act, 2000; National Council on Disability, 2011). Additionally, DD councils are obligated to honor the principles of the Developmental Disabilities Act (DD Act) through the involvement of people with developmental disabilities as council members, serving in leadership roles where they can demonstrate their competence and capacity to make decisions (DD Act, 2000). The paid leadership position for a DD council is provided by the executive director (DD Act, 2000). DD council executive directors implement the legislative mandate to include people with developmental disabilities in council work; however existing strategies and actions result in less than meaningful participation on boards, committees, and councils by people with developmental disabilities (Caldwell, Hauss, & Stark, 2009; Radermacher, Sonn, Keys, & Duckett, 2010) and a lack of leadership guidance support materials exists (Frawley & Bigby, 2011; National Council on Disability, 2011).

Throughout history, people with developmental disabilities have not been afforded equal opportunities to participate in society (Mayer, 2012). Current research demonstrates a lack of participation by people with developmental disabilities in social and political structures (Bess, Prilleltensky, Frawley & Bigby, 2011; Mayer, 2012). This lack of participation contributes to further inequality and the marginalization of people with developmental disabilities (Caldwell et al., 2009; Frawley & Bigby, 2011; Radermacher et al., 2010). Moreover, as meaningful involvement in DD council work can strengthen feelings of self-determination, a core principle of the DD Act, the preparation of DD council executive directors to support the social inclusion of members with developmental disabilities is vital to address.

Although researchers explored the perspectives of people with disabilities regarding inclusion processes in social and civic structures; an exploration of council leaders' perspectives of knowledge, supports, impact, and preparation strategies related to the inclusion of members with developmental disabilities is needed, as leaders are responsible for implementing inclusion processes for people with disabilities on councils (Bess et al., 2009; Caldwell et al., 2009; Frawley & Bigby, 2011; Harris et al., 2012). Information about DD council executive director perspectives regarding current knowledge, supports, impact, and preparation strategies may allow for the development of leadership guidance support materials (Bigby, 2011). This information may ultimately be used to provide DD council executive directors with knowledge and information about implementation processes, and the provision of effective leadership to their staff and DD council membership at large as they operationalize the intent and purpose of the Developmental Disabilities Assistance and Bill of Rights Act of 2000 (DD Act).

Introduction sample #3 (Prior, 2015). Motivated employees are good for business because they effectively work to reach organizational objectives (Mathison & Vinja, 2010). Lack of motivation among employees can impair organizational success because unmotivated workers perform with less engagement and negative attitudes that can impede the attainment of organizational goals (Deci & Ryan, 2014; Mackenzie & Peters, 2014; Tews, Stafford, & Michel, 2014). Maintaining employee motivation continues to be an important issue for most organizations (Delia & Georgiana, 2013) and improving motivation is especially important in the hospitality industry because more than half of the workers are unmotivated (Kara, Uysal, Sirgy & Lee, 2013; Lee & Ok, 2014; Tews et al., 2014).

In an effort to improve motivation among employees, hospitality managers and human resource planners strategize to provide effective reward programs and customized incentives (Pechlaner & Volgger, 2012; Tracey, 2014). Extrinsic rewards, such as salary and financial bonuses, are frequently used to motivate workers because such rewards give employees tangible reasons to perform. Intrinsic rewards, like recognition and promotion, are used less frequently, but they also motivate employees because they provide psychological satisfaction and meet needs that originate within the employee (Chileshe & Haupt, 2010; Furnham, Eracleous, & Chamorro-Premuzic, 2009; Kara et al., 2013). Empirical evidence suggests intrinsic and extrinsic rewards are both effective for improving employee motivation, especially when the appropriate reward is allocated to match the specific behavior and preference of the employee (Harris & Ogbonna, 2012; Laurie & Cherry, 2013; Lee & Ok, 2014). Still, other researchers disagree about how to motivate employees overall. Whereas some researchers have suggested motivation is increased by developing a customizable incentive plan with plenty of intrinsic rewards (Halkos & Bousinakis, 2010; Kumar & Raghavendran, 2013), others argued for certain employees extrinsic rewards are most effective for energizing work behavior (Tan & Waheed, 2011). Still other researchers argued organizational factors (Patnaik, 2011; Pettigrew, 2012) and leadership style supersede all rewards for motivating employees (Ballaro & O'Neil, 2013; Kara et al., 2013). Based on the disagreement about reward efficacy and the lack of a set formula for what motivates workers, information about motivation among hospitality employees is needed before strategies to increase can be improved. In particular, more understanding is needed about the individual needs of employees in this industry (Mackenzie & Peters, 2014; Tews et al., 2014).

According to Herzberg et al.'s (1959) motivation-hygiene theory, in order for extrinsic and intrinsic rewards to be effective, they must align with the changing needs of workers while preventing a state of dissatisfaction for the employee (Halkos & Bousinakis, 2010; Hao & Zihanxin, 2011). Although researchers identified organizational factors and effective leadership styles are important for motivating hospitality workers (Kara et al., 2013; Tudor, 2011), improving work motivation occurs from having the appropriate mix of extrinsic and intrinsic rewards for the worker so that dissatisfaction is reduced (Chileshe & Haupt, 2010). Research is needed to extend Herzberg et al.'s (1959) motivation-hygiene theory to a new population by examining psychological and physiological needs among hospitality workers.

Introduction sample #4 (Sylver-Foust, 2015). An organization's achievement hinges on leaders' ability to utilize resources, which increases the likelihood for successful accomplishment of the organizational mission (Ciulla, 2006). A leader is defined as an individual who can influence others to sacrifice their personal dreams and pursue a collective purpose through the demonstration of leadership (George & Sims, 2007). Explicit behaviors leaders manifest have been shown to both negatively and positively impact employees' perspectives and productivity (Rooke & Torbert, 2005). Specifically, ineffective leaders often demonstrate a lack of leadership and behaviors that employees perceive as unsupportive and deficient, which often affect organizational effectiveness, insofar as decreasing employee satisfaction and organizational commitment (Ciulla, 2006; Freedman, 2012).

Some researchers suggested leaders should be required to demonstrate the collegial leadership style (CLS), as a method for improving organizational effectiveness (Barth, 2006). Leaders, who demonstrate the CLS improve employee skills, invoke trust, motivate employees, and promote a positive culture with the CLS dimensions collegiality, distributed power, and facilitative leadership (Brundrett, 1998; Howze, 2003; Shrifian, 2011). Although the majority of research on the CLS has been conducted in academic cultures such as primary schools, universities, and libraries (Akert & Martin, 2012), some research on the topic has been conducted in hospitals, restaurants, and Roman Catholic dioceses (Adhikari, 2010; Lazega & Wattebled, 2011; Padgett, 2013). The research results on the topic are mixed with some researchers maintaining the CLS is excessively complex and time consuming; thus, suited for academic and professional cultures (Thorpe & Kalischuk, 2003). Conversely, other researchers suggested the CLS is suitable for all organizational cultures, as it fosters accountability, creativity, and productivity (Singh, 2013). Research on leaders' utilization of the CLS in federal agencies has not yet been conducted, but is needed to understand its impact (Joaquín & Park, 2013).

The organizational cultures of the United States (US) federal government include over 2.1 million employees across all fifty states and is regarded the largest employer in the US (Department of Labor [DOL], 2012). Based on the opinions of all 1.6-million federal employees surveyed, employee satisfaction and commitment have deteriorated the last three consecutive years with a rating of 57.8%, (Partnership for Public Change [PPC], 2013). Leadership effectiveness has been the critical element that drove the decline in employee satisfaction and commitment as it has been the lowest scoring constituent with an average rating of 51.8% (PPC, 2013). Indeed, the primary reason federal government employees left their job was due to ineffective leadership (US Government Accountability Office [GAO], 2012). Strategies to facilitate effective leadership in the federal government are clearly needed; however, before suggestions for improvement can be made research is called for about the efficacy of the CLS within other populations (Singh, 2013).

Introduction sample #5 (Ulmer, 2016). The emphasis on the accountability in education in the United States has received great attention since the enactment of No Child Left Behind legislation in 2001. As a consequence of having a de-federalized education system, it is important for a process to exist to determine the credibility of institutions of learning (Statler, 1961; Supovitz, 2009). School accreditation emerged as the tool for determining credibility and trustworthiness in institutions of learning.

In the last decade, schools and school districts have increasingly been challenged in maintaining accreditation. For example, in 2008 Clayton School District in Georgia became the first school district to lose accreditation since Duval County School System in Florida in 1969. Then, in January 2011, Burke County School District in Morganton, NC, lost accreditation (AdvancED, 2011, sec. News Release). Also in 2011 Kansas City Public Schools were classified unaccredited, and by 2012 two additional school districts in Missouri had lost accreditation and 11 school districts had been placed on provisional accreditation (Missouri Department of Elementary and Secondary Education, 2012).

Although many variables influence accreditation, such as data-informed instruction (Ingvarson & Rowe, 2008) and comprehensive assessment systems that drive school-improvement endeavors (Bernhardt, 2009), teachers are the common variable that connects other variables (Fullan, 2008). Additionally, teachers have been shown to be critical in helping achieve desired educational outcomes (DuFour, DuFour, Eaker, & Karhanek, 2010), implementing educational plans to drive change (Gray, 2009), and ensuring that continuous-improvement endeavors become embedded in schools (Boonen, Van Damme, & Onghena, 2013). In particular, teacher attitudes toward any facet of education, environment, or culture have been found to effect student achievement (Stronge, 2007; Wilkerson & Lang, 2007). Researchers also suggested teacher attitudes toward the accreditation process (Wood, 1999) and teacher attitudes about professional development (e.g., Torff & Sessions, 2009) might effect accreditation outcome scores. However, the empirical research is inconclusive on how teacher attitudes toward accreditation process, the vehicle to ensure educational quality, and professional development, the mechanism to implement the accreditation process, and the interaction between these two variables exist on actual accreditation outcome scores (Boonen et al., 2013; Singh & Stoloff, 2008).

Information is also needed to inform Appreciative Inquiry (AI) Theory: a theory based on the premise that positivity produces a positive effect. If this AI premise is consistent in education accreditation, then one positive variable in the educational process, such as teacher attitudes, should positively effect accreditation (Levine, 2011; Miller, Drill, & Behrstock, 2010). Although AI has been observed as a positive practice concept for evaluation (Preskill & Catsambas, 2006) and researchers indicated that AI added value to the accreditation process in higher education

(Thibodeau, 2011), information is needed to determine if positive teacher attitudes toward accreditation processes and professional development effected accreditation outcome scores at the K-12 level (Miller et al., 2010).

Background Section

I like the think of the Background Section for Chapter One to be a mini lit review, but I mean really mini. When a student is struggling with trying to figure out what information to include in this section I tell them (if it is before they developed their lit review) to draft an outline for their future lit review. Then instead of having a whole section about the lit review outline section, have one paragraph about it for this background section. Present the paragraphs in the exact order as you plan to do in the lit review.

At the school I currently teach, students' don't develop their Background Sections until a mini lit review has been established, so for these students, I instruct them to just develop about one paragraph for each main section in the mini lit review and present the information in order of the lit review. As with the introduction section, most sentences in the Background Section will be cited. Each paragraph will be about one main idea. Each paragraph will have a topic sentence. Each sentence should only about one idea. Each sentence in the paragraph should logically connect to the previous one, and the order of sentence presentation should go from general evidence/information to more specific information at the end of the paragraph.

Summary of Chapter One

Some schools call for a summary of Chapter One, some do not. Again, check your school template to make sure. If you don't have a template it is a good idea to get a couple of your chairs favorite dissertations (preferably they have chaired) to use as a model. Then if you develop your proposal like your chair's fav she really can't argue with you about why you did or did not include a certain section. You can just say you were following the sample. If you need a summary, as with all chapter summaries in the dissertation, make it clear and concise. I suggest only one or at most two sentences from each section in the chapter.

Remember you can't copy and paste the sentences into the summary, but you can easily redraft them with the most important information needed. Based on what we have covered and what I predict will be needed for your dissertation proposal you should include: one sentence about the topic in general (from the intro), one sentence about the general problem, one sentence about the specific problem, the copy and pasted main purpose statement sentence, one sentence about data collection and analysis (if you included that in the purpose section), one sentence about the theoretical framework, and one sentence about the significance of the study.

The majority of feedback requiring revisions for summaries is that committee members feel they are unfocused and too long. If a chapter summary is more than one page you can be pretty sure it is too long. Only include information you covered in the chapter in the summary - do not present any new information - as that is not a summary :) That should do it for Chapter One of your Dissertation Proposal! Onward to the lit review!

CHAPTER 6: The Literature Review

The literature review chapter of your dissertation will most likely be the longest (in length contributing to the document), and will take the longest to develop. It is an important section! This section also really distinguishes students in terms of their technical/academic writing skills. In the previous chapters of this text about the dissertation front matter we had templates and specific instructions to follow. I find that even students with poor technical writing skills can develop a sufficient front matter without needing much editing assistance from me. That is not the case for the lit review.

Right away, when reading your lit review, it will become apparent to your chair if you have problems with academic writing and quite possibly nothing will be more frustrating to them. As a member of the dissertation chair club. I can tell you the thing we find most challenging is a student's lack of skill with technical/academic writing (and incorrect use of APA style) when we are trying to assist that student with the finalization of their lit review. It is challenging to be sitting in front of a 40 page review of the literature and not being able to make it through a sentence without having to guess what the students means to say with their writing. I haven't seen anything result in chair burnout quite like this problem. When a chair gets a student who is good at technical writing - and it is time for a lit review review - we feel like we won the lottery. If I can suggest anything it will be to make sure you take time to hone your academic writing and APA skills for this lit review section. Please see my additional resources section for more info about scholarly writing. It will REALLY behoove you to hone these skills before you ask your chair to review a large piece of your lit review work. Moreover (and this is not the best news, but it is interesting) I have seen significant design problems go unrecognized because a group was bamboozled by excellent writing skills.

It is true that you most likely entered grad school without the requisite academic writing skills. We are taught to write differently in high school, college, and for most grad school classes. The dissertation requires a completely different type of writing - scientific/academic/technical writing (scholarly writing). As I mentioned earlier, such skills will not likely be taught during your grad school classes, so where will you acquire these coveted skills. You can pick up on this style of scholarly writing when you read empirical study write -ups (research articles) published in peer reviewed journals (not other's dissertations published in ProQuest by the way, and/or not even your text books). You can review information about scholarly/technical/scientific writing on your own outside of your dissertation courses (see my additional resources appendix for several recommendations about scholarly writing and APA style). You can work with your schools' writing services team (most schools have these), you can hire an editor from an outside company, or you can rely on your chair to point out what is not scholarly and how to fix it. I do not mind when my students select the chair option (I do feel like it is part of my job to teach technical writing skills). Still I can tell you as we (me and the student unskilled in technical writing) go back and forth with the comments, revisions, more comments, more revisions, about their writing we can spend months to in some cases years on just this one component. The variability comes from how quickly the students can grow from the feedback. Some students consistently make use of the Oxford comma (WHICH IS MANDATORY IN APA STYLE!!!) after the first time I mention it in a comment. Other students can get this same exact comment 15 times and still not incorporate it into their skill set. I am not sure what causes the variability - but I think it is responsible for the chair frustration and extra time for projects (when chairs are charged with the technical writing training). I include information about other technical writing hot spots chairs find frustrating in my long lit review sample below.

It will behoove you to do some research on technical writing before turning in your lit review to your chair and to proof your work to make sure it is the best version it can be. I promise things will go a lot faster if your chair and committee think you can write well (scientifically). That seems to be a fact. If your technical writing skills are really poor and your chair notes this on more than three occasions - and your work with my suggested resources are not resulting in growth - do yourself a favor and check with your school to see how they can help. You may take a writing class, they may offer writing coaching, and they may have other resources you find it easier to connect with. If you begin to feel like the writing part may become a deal breaker for this whole thing, then by all means ask your chair if they would allow you to use an editor. Some chairs don't like when students work with outside services. Some insist on it. It would be good to get your chair's opinion. In the end though it will be your decision and with most things in life - you have to do what you have to do.

The Timing of it All

Should you start the project by developing the lit review first, or the front matter first? When I started coaching I wanted the student to do what they felt most comfortable with. Over time I noticed those starting with their lit review were taking one or more years longer to complete! I then noted this observation for students and recommended we work on the front matter first. Some readers may be questioning, how the heck can I write the front matter if I haven't done the lit review. Smart readers.

Here is the strategy I recommend, as you read the first five empirical research articles (remember that whole thing from Chapter Two of this book), use the article critique categories to write down the answers/notes (remember most of the information called for on the review form can be used in the study write-ups needed for the lit review). This obviously won't be enough for an entire dissertation literature review, but if you read the most current five articles on the topic (and focus on the critique categories) you will likely develop a pretty decent understanding of the literature (from the current study discussed in the literature as well as the study author's literature review). It is also likely you will need to read two or more sets of *five more articles* when you are developing your problem statement, so you could arrive at this juncture (this one I am suggesting) having read about 15-20 articles on your topic. Remember these are current articles and other important ones you found (through the reference sections of the current articles). I am certain 15-20 articles are enough to develop a decent outline for your literature review.

Why start with an outline? Another good question. I like the outline because it will allow your chair an opportunity to provide early feedback on the sections you are planning. Once you get their buy in - it will be protective for you! If they "sign off" on the outline you can feel better about developing a significant chuck of information about it. Chairs are not always out to get you anyway. It is likely your chair has some good suggestions about additional sections when they see your outline. Another reason I like the outline is to help students see early on that the organization for the lit review should be a presentation of general ideas first and then get closer and closer to the specific variables (funnel) in the proposed research (with a real focus of why additional research is needed).

REMEMBER - the purpose of the lit review is to provide a critical analysis of the empirical literature related to your topic, so the reader can appreciate the need for additional study. The format is also to SHOW (what research is needed) and not just TELL (what research is needed). You SHOW this by providing a review of the literature, or pointing out gaps/weaknesses with the current studies on this topic to justify of your line.

Once the lit review outline is commented on and "approved" by your chair enter those main headings into a blank Word doc (oh yeah, type lit review on the top heading too - it just makes you feel good) and let's get started. We can sit around for two weeks or two years contemplating this lit review step. It is up to you. When you sit down to write it you will see it can get done rather quickly. As with most dissertation things - the longest part is the contemplating and procrastinating. We contemplate because we don't know how to do these things - not any more with this book! We procrastinate because we don't think it will be good enough - not any more with this book! Let's just keep going with these concrete actions and get this dissertation done already!

From Outline to Text

This is my favorite strategy, so I'm sticking with it, and sharing it here. Once you have the headings in the Word doc get a binder and develop a section for each of your lit review sections. If you have a lot of articles, get a binder for each section! If you are not a fan of binders, or printing articles, create folders on your computer instead of binders (how old is she anyway you are thinking now!). I am young, but old school - I like to print out the articles and the critique forms - sheesh.

Decide which section you are going to work on today. Make a plan. I have scheduled 1 hour for dissertation writing today (this is you talking). I will work on the xx section. Now, sit down and start doing it. You don't have to re-read the article. The notes about the article have already been taken! Review the notes and copy and paste the info into the Word doc section. This only works if you didn't copy your answers to the critique questions verbatim from the article. Because of this - I suggest students answer the review critique questions in their own words (it will be easier to think of your own words at this point anyway), so you can just copy and paste into the lit review). Do this for a few of the articles in the binder. Add some sentences to string things together. Try to synthesize the articles and organize it so the section in total makes sense.

If you don't finish with the entire section during that work session, jot down your stopping point on a post it (I left off discussing xx - remember to include xx tomorrow). I am a big fan of writing myself these place-keeping notes and putting them on the top of my work folder. Then tomorrow, or your next work session (it should really be tomorrow :) check out your post it note to yourself, sit down, and go. I find this post it left off point reminder strategy really works to minimize the *warm up period* that is sometimes needed when warming up to difficult tasks.

If you are consistently feeling the need to clean your desk, or organize your office before you can write (which is a warm up task I think), then be sure to add that time in to your "dissertation work time." I think you know what I am getting at! Okay, let's keep writing. What about 30 minutes a day? What about one hour a day? What about one hour every other day? What time is it easiest for you to write? Figure everything out and make a plan and then just do it. You will be so happy when it is done. Not working on it is stressing you out and making you anxious. Remove all of that non-working time and stress and let's just keep writing. You can do it!

Hot Spots and How to Avoid Them

1. A common mistake dissertation students make is to provide "infomercial type" information on their topic, or present information about how to solve their identified general problem in the lit review (if we know how to solve the general problem then why do we need your study - why don't we just go out and do the things these other authors are suggesting to solve the problem). This type of information does not justify additional research, AND it even suggests that no more research is needed - so it's like a deal breaker for your project. Still, each and almost every student sends me a first lit review draft of an infomercial about how to solve a problem.

REMEMBER: The purpose of a literature review is to provide a critical analysis of the research (by pointing out weaknesses that relate to your study) that will allow the reader to see why more research is needed. You can provide some background material for things that are essential for the reader to know, but this is not a term paper, story, or infomercial.

The lit review is a review of the empirical literature (a critical and synthesized review) that allows the reader to see what research is needed. Not what needs to be done to fix a problem, or what other researchers' recommended should take place to fix a problem (based on their findings), but what problems are there with the existing literature...that require additional study. That is the purpose of the lit review - to provide a justification for your particular study.

2. Still, when you point out a gap or weakness, make sure it is related to your study, otherwise you will lead the reader to think that different research, from what you are proposing is the next step in the research process (e.g., If you are not including gender as a variable in your study then do not point out weaknesses that researchers did not consider gender and write that more research about gender is needed). You would be surprised how frequently this happens!

3. Sometimes during a writing work session it is important to just get some information out of your head/the critique notes and onto the computer. Then go back and make it really presentable. Here is how:

The most important thing you can do as you draft your lit review is follow the MEAL technique. In the MEAL technique a paragraph should begin with a Main idea: Topic sentence stating the focus of the paragraph (no citation). Evidence: Paraphrase from source(s) to support the topic sentence. Analysis: Explanation and evaluation of the evidence cited and its relevance in the student's own words. Lead out: Wrap-up for the paragraph, leading the reader to transition to the next paragraph (and the next point/topic sentence). It is essential you use the MEAL technique for the development of your lit review.

4. Organization of the overall lit review seems to be a stumbling block for students. Envision the presentation of the chapter/information as a funnel. Begin broad (general information sections) then the specific sections (closer to the topic). You can organize the sentences within each paragraph like this as well - general sentences appear first in the paragraph, then present more specific sentences toward the end of the paragraph.

    5. The next most common stumbling block is a lack of a topic sentence for a paragraph (we just went over this in the MEAL section - I know. But when you know what I know you will say this more than once!). The next stumbling block is when the topic sentence does not reflect all of the sentences in the paragraph. The next is when each sentence doesn't logically connect with sentence right before it. The next is when a paragraph is about more than one main idea and/or when a sentence is about more than one main idea. Make it a priority to master these ideas and make your written work reflect them.

    6. Each sentence also needs to be proofed for clarity and grammar. I hate to say it and hate to focus on it, but it just really does matt. Another problem is when the information you are writing makes sense in your head (because you know all about it), but it the words you chose to put down don't clearly capture your points. Because of this you have to step away from your work (return to the section the next day) and proof it from the **readers' perspective** and make sure that the information is clear, succinct, and correct.

> **Comment [JB]:** Notice my use of the Oxford comma before "and" here. The use of the Oxford comma is essential in APA style and chairs get irritated when they have to add these for you

    7. Each sentence also needs to be proofed for APA style problems. APA style problems really stick out in the literature review. I will point out some of the most common errors I see in the margin comments of the lit review samples that follow. For a great review of the most popular list see Onwuegbuzie, Combs, Slate, and Frels (2010). Dissertation students are not the only ones who make APA style errors. It is actually a bit concerning how many published authors have seemingly not read the manual. Please read the manual!

    8. You should not mention yourself (as you, or as the researcher) at any time in the dissertation), this is my and other old school writer's preference. For sure you don't want to mention yourself or even anything about your study in the lit review. Your research hasn't been

conducted yet; you can't review it :) Don't mention your future study at all. You will repeat your main purpose sentence in the introduction to the lit review, but that is it for you mentioning your study in the lit review. You can note that additional research is needed (frame it that way), what type of additional research is needed and why, but DO NOT write - my study is going to be on, or that's why this project on xx is needed.

Some samples follow. The first sample is only minimally synthesized with other research and it is intended to be an example of an experiment write-up. It includes a lot of information about the published experiment's method, because this student wants to expand on the explained research and needs to point out the study weaknesses - that prompt the need for more study. When your study plan is very similar to a published study you should point out that study weaknesses, so to lead your reader to see additional research (besides the published info you are critiquing is needed). In those cases you can provide specific details about published research and their methods.

Samples

Lit review sample #1 - **study write-up.** Not all researchers corroborated Smith and Jones' (2011) findings. Lee (2012) conducted a case study and used qualitative and quantitative data to reveal elementary teachers perceptions about VAM as a teacher evaluation tool as well as the overall evaluation process. Participants were teachers from an urban public school district who responded to teacher efficacy ratings based on VAM scores published in a Los Angeles newspaper. In the initial phase of the study 23 of the 376 participants who submitted comments to the newspaper database completed a study questionnaire about VAM approaches to evaluation. The questionnaire responses and newspaper database comments were reviewed to inform the second and third phases of the study which involved one-on-one interviews (18 participants) and four focus group sessions to garner information for content analysis on teacher's perspectives on administration's role in evaluation, teacher efficacy, and how to measure it. The questionnaire included six open ended (qualitative) and three closed ended (quantitative) questions to reveal the extent of agreement or disagreement with VAM components, the understanding of the purpose of evaluation, and teacher evaluation in general. The semi-structured interview guide, used for the one-to-one interviews, were designed to encourage a dialogue on pros and cons of VAM, definitions of teacher efficacy, and feelings about their evaluation process. Finally, the focus group protocol included talking points to encourage a dialogue on effective evaluation approaches and alternatives. The findings from the qualitative database review of newspaper comments suggested 77% of the comments were negative toward or disagreed with VAM approaches (Lee, 2012). Based on the questionnaire findings, it was noted 67% disagreed with their VAM ratings,

90% disagreed with the usage of VAM approaches to some extent, and 57% of the teachers believed VAM should be included in the evaluation component to only the smallest extent (0-10%). Lee reported teachers noted the purpose of teacher evaluation was to help improve teacher practice. In Lee's analysis of the relationship between value-added rating and the school's Academic Performance Index (API) a small positive correlation was revealed. That is API score was correlated with a school growth as measured by value-added ratings. Corroborating Despain and Juarez-Torres (2004) finding that half of their respondents did not support their current observation based evaluation system, Lee (2012) found approximately 60% of the teachers reported their current Stull evaluation (performance based/observational) process as unhelpful or only somewhat helpful.

Some limitations of Lee's (2012) research were most teachers interviewed had more than 10 years of teaching experience, those who responded to the study invitation had higher VAM ratings and were from schools with high scoring students, and the entire population of teachers may have been surprised, offended, or "felt attacked" by the publication of their and their students test scores out of context for the public to review (p. 102). Although multiple data collection sources adds to the validity of Lee's research, mainly qualitative data was used for analysis and a quantitative investigation with a more representative sample would be informative. Additional research with a larger and more representative sample was called for to represent an even larger voice in evaluation reform (Lee, 2012). Finally, although an excellent question was asked about the purpose of evaluation in general, and the majority of responses focused on student growth, and it was unclear from the data whether or not the teachers felt their current Stull approach or a different VAM approach would be more indicative of student growth (Lee, 2012). Information is needed about teacher's perceptions of the purpose of VAM approaches as compared to traditional performance based approaches. If there is a discrepancy between teachers' perceptions about the purposes of the two approaches, then such a discrepancy may be contributing to the lack of support for VAM approaches evidenced by Lee.

This next sample (#2) is a little more synthesized and contains some general information, but still very detailed published study information in some places. What do you think?

Lit review sample #2 - another study write-up. Performance based teacher evaluation methods can consist of informal classroom observations, review of lesson plan evaluation, faculty interactions, student performance ratings, administrator interactions self-reflection exercises, and other formal and informal observations (Marshall, 2009). Most states and districts across the country have implemented either standardized or unstandardized performance based evaluation procedures. Researchers gathered information on how teachers perceive such performance based evaluation procedures. The existing research on this topic is mostly in the form of doctoral dissertations, and the results of the published research have been mixed. For example, the dissertation work of Giliya (2006), Batchelor (2008) and Robles (2007) demonstrated negative teacher perceptions, whereas other's dissertation work showed positive teacher perceptions toward evaluation (Clayton, 2008; Kelly, 2006). Still other dissertation researchers found mixed results (Astor, 2005; Lansman, 2006). The few recently conducted peer-reviewed investigations on the topic of teacher perceptions toward evaluation and some of the dissertation research will be reviewed.

Despain and Juarez-Torres (2012) used a mixed methods research approach to investigate public school teachers' and administrators' perceptions about observation as an evaluation tool,

72

and how such perceptions impacted performance. Sixteen teachers and 16 administrators representing varying campus levels from an independent school district that used an observational teacher evaluation system completed an online survey questionnaire. The questionnaire had three parts and was designed to ascertain minimal demographic information (quantitative data), Likert-type responses to questions about perceptions of the evaluation process (quantitative data), and two open-ended questions about views on changes suggested for their observation type evaluation system and important aspects of the system (qualitative data). The 10 Likert-type response questions garnered information on the adequacy of the observation time, the impact of observations on student growth and learning, agreement with observational approaches for evaluation, and perceptions of whether or not the observations truly reflected reality. For the quantitative data, Despain and Juarez-Torres found half of the teachers and administrators agreed with the statement about the amount of observation being adequate and the other half did not.

This result about adequacy of observations was not corroborated by the thesis work of Batchelor (2008) who demonstrated a lack of positivity about teacher observation with a sample of 87 teachers. Interestingly, in Batchelor's comparison between a test school district, which had recently adopted a standards-based evaluation model (test group), and a school district that did not have a standards-based evaluation model (control group), teachers from the control group were more likely to report their evaluation systems were more professional and thorough. Batchelor also demonstrated no differences between the test and control group on questions about evaluation standards being clearly explained, and teacher's perceptions that evaluation helped them to improve as an educator, which both statements were likely to be agreed with.

The views of teachers as compared to administrators were not always aligned. Despain and Juarez-Torres (2012) indicated administrators reported teacher observations had a positive effect on student learning, but teachers disagreed. Teachers and administrators also disagreed about the whether or not the classroom events revealed during observation evaluation mirrored reality, with teachers more likely to indicate such observations did not reflect reality (Despain & Juarez-Torres, 2012). Also noteworthy was teachers' lack of support for their current teacher evaluation practice, and the administrations agreement with it. Despain and Juarez-Torres' qualitative results also revealed teachers thought student performance, content knowledge, and increases in observation time were the most important teacher evaluation aspects. Interestingly, although teachers thought student performance was essential in evaluation, administrators did not echo this sentiment. Based on only 50% of agreement with observation processes for evaluation, Despain and Juarez-Torres recommended additional research was needed to determine if this a need for concern, and also to identify problems with observational approaches to evaluation. The researchers also recommended additional information be collected on demographic factors that may play a role in perceptions on evaluation, as well as inquiry on the dichotomy of teacher and administrator perceptions (Despain & Juarez-Torres, 2012).

Lit review sample #3 - it's a whole lit review! (Prior, 2015). The general problem is hospitality workers lack motivation, which can lead to poor job performance and increased employee turnover (Mackenzie & Peters, 2014; Tews et al., 2014). Researchers disagree about how to best improve motivation among hospitality workers, and the area of reward management adds more ambiguities to work motivation research (Degan, 2013). While some researchers argued only intrinsic rewards will truly motivate (Halkos & Bousinakis, 2010; Herzberg, 1968; Kumar & Raghavendran, 2013) other researchers demonstrated extrinsic rewards are most essential to drive work behavior (Jeacle & Parker, 2013). Before incentive plans can be developed or improved, information is needed about which worker needs so that rewards can effectively motivate (Kara et al., 2013; Tracey, 2014). Specifically, research is needed about hospitality workers' point of view regarding their physical and psychological needs. Accordingly, the purpose of this qualitative, multiple-case, holistic study is to explore the physical and psychological needs of employees in the hospitality industry.

An integrative literature review was undertaken to locate current research that has been used to examine the way rewards are used to motivate employees. A search of electronic databases of business and psychology library journals, like ProQuest and PSYCLINE, were accessed in order to allocate studies on this topic. The keywords used to search for general articles included work motivation, work rewards, hospitality employees, content theories, process theory, and individual differences. The search was narrowed to locate studies within the last five years and then within the last three years. The key search words were narrowed to include work incentives, dissatisfaction, and employee needs. The remainder of this section presents information about motivation, hospitality workers, rewards, motivation-hygiene theory, and managing rewards.

Work Motivation

Work motivation refers to the influences that promote positive work-related actions (Ankli & Palliam, 2012). Work motivation is a multifaceted subject and understanding work behavior and the sources behind motivation is complex (Gneezy, Meier, & Rey-Biel, 2011). Motivation is frequently studied because unmotivated workers can impair organizational success (Mackenzie & Peters, 2014; Zhang & Qi, 2014). Low motivation among employees can lead to work disengagement, decreased morale, deviant work behavior, and high employee turnover (Deci & Ryan, 2014; Gneezy et al., 2011; Tews et al., 2014; Tracey, 2014; Zhang & Qi, 2014). Work motivation has been studied empirically for over 100 years from many different theoretical lenses (Muchinsky, 2012). Theories of motivation are categorized as content theories, which focus on *what* motivates, and process theories, which focus on the *process* of motivation (Bell & Martin, 2012; Fichter, 2011; Shin, 2013). Bassett-Jones and Lloyd (2005) argued understanding *what* specifically motivates workers is essential because each person comes to work with diverse psychological and physical needs that change over time. In contrast, Gneezy et al. (2011) and Rose and Manley (2012) argued the process of motivation, or how workers are moved, is most important for effective reward management.

Employee needs can be categorized as psychological (intrinsic) and physical (extrinsic); consequently, the factors to motivate are classified as intrinsic and extrinsic motivators (Linz & Semykina, 2012). Intrinsic motivators refer to incentives that target psychological meaning attained from work, such as recognition, skill development, job content, personal achievement, and being treated in a considerate manner (Chileshe & Haupt, 2010; Zeffane, 2010). In contrast, extrinsic motivators refer to tangible incentives that target physical provisions attained from work, which includes rewards such as pay, fringe benefits, job security, and work environment (AlBattat & Som, 2013; Jeacle & Parker, 2013). The effectiveness of both extrinsic and intrinsic motivators was shown to be dependent on what employees needed at different times (Tracey, 2014). However, Herzberg (1968) argued intrinsic motivators improved motivation; in particular, *job enlargement*, the horizontal expansion of job duties, and *job enrichment*, the vertical extension of job duties, can motivate workers through challenging work (Bassett-Jones & Lloyd, 2005; Deci & Ryan, 2014).

Extrinsic motivators improved motivation among employees who had coping styles that allowed them to cognitively justify perceived inequalities or imbalances (Oren & Littman-Ovadia, 2012). However, Herzberg (1968) noted the overuse of extrinsic motivators pulled from work motivation because employee demands escalated and the desire for extrinsic reward became insatiable (Herzberg, 1968). Further, intrinsic rewards were shown to boost worker motivation, even during economic hardships or times of decreased extrinsic incentives (Amabile & Kramer, 2012). All rewards function with fluctuating strengths for different workers in different situations, but it still remains unclear what workforce needs are in order to be motivated (Deci & Ryan, 2014; Degan, 2013).

Hospitality Workers

The hospitality industry in the United States is one of the largest job sectors with more than ten million employees contributing to the economy (Shierholz, 2014). Employee motivation continues to be an important area of study because more than half of the workers in this job sector are unmotivated (Lee & Ok, 2014; Tews et al., 2014; Zhao et al, 2013). Most hospitality workers do not receive any benefits and 17% of restaurant workers have been found to live in poverty (Shierholz, 2014). Because these workers have substantially lower hourly wages than workers in other job sectors, understanding the individual intrinsic and extrinsic needs that underpins motivation can help improve these jobs.

Work motivation in the hospitality industry. Managing rewards in the hospitality industry is a complex matter because the pay is often low, the work is labor intensive, and promotion options are limited (Tudor, 2011). Compared to other service sectors, the restaurant, hotel, and lodging job sectors have difficulty retaining skilled workers because employees do not have the right extrinsic and intrinsic rewards to keep them motivated to stay long-term (Kim et al., 2013; Lee & Ok, 2014; Mackenzie & Peters, 2014). Also, the ongoing changing needs of employees in this industry means motivational factors do not have the same impact across all work environments (Kukanja, 2013).

Reasons for low motivation in hospitality workers. More than half of all restaurant employees are unmotivated (Shierholz, 2014), but the reasons for lack of motivation is unclear. Kukanja (2013) reported demographics, including, age and gender, were important factors that determined how and if rewards motivated employees in the hospitality industry. However, Tews et al. (2014) demonstrated little opportunity for advancement and low wages were the primary challenges that all hospitality workers faced, regardless of demographics. Kara et al. (2013) suggested employee motivation among hospitality workers was low because of incompetent leadership and resulted when managers were not able to maintain an equitable work environment. Tudor (2011) also found inequitable workplace conditions de-motivated hospitality workers and an unpleasant work environment was a major source of turnover.

Effects of low motivation in hospitality workers. Low motivation among hospitality workers leads to negative job outcomes such as poor job performance, lack of engagement, and high turnover (Vasquez, 2014; Zhao et al., 2013). Also, unmotivated hospitality workers are shown to have lower check sales and work with diminished helping behaviors (Kim et al., 2013). Organizations and individuals both suffer from unmotivated workers because it is costly to the organization to have ongoing employee turnover or negative work behavior and it is also costly to the worker who frequently changes jobs (Tews et al., 2014). The impact of unmotivated workers is also felt in the community because ongoing decreased motivation can result in counterproductive work behavior and acts of sabotage (Deci & Ryan, 2014; Lee & Ok, 2014; Zhao et al, 2013).

Strategies to mitigate low motivation in hospitality workers. Developing incentive plans to ameliorate motivation among hospitality workers is not an easy matter because motivational factors do not have the same outcomes across different settings (Kukanja, 2013). It is unclear if employees want and need more extrinsic or intrinsic motivational factors. Some researchers argued intrinsic motivational factors are the most important to consider because they help to develop psychological growth among workers and allow for personal growth, which in turn increases motivation (Krug & Braver, 2014; Salman & Khan, 2014). Indeed, Tudor (2011) found hospitality employees were motivated by intrinsic rewards like recognition, games at work, and a pleasant work environment, in spite of decreased rates of pay. In contrast, AlBattat and Som (2013) demonstrated extrinsic factors were most important and argued that dissatisfaction, which is associated with low motivation among hospitality workers, was reduced when managers improved working conditions and ensured equitable pay.

Even though there are ambiguities about effective motivational factors for hospitality workers, all employees need both intrinsic and extrinsic rewards in order to stay motivated at their job (Muchinsky, 2012; Shin, 2013). However, determining which rewards will be most effective is complex because motivational factors are most efficacious when they align with employee values and preferences (Ryan & Deci, 2000; Tracey, 2014). Some hospitality employees prefer advanced job opportunities while others find inspiration from competent leadership and a positive work environment (Kim et al., 2013; Tudor, 2011). More information is needed about worker needs and preferences, which can be better understood through a qualitative inquiry. Specifically, research is needed from the hospitality workers' point of view about their motivational preferences, which can assist hospitality managers and human resource planners to strategize effective reward programs (Kim et al., 2013; Tews et al., 2014; Tracey, 2014).

Motivation-hygiene Theory

Workers have different reasons for performing at work and rewards offered need to be desirable or have value to the individual in order to motivate; however, motivation and satisfaction will be encumbered if workers are dissatisfied, no matter how desirable the reward or incentive (Tan & Waheed, 2011). The motivation-hygiene theory (Herzberg et al., 1959) is a need-based model that provides a comprehensive theoretical lens to explain the duality that exists between worker satisfaction and dissatisfaction at work. Most motivation theories differentiate between intrinsic and extrinsic rewards, but fail to distinguish the states of satisfaction and dissatisfaction, which underpins all work effort no matter how much talent, organizational support, or incentive plans are in place. The motivation-hygiene theory highlights the dual nature of satisfaction and dissatisfaction, where "the opposite of job dissatisfaction is not job satisfaction, but no job satisfaction" (Herzberg, 1968, p. 58). Workers have two different sets of needs that must be fulfilled from work. One set of needs involves the intrinsic motivating factors that satisfy while the other set involves the human drive to not be dissatisfied (Bassett-Jones & Lloyd, 2005; Herzberg et al., 1959).

The motivation-hygiene theory is also referred to as the *two-factor* theory because it presents a two-step process to need fulfillment where employees must first have reduced states of dissatisfaction before they can be motivated by intrinsic rewards. This is different from Maslow's (1970) hierarchy of needs, where needs are ranked and then build from high to low to suggest satiation of ordered needs, but this ordering of lower and higher needs does not apply to all workers (Navarro, 2009). Further, the hierarchy of needs fails to consider dissatisfaction and fails to address how extrinsic rewards help reduce dissatisfaction among employees, which then contributes to becoming more motivated at work (Chileshe & Haupt, 2010; Hao & Zihanxin, 2011). The two-step process embedded in the motivation-hygiene theory suggests that extrinsic rewards, or *hygiene*, like salary, policies, and status only satisfy needs temporarily while they move behavior, but meeting psychological growth needs is what really satisfies workers, which can only come from intrinsic rewards, or true motivators, that come from within the job and work itself (Herzberg et al., 1959; Lanfranchi et al., 2010;. Extrinsic rewards are part of the recipe for motivational success because they move behavior as they meet very real needs to live, survive, and avoid pain, but only intrinsic variables have been shown to motivate workers in ways that lead to satisfaction (Chileshe & Haupt, 2010; Fichter, 2011; Pinto, 2011).

Job dissatisfaction. Employees have the potential to be motivated by intrinsic factors when hygiene reduces dissatisfaction, so that physiological growth and achievement can fulfill needs

(Herzberg et al., 1959; Malik & Naeem, 2012). According to Herzberg et al.'s (1959) motivation-hygiene theory, job satisfaction and job dissatisfaction are not opposites of each other; instead, both states are a result of separate factors, where intrinsic rewards or motivator factors lead to satisfaction and where extrinsic rewards, or hygiene factors, serve to remove dissatisfaction. Employees working with high states of dissatisfaction can still be productive, but ongoing increased dissatisfaction could lead to turnover intention and negative job behavior, which in the long run pulls from organizational and employee success (Chullen et al., 2010; Harris & Ogbonna, 2006).

Job dissatisfaction was examined in recent studies and even though Herzberg (1968) argued ongoing dissatisfaction interfered with intrinsic motivation, the state of being dissatisfied is not always bad for workers when it comes to job output. For example, creativity output is sometimes higher during tense, dissatisfied states (Andersen & Kragh, 2012). Also, dissatisfied employees are more creative at work because a certain level of displacement can foster resourcefulness (Amabile & Kramer, 2012). However, factors that lead to job dissatisfaction are context specific for different workers (Tracey, 2014) and some job factors, like working conditions, salary, colleague relations, may contribute to both job satisfaction and job dissatisfaction depending on the set of conditions for the worker (Tilman et al., 2010).

It is important to note again that the opposite of satisfaction is *no* satisfaction and the opposite of job dissatisfaction is not job satisfaction, but *no* job dissatisfaction (Herzberg, 1968; Sachau, 2007); consequently, it is not always easy for quantitative inquires to distinguish the difference between these states with participants. However, qualitative inquiries, where the researcher becomes an essential part of the instrument (Frels & Onwuegbuzie, 2012) can better explore satisfaction and dissatisfaction separately while uncovering data about worker's hidden motivations, feelings, emotions, and unique perspective, which is not always attainable through questionnaire data collection (Chenail, 2011; Degan, 2013). Organizations may still be successful, or at least productive, with dissatisfied employees (Amabile & Kramer, 2012), but more research is needed to expand and clarify the concept of job satisfaction and motivation as separate from the factors that lead to job dissatisfaction (Andersen & Kragh, 2012; & Gutnick, Walter, Nijstad, & De Dreu, 2012).

Misunderstanding the motivation-hygiene theory. The motivation-hygiene theory receives frequent criticism around the role that hygiene, or extrinsic reward, factors play at work (Sachau, 2007; Smerek & Peterson, 2006). Many times the criticisms are due to misinterpreting the theory and overlooking Herzberg's posit that two sets of needs must be fulfilled in order to experience satisfaction and work motivation, which involves intrinsic rewards to motivate and extrinsic rewards, or hygiene, to prevent dissatisfaction (Chileshe & Haupt, 2010). The misunderstanding of the motivation-hygiene theory is assuming that it can be used to argue that money does not motivate work behavior (Sachau, 2007; Zeffane, 2010). This theory does acknowledge the powerful role of pay, but the theory differentiates psychological enrichment from physical enrichment (Herzberg et al., 1968; Tilman et al., 2010). According to the motivator-hygiene theory, extrinsic incentives *move* work behavior, but these rewards cannot inherently motivate because only intrinsic rewards can meet psychological needs that truly motivate (Tan & Waheed, 2011; Zeffane, 2010). The confusion could have been reduced if Herzberg referred to motivators as intrinsic motivation and to movers as extrinsic motivation.

Rewards

Rewards are the incentives and recompenses offered to an employee in return for pre-determined work or service (Delia & Georgiana, 2013). Rewards are categorized as either intrinsic, which refers to intangible recompenses like recognition, or as extrinsic, which refers to tangible recompenses, like pay. Both intrinsic and extrinsic rewards are inseparable from the world of work (Sachau, 2007; Tudor, 2011), but there is not a set formula for what workers need in all settings and so rewards and incentive plans are more effective when they can be customized (Deci & Ryan, 2014).

Intrinsic rewards. Intrinsic rewards are non-tangible recompenses for work that help to give an employee satisfaction by meeting psychological needs. According to motivation-hygiene tenets, intrinsic rewards are referred to as *motivators* because they are the intangible factors that inspire and energize a worker from within; consequently, motivators can be added to job content to add meaning, responsibility, and psychological growth for the employee (Chileshe & Haupt, 2010). In contrast, extrinsic rewards are viewed as external job recompenses, and according to motivation-hygiene tenets, extrinsic rewards are referred to as *hygiene*. Intrinsic rewards specifically help employees fulfill needs for meaning and purpose in a way that extrinsic rewards can never assuage (Harunavamwe & Kanengoni, 2013; Pinto, 2011). Boachie-Mensah and Dogbe (2011) and Tews et al. (2014) found intrinsic rewards were more effective than pay alone to improve employee motivation.

Intrinsic rewards are used to cultivate a sense of validation for the employee while allowing the work itself to give workers a personal sense of meaning; consequently, the task is part of the reward, rather than just the productive outcome of the task (Salman & Khan, 2014). Tews et al. (2014) found a pleasant work environment that allowed hospitality employees to bond with other employees could buffer jobs with low wage offerings. However, not all employees attain satisfaction through intrinsic rewards. Tan and Waheed (2012) demonstrated intrinsic rewards were not motivating for workers who had the mediating effect of the *love of money*, because for these workers extrinsic rewards were the primary behavior driver. However, it remains unclear if there were additional unspecified employee needs that made the extrinsic rewards more effective for those workers.

Intrinsic rewards can help keep employees stay committed and engaged with their job tasks (Gneezy, Meier, & Rey-Biel, 2011; Linz & Semykina, 2012). Intrinsic rewards are also essential because they help satisfy workers' direct needs for satisfaction and pleasure. Herzberg (1968) advised managers should design reward systems in a way that keeps extrinsic rewards, or hygiene factors, separate from intrinsic rewards, but both have an important function in the workplace. Rewards need to be managed to balance out the excessive use of extrinsic rewards, so that employees attain need fulfillment (Deci & Ryan, 2014), but more research is needed to explore worker needs in order to identify the types of intrinsic (psychological) rewards that are most effective.

Extrinsic rewards. Extrinsic rewards refer to the tangible remunerations for work effort and they are referred to as *hygiene* because they function to preserve wellness in a hygienic manner as these rewards provide the basics for human existence (Herzberg et al., 1959; Sachau, 2007). Extrinsic rewards are aligned with work effort, as opposed to job content, because such incentives involve the use of tangible perks, incentives like money, and enriched benefits to get an employee to perform or accomplish work goals (Trevor et al., 2012). Extrinsic rewards provide money, benefits, and other monetary essentials that help meet basic employee privations, which then reduce dissatisfaction. However, extrinsic needs fall short when used as the sole motivator for work behavior because they are unable to meet psychological needs and cannot provide meaning, purpose, and growth from work.

Herzberg (1982) warned if managers overused extrinsic rewards to drive work behavior, it could compete with the attainment of meaning and growth because the need for extrinsic rewards escalates, and while doing so, more and more extrinsic rewards are needed to keep driving the same behavior, which could lower employee motivation and deplete company resources

(Herzberg, 1968; Sachau, 2007). Tan and Waheed (2011) suggested managers who rely too heavily on extrinsic incentives to motivate will only have short-term success because it does not meet employee psychological needs for meaning and growth. Reward systems in the workplace are more effective when extrinsic rewards, like money and benefits, are viewed as ways to reduce states of dissatisfaction, while intrinsic rewards are regarded as ways to inspire and motivate workers (Chileshe & Haupt, 2010).

Extrinsic rewards, or hygiene, are necessary job rewards because they are essential for meeting basic worker needs that prevent or reduces dissatisfaction from work (Herzberg et al., 1959; Herzberg, 1968; Linz & Semykina, 2012; Marques, 2011). If an employee is dissatisfied from not having adequate extrinsic rewards, it is difficult to become psychologically motivated from intrinsic rewards like recognition, validation, or personal growth (Redmond, 2010; Salman & Khan, 2014). Extrinsic rewards will always play an important role in work motivation because they are incentives that drive behavior and meet needs to prevent dissatisfaction for employees, so long as the rewards are perceived as fair and appropriate to the worker (Bell & Martin, 2012).

In general, both intrinsic and extrinsic rewards have been shown to be effective and necessary to motivate work behavior (Andersen & Pallesen, 2008; Shin, 2013). However, not all employees value the same rewards at the same time. For example, Tan and Waheed (2011) demonstrated *love for money* mediated the relationship between job satisfaction and pay for employees, regardless of their needs. Sales employees that *loved money* appeared to be more motivated by extrinsic rewards than employees who did not have the same preference for money (Tan & Waheed, 2011). Also, Mustata et al. (2011) reported extrinsic rewards were valued more by entry-level employees who had more pressing financial needs than established accountants, which further highlighted the changing needs of workers. Even though it is clear employees working in different job sectors, within a variety of different organizational settings, value both extrinsic and intrinsic rewards, it is also clear that employee preferences for rewards is continuously changing (Krug & Braver, 2014; Tracey, 2014) and research is needed to uncover workers' point of view about their physical and psychological needs (Kara et al., 2013; Tews et al., 2014).

Reward Management

The area of rewards management is complex because workers are inspired by different rewards at different times in their career. Compensation plans and work incentives fall into the hands of the manager. Gneezy et al. (2011) argued the effectiveness of all rewards depends on how the incentives are designed, distributed, and then withdrawn. Some employees are more stimulated by intrinsic motivators while others are more motivated by extrinsic rewards. Boachie-Mensah and Dogbe (2011) found manufacturing employees performed better when leaders had a supportive managing style and properly recognized consistent work. Ballaro and O'Neil (2013) reported managers had more success motivating workers when expectations were clear and when rewards were deemed fair. In contrast, Redmond (2010) showed managers who used intrinsic rewards were not as motivating as those with the use of extrinsic rewards deployed in reinforcement based leading styles.

Extrinsic rewards can have a positive effect on intrinsic motivation when goals and rewards are directly related to achievement of the performance goal (Tadajewski & Jones, 2012); consequently, goal-setting is the most frequent strategy associated with rewards management because it allows work behavior to be focused, measured, and then rewarded accordingly (Anderson et al., 2010). However, a heavy emphasis on objectives and goal attainment can have a negative impact on motivation (Bell & Martin, 2012). If the managerial focus is too heavy on meeting organizational goals, the objectives can pull from the meaning and pleasure from the work itself. For example, Amabile and Kramer (2012) demonstrated when managers were trying to

> **Comment [J]:** Excellent summary at the end of this section to suggest the need for this particular research project.

reduce operating costs to save the organization money, they did not realize this pursuit was pulling from job meaning among employees; consequently, the small cost savings that occurred came at the expense of lowered morale and decreased motivation. Leaders have the responsibility to help inspire and provide a sense of meaning, cause, and purpose to employees (Amabile & Kramer, 2012; Jackson, 2012); consequently, effective managers will go out of their way to manage and customize rewards effectively in ways that helps both the organization and employee succeed (Pater, 2011).

Customized rewards. Although it has been established that employees differ in how they choose to be compensated for their skill and performance (Schaufeli, 2006; Tilman, Feliccia, & Tilman, 2010; Vasquez, 2014); what is unknown are which context specific needs interplay with intrinsic and extrinsic rewards (Delia & Georgiana, 2013). Determining rewards for individual employees is not an easy matter because even though both types of rewards are needed, rewards *function* in different ways at different times across different populations. Chileshe and Haupt (2010) found construction workers did not respond the same way to rewards because older employees were more motivated by recognition than younger, entry-level workers (Chileshe & Haupt, 2010). Similarly, van Veen-Dirks (2010) found reward relevance was different among production managers, and argued incentives, regardless of being intrinsic or extrinsic, were most effective when the incentives addressed differing economic and growth needs of employees (van Veen-Dirks, 2010).

Rose and Manley (2012) found extrinsic rewards were equally effective as intrinsic rewards when the reward was modified with employee preference and relevance. However, other studies showed even when customized, extrinsic rewards were ineffective at motivating workers in the long-term (Hu, Schaufeli, & Taris, 2013; Tan & Waheed, 2011; Tudor, 2011). The conflicting findings further support the need for more research about how employees determine which rewards matter and when. Kumar and Raghavendran (2013) argued that both intrinsic and extrinsic rewards motivate workers, but the effectiveness of a reward depends on the workers' feelings about a reward, which is called their emotional wallet. This argument is similar to what other researchers have suggested for customizing rewards, which is to align incentives to preference of rewards rather than just assigning standard rewards (Gneezy et al., 2011; Harunavamwe & Kanengoni, 2013; Jackson, 2012; Jones et al., 2013). While it is clear from the research motivation can be increased by developing customizable incentive plans (Halkos & Bousinakis, 2010; Kumar & Raghavendran, 2013; Redmond, 2010), what remains unclear is what workers in today's workforce prefer and need. In order to design reward programs that reduce dissatisfaction and give employees a sense of meaning from the work itself, an in-depth exploration of hospitality workers' point of view about their physical and psychological needs is needed (Kara et al., 2013; Kukanja, 2013; Tews et al., 2014).

Challenges for leaders. The challenge for leaders is to decipher when different rewards do and do not work within their organization (Gneezy et al., 2011). If a leader uses a reward that does not align with what an employee wants or needs at the time, the reward will be less productive (Boachie-Mensah & Dogbe, 2011; Tan & Waheed, 2011). While some employees are motivated by extrinsic rewards, other employees may find that their motivation is impeded when these overused and standard rewards, like pay raises or enhanced benefits, are generically distributed (Simintiras, Ifie, Watkins & Georgakas, 2013). Even though extrinsic rewards are important and needed to move behavior, employees are human beings, and as such, they need rewards managed in a way that allows psychological growth from their work, which is only attained through intrinsic rewards (Halkos & Bousinakis, 2010; Herzberg et al., 1959; Sachau, 2007).

Using intrinsic and extrinsic rewards in most organizations poses special challenges for leaders because while managers may have the authority to delegate rewards, many do not have the freedom to customize rewards within their organizations (Jones et al., 2013; Miah et al., 2012). Some managers never even think about customizing rewards because of work limitations and restrictive policies (Jeffery, 2005; Jones et al., 2013). Other managers lack awareness about the advantages of customizing rewards (Vasillopulos, 2011), because even though human needs are universal, employees still respond to different rewards in different ways at different times, and effective managers are aware of this and manage rewards accordingly (Patnaik, 2011; Tuggle, 2010).

Leaders can overcome challenges with rewards by learning about the needs and preferences of individual employees and then staying in tune with how those needs change over time (Degan, 2013; Pater, 2011). Due to the fact employee changes are ongoing, research is needed to explore the preferences and motivators of new populations. The review of the literature revealed that successful leaders are not just supportive of employees, but they are also in tune with what employees need and want in the area of rewards (Fernet, 2013). Effective reward management occurs when leaders are willing to actively assign rewards that align with changing needs in order to help both the employee and the organization (Degan, 2013).

The majority of reward management and work motivation studies are quantitative inquiries (Oren & Littman-Ovadia, 2012; Simintiras et al., 2013; Teti & Andriotto, 2013) and while these objective quantitative studies provide useful data about relationships, predictions, and potential causal factors, the findings are limited because they cannot capture the individual experience or contextual factors that impact what employees need and want for motivation. Findings from current quantitative studies (Clark et al., 2010; Oren & Littman-Ovadia, 2012; Waters, 2012) have been used to suggest that the cognitive processes employees use to respond to rewards are important because they filter and influence which rewards motivate. However, quantitative inquiry cannot always detect context or personal point of view that is also important to understanding worker motivation (Degan, 2013).

A qualitative examination can provide details that quantitative studies are unable to delve into because inductive investigation allows employees to clarify and elaborate answers. For example, Clark et al. (2010) used a quantitative investigation to study worker perceptions of equity and argued that perceptions of pay fairness among employees was multidimensional and suggested that more explorative data was needed to examine the reward influencing differences among workers. Similarly, Waters (2012) conducted a quantitative investigation on worker attitudes and demonstrated that organizational gratitude predicted increased job satisfaction. However, employees have different individual experiences with gratitude and quantitative inquiry does not provide information about motives; consequently, a qualitative assessment can be conducted to allow data to be described and expounded upon for meaning

A qualitative description of the employee experience may provide more understanding about the way motivation interplays with employee perceptions and meaning. Voigt and Hirst (2014) have found among banking employees, intrinsic rewards like promotion and recognition only functioned to reduce turnover intention in employees that were grouped as high performing. The quantitative findings were used to suggest there was reduced intention to leave from high-performing employees, but limitations to these findings came from the lack of a detailed description of the personal experience of all employees, which cannot be attained through quantitative assessments. Employee cognitive processes at work might function in conjunction with the need to attain underlying need fulfillment, but in order to discover specific context factors that impact different individual and organizational outcomes qualitative research is needed (Cooper & Schindler, 2012; Tracey, 2014).

Objective, quantitative studies are not able to uncover the rich, contextual data that is needed for understanding and interpreting the psychological and physical needs of employees

(Pratt, 2009). Qualitative research can be used to better understand the perceptions that mitigate underlying worker needs, like that of avoiding pain or attaining meaning and growth through work (Degan, 2013). However, there are a limited number of qualitative studies in the area of work motivation research, and even fewer in the specific area of rewards (Cusumano, 2010; Degan, 2013) and more research is needed. The few qualitative studies on these topics address leadership behavior (Williams, Campbell, McCartney & Gooding, 2013), ethics in rewards (Tadajewski & Jones, 2012), ineffective rewards management (Rasch, Shen, Davies, & Bono, 2008), and goal attainment (Anderson, Dekker, & Sedatole, 2010), but have failed to address the context specific needs of workers. The contextual outcomes with qualitative assessment also offers the advantage of being meaning laden, which cannot be obtained through quantitative inquiry and objective statistics with frequencies about variables (Cooper & Schindler, 2012). The explorative strengths of qualitative research can help reduce current ambiguities about reward reception while it increases basic and deeper understanding of employee behaviors and responses to different rewards (Degan 2013).

Summary

Employee motivation is a complex matter, but understanding this multifaceted issue is critical for organizational and worker success, which is why this topic has been a popular area of research for more than seventy years (Muchinsky, 2012). Employee motivation can be improved when organizations offer an appropriate mix of extrinsic and intrinsic rewards, so that dissatisfaction is reduced (Chileshe & Haupt, 2010; Herzberg, 1968). However, there is much ambiguity about the most effective rewards for hospitality workers (Kim et al., 2013; Kukanja, 2013; Tews et al., 2014). Some rewards target intrinsic, psychological needs like increased job fulfillment, recognition, and advancement opportunities (AlBattat & Som, 2013; Harris & Ogbonna, 2006), whereas other rewards focus heavily on extrinsic needs in order to improve employee motivation through monetary perks and pay (Chullen et al., 2010; Tews et al., 2014; Tudor, 2011).

The general problem is hospitality workers lack motivation, which can lead to negative job behaviors and unnecessary costs to organizations from high turnover and counterproductive employee behavior (DiPietro et al., 2014; Lee & Ok, 2014; & Zhao et al., 2013). Researchers disagree about how to best improve motivation among hospitality workers, and more information is needed about hospitality workers' point of view regarding their extrinsic (physical) and intrinsic (psychological) needs. Research is needed to examine the needs of employees working in the hospitality industry. The ramifications of low motivation can lead to decreased performance and engagement (Cole et al., 2012; Deci & Ryan, 2014). Low motivation can also lead negative job behaviors like sabotage or turnover, which brings unnecessary disruption and costs to organizations and employees (Tews et al., 2014; Zhao et al, 2013).

The review of the literature revealed an imbalance in the current literature because the majority of work motivation studies are quantitative inquires which pivot from predominately post-positivist worldviews using deduction (Corley & Gioia, 2011; Degan, 2013; Ghostal, 2005). Quantitative studies are robust and useful, but because they measure relationships and serve as confirmatory research, such studies are not able to explore context. When issues are unclear, a thick description is needed to provide insight and understanding, which is needed in the area of rewards management (Degan, 2013; Tracey, 2013).

Based on the disagreement about reward efficacy and the lack of a set formula for leaders to follow while managing rewards, information about employee needs is required so that strategies to increase motivation can be improved (Linz & Semykina, 2012; Mackenzie & Peters, 2014; Tews et al., 2014). Employees are best motivated when basic needs are met to prevent dissatisfaction and when the work itself offers a sense of meaning (Chileshe & Haupt, 2010; Hao

& Zihanxin, 2011; Mustata et al., 2011), but information in new populations is needed. More understanding in this area can also help to mitigate negative job behaviors like sabotage (Lee & Ok, 2014; Tudor, 2011) and findings can contribute to the discussion about need fulfillment, so that specific reward strategies can be developed in order to better meet the needs of workers in the hospitality industry (Kim et al., 2013; Kukanja, 2013; Tews et al., 2014).

CHAPTER 7: The Method Chapter

Hopefully your school has a template or at least some guidelines for Chapter Three of the dissertation - the Method Chapter. When I would work with a client who didn't have such a guide I would ask them to obtain a sample dissertation from their chair. Sometimes the chair would send them a dissertation they liked, sometimes they didn't. When they didn't I suggested the following structure for this chapter.

More than any other section your Method Chapter will change significantly from the proposal stage to the dissertation manuscript stage, so you will need to revisit this dissertation chapter and make sure to move all verbs about the study from future tense (in the proposal) to past tense in the final dissertation manuscript, because the study will be already conducted for the latter. I will vary the samples and point out situations where you want to catch these things. Maybe 80% of dissertations come back with committee comments to "don't forget to change to past tense," because a student forgot, or missed a few. Even if you don't forget - it seems to be the case that you will need to read the document in its entirety so many times (one sentence at a time) to catch all of them. At a time when the last thing you want to do is reread your proposal, this can be a little frustrating. STILL, it will really put your committee in a good mood (and think you really have your act together - which will set the stage nicely for when they read your results chapter :) if they are reading your dissertation manuscript and you have been thoughtful enough to change all verbs from the proposal (chapters 1-3 to past tense)!

Introduction to the Method Chapter

Here you can include one or two sentence about the general problem. One sentence about the specific problem, and then one restating the purpose sentence. You can also include a restatement of the research questions in this section. This intro section can be about one page.

Research Method and Design

In this section provide one paragraph (just three sentences) about the method you are proposing (qualitative or quantitative) and why it is most appropriate for this study/topic.

Then develop one paragraph (three sentences) about the design you are proposing and why it is most appropriate for this topic/study.

Sample #1 - qualitative method/case study design (Prior, 2015):

A qualitative method is proposed for this inquiry to explore perceptions about psychological needs. It has been established that psychological needs are factors which cannot easily be measured with standardized quantitative inquiries (cite). The xx literature is plentiful with research characterizing employee needs in an objective manner (cite); however qualitative research was needed to learn about perceptions of hospitality employees (cite).

A multiple-case, holistic design is proposed. A case study design was chosen to allow for the exploration of information about perceptions. A multiple case was considered more appropriate than a single case to garner perception information from employees within different restaurant settings and to then examine any differences within and between cases. The comparisons drawn from the findings can help identify the extrinsic (physical) and intrinsic (psychological) needs of employees in the hospitality industry. A multiple case study can be more robust and have stronger external validity than a single case because it allows comparisons to be made between settings in order to identify similarities and contrasting results (Baxter & Jack, 2008; Yin, 2009). A holistic case study was chosen because there is a single unit of analysis for each case, which is employee needs. No subunits were identified, so the holistic design was selected; however, as data unfold during the study the unit of analysis may need to be reexamined to match the discovery of any new information (Yin, 2009).

_____

Sample #2 - quantitative method/causal comparative design (Lawless, 2016):

A quantitative approach was chosen to analyze the relationship between self-efficacy and successful Lean Six Sigma implementation. Quantitative data is useful in that it may be used to make unbiased inferences based solely on the available data (Howell, 2010). This statistical rigor contributes to a greater degree of confidence that links between efficacy and Lean Six Sigma implementation success are not due to bias or random chance. This approach was preferable to the qualitative approach in this study, as the researcher did not aim to explore potential variables, which may contribute to Lean Six Sigma success, but rather, to determine the statistical relationship between variables. While qualitative research provides rich, thick descriptive data pertaining to a case, phenomenon, or event, quantitative research is able to make inferences, which may potentially be extrapolated, to a larger population (Tabachnick & Fidell, 2012).

A causal comparative research design was used for this study. The causal comparative methodology is focused on determination of an existing difference between groups of individuals when the independent variable is not manipulated (Pagano, 2009). This difference may then be described as significant or non-significant, and descriptive statistics may be used to detail these findings. A causal design entails data collection after some intervention has taken place, where data is collected only once for each participant (Pallant, 2010). This data collection method provides a snapshot of the variables of interest so data may be examined, as it exists at the time of

> **Comment [JB]:** Future tense for the proposal.
>
> **Comment [JB]:** Past tense for the final dissertation manuscript.

collection. The goal of the causal comparative design was to assess differences in the study's outcome variables (Lean Six Sigma success) between leaders with high versus low self-efficacy. Because random assignment to groups was not possible, a true experimental design was not appropriate (Tabachnick & Fidell, 2014). Rather, differences were assessed between groups which were pre-existing due to natural differences in self-efficacy. The use of this causal comparative design allowed for understanding about the influence of the independent variable on the dependent variables after the event has already occurred.

Operational Definition of Variables (this section will usually only be included for quantitative method studies)

I like to include this section, so there are no questions about the study variables in a quantitative study. You don't need to discuss how you will measure each variable here (save that for the upcoming materials/instruments section). In this section provide an opening few sentences by noting the variables for the study. Note in a qualitative method study you won't have variables, so you won't need this section.

Motivation (dependent variable). Here provide a general definition of the variable of student age (with a citation). Then note how you will measure it in your study. Make the third level heading look just like this with the variable name as the heading. You can also indicate what type of variable it is (independent/dependent/control) as I did in a parentheses in the heading, or the first sentence can read... "Motivation is the dependent variable in the current study."

Student age (independent variable). Here provide a general definition of the variable of student age (with a citation). Then note how you will measure it in your study.

Population

In this section about the study population provide information about the population you plan to extend your results to. Students (and some chairs) get confused about what goes in this section (about the study population) and mistakenly include information about the study sample. What we really need is information about the general population. Then provide some general

> **Comment [JB]:** See all the changes to past tense that were needed (to move from the proposal to the final manuscript). Would you have caught all of them?

population characteristics. Here is a sample. Note how there is no discussion specific to this particular study sample.

Sample #3 - population (Prior, 2015). The population for this study is restaurant employees working in the hospitality industry. The hospitality industry in the United States is one of the largest job sectors with more than ten million employees contributing to the economy (Shierholz, 2014). More than half of restaurant employees have been shown to be unmotivated, which can lead to lead to negative job behaviors and increased turnover (Lee & Ok, 2014; Malik, 2010; Zhao et al., 2013). The most predominant job in the hospitality industry is that of waiters and waitresses, which accounts for 23.3% of all restaurant positions (Shierholz, 2014). Most of these workers do not receive any benefits and 17% of restaurant employees have been found to live in poverty (Shierholz, 2014). Because these workers have substantially lower hourly wages than workers in other job sectors, and because turnover remains high, understanding the changing needs that underpins motivation can be used to help improve these jobs.

> Comment [JB]: Please note no discussion about the sample at all in the population section. Because of this - this population section will not need to change at all when you move from the proposal stage to the final manuscript stage (after the research is conducted).

Sample

Now here in the sample section you can provide information about your particular sample. For the proposal include information about the group from where you will recruit and provide some sample characteristics for that particular group. You should include the sample number. Identify the a priori sample size calculator you used to arrive at this number (for quantitative method studies), include a sentence about saturation for your qualitative study.

Include a sentence about how will identify individuals from the sample and how you will select them to invite them to participate. You should note if you will use random selection, snowball sampling, or some other technique to identify and recruit for your study. If there are particular sample characteristics (different from the population) then you can note that here.

For the dissertation manuscript you will come back to this section specifically and make many changes. In addition to changing discussions from future to past tense (because the study will have already been conducted), you can update this sample section to include information about your actual sample. What number did you end up with for the sample? What were the actual sample characteristics (how many males, females, education, etc.)?

Sample #4 – sample section for the proposal phase (Prior, 2015). The sample will include 15 hospitality employees from the east coast of the United States, which will include five employees from three different restaurants. The employees participating in this study will include waiters and waitresses employed in a full-service, causal style eatery working at least thirty hours per week. Each participant will have at least five years experience in this industry and will not have any supervisory or managerial role. The sample and setting will be purposefully selected to ensure participants are varied enough to represent the central phenomenon under investigation. Purposive sampling was selected for this study because the central questions only apply to experienced employees who have a minimum of 5 years of experience in causal dining eateries on the east coast of the United States. Participant willingness and availability will also be a factor, but this type of non-random sampling can help provide a cost-effective, time efficient subset of the larger employee population working in the hospitality industry (McGuinness & Hutchinson, 2013). Disadvantages of non-random purposive sampling pertain to the fact that many accessible employees will not be able to participate and the selected group may not in fact represent the population being studied (Yin, 2009). The sample of participants in qualitative studies should be homogeneous (Johnson & Onwuegbuzie, 2006) and because the individual experience of each employee will be used to derive meaning, the predetermined parameters of five years experience can help ensure the sampling is not too narrow to provide rich, in-depth information about the needs being examined (Frels & Onwuegbuzie, 2012).

Sample #5 – same sample section but for the final dissertation manuscript phase (Prior, 2015). The sample included 12 restaurant workers from four different restaurants, and the only requirement was to have at least three years of experience in the restaurant industry. The employees that volunteered to participate were nine females and two males who all worked at least thirty hours per week at a casual dine-in restaurant on the east coast of the United States. The sample included a host, hostess, servers, and bartenders. Each participant did not have any supervisory or managerial role, but two employees had dual roles at their job, one worked as a server and bartender and the other worked as a bartender and trainer.

Purposive sampling was selected for this study because the central questions only applied to experienced employees who had a minimum of three years experience in this area of work. Participant willingness and availability was also a factor, and this type of non-random sampling can help provide a cost-effective, time efficient subset of the larger employee population working in the hospitality industry (McGuinness & Hutchinson, 2013). Disadvantages of non-random purposive sampling pertain to the fact that some potential participants were not be able to participate and the selected group may not in fact best represent the population being studied (Yin, 2009). The sample of participants in qualitative studies should be homogeneous (Johnson & Onwuegbuzie, 2006) and because the individual experience of each employee will be used to derive meaning, the predetermined parameter of three years experience in this field helped ensure the sampling was not too narrow to provide rich, in-depth information about the needs and viewpoints under investigation (Frels & Onwuegbuzie, 2012).

Instrumentation

Here you provide information about the instruments/materials you will use for data collection. In a **quantitative** method study, you will most likely use already published instruments

> **Comment [JB]:** Note the updates from the plan to what actually happened.

to garner data for a study variable. The only thing you have to worry about if you use a published instrument is getting permission to use the instrument from the author or publisher. Students often think this is a challenging feat, but it is not. You just identify who to send the permission request to and send an email. It is actually much easier than developing questions, pilot testing, and establishing reliability for your researcher-created questionnaire.

Develop a third level heading for each instrument. Note in the first sentence what variable that instrument will be used to measure. Then provide information about the instrument including how participants will respond and how you will calculate their scores. Then provide information about the reliability and validity of the selected instrument (with citations) if it is available.

If you are developing an instrument for your **quantitative** method study you should write about how you developed the questions (for the researcher-developed questionnaire) and then address information in the above paragraph. You can note that your instrument will be **pilot tested.** In a pilot test you will identify a group of individuals similar to your sample, but not your sample, to test out your questions. You can use the pilot test data to establish the reliability of your researcher-created instrument. You will likely run an internal consistency reliability analysis on the pilot data to demonstrate this researcher-created instrument's validity. Still, really try to find an already published instrument others use to garner information about your study variables. It will be easier and be more likely to be approved by your school in the first round of review. It is also common for schools to require a separate Internal Review Board (IRB) application for a pilot study.

For **qualitative** method studies you will also have an instrumentation section as you will likely develop an **interview guide** for data collection. In a qualitative method study you will likely run a **field test** (instead of a pilot test) of your interview guide questions. In a field test you share your proposed questions with experts in the field to get feedback. You could ask the experts to indicate if the questions will likely yield rich and detailed information and ask them to make recommendations. You will likely not have to get permission from your school's IRB for a field test as the people participating in this field test are not like your sample, but are experts in the field.

Sample instrumentation section for qualitative study - instead of this heading I have here, yours would be "interview guide" (Prior, 2015):

Interview guide. Data collection will consist of qualitative interviews facilitated by a researcher-developed interview guide (see Appendix A). The interview guide will consist of four sections with different questions designed to elicit information about employee preferences for rewards and satisfaction with work. The questions for the interview guide were developed for this study by examining existing protocols and interview checklists used in similar qualitative retail studies (Carsten, Uhl-Bien, West, Patera, & McGregor, 2010; Cooper, 2012; Herzberg et al., 1959; Herzberg, 1965). The interview guide will include space for interviewer comments and reflective notes, along with a flow chart to help monitor answers and categorize themes during and after the interview (Cusumano, 2010; Rose & Manley, 2012). The interview guide will be used as a tool to ensure that the researcher stays within the allotted time, which is approximately ninety minutes. The guide is also used to help prevent the researcher from becoming suggestive about rewards or anything else during the interview process. The interview questions will be field-tested with three experts in hospitality (i.e., worked in the industry for at least five years in a managerial capacity) who are not participating in this research study. The expert feedback will be used to improve the questions as needed.

Sample instrumentation section for quantitative study - instead of this heading I have here, yours would be "Lean Six Sigma implementation success rate checklist" (Lawless, 2016):

Lean Six Sigma implementation success rate checklist. The dependent variable is Lean Six Sigma implementation success rate. In the current study, Lean Six Sigma implementation success rate, operationalized as OEE score, was measured with a researcher-created checklist to evaluate an organization's OEE (see Appendix A). The checklist consisted of 5 questions that confirmed the leader's familiarity and participation in Lean Six Sigma techniques, as well as collected information about the three areas needed to derive an OEE score. The checklist was completed by the leader, who had the option to report the OEE directly, or to report about the three aspects of OEE (i.e., losses in quality, performance, and equipment availability). If the business leader reported the three aspects of the OEE individually, the researcher calculated the total OEE score for the organization.

Leader Efficacy Questionnaire (LEQ). The independent variable, perceived leader efficacy was measured with the LEQ (see Appendix B), and participants were designated as high or low in leader efficacy depending on their overall LEQ total score. The LEQ is based on leader self and means efficacy theory and was developed by Hanna and Avolio (2013). The LEQ consists of 22-prompts, where each prompt must be rated on a scale of 0 = not at all confident, to 100 = totally confident. Examples of prompts include "As a leader I can energize my followers to achieve their best" and "As a leader I can rely on my peers to help solve problems." This assessment takes approximately 5-10 minutes to complete. A total score is calculated as the mean of the 22 items, and represents a leader's overall efficacy with regard to each of these subscales (Hannah et al., 2012).

The LEQ has been validated across several diverse study samples (Bandura & Wood, 1989; Hendricks & Payne, 2007; McCormick et al., 2002) and has been shown to predict outcomes such as ratings of leader performance (Chemers et al., 2000), motivation to lead others (Luthans & Peterson, 2002), and highly effective leadership styles, such as transformational leadership style (Finn et al., 2007). Research has shown mentoring and targeted leader development programs can promote leader self-efficacy as well as means efficacy (Finn et al., 2007). To date, there has been no other leader efficacy measure validation encompassing the same spectrum as the LEQ which includes convergent, discriminant, and predictive validity tests. This full range of areas is required to properly validate a measure. Leader efficacy (as measured by the LEQ) has been linked with both prior leadership experience ($r = .41$) and attempting to assume leadership positions ($r = .60$) in a study conducted by McCormick et al. (2002). In a 1999 study, McCormick also assessed the test-retest stability, and found this instrument provided stable results over time ($r = .80$).

Data Collection

In the data collection section, provide information (in order from start to finish) about the steps involved in data collection. Again, there will be quite a big difference between this section for the proposal with all information appearing as the plan in future tense, and the final dissertation manuscript that will serve as a record of what actually happened during your data collection process. This section typically opens with a sentence about the IRB and follows with other specifics in order. Here is what to plan for - for the proposal phase......

Prior to the collection of data for this study, approval from the xx University Institutional Review Board (IRB) will be obtained. Next, a letter of permission to conduct the study (see Appendix X) will be hand-delivered to xx. Once site approval has been obtained, a group of potential participants will be identified and invited to participate by letter of invitation to participate in the study (see Appendix X). The letter of invitation will describe in detail the purpose of the study, information about the researcher and contact information, the possible benefits and risks of participating in the study, the time it will take to participate, and will include informed consent information. Once an individual agrees to participate they will be asked to execute an informed consent form (see Appendix X) and instructions about how to complete the study questionnaire (for a quantitative method study), OR for a qualitative method study, how to set up the qualitative interview will be provided. Any other notes important about data collection should be included in this section (e.g., how the participants will be randomly assigned to conditions, where the qualitative interview will take place, will it be recorded, etc).

After the proposal is approved and after you completed your data collection (maybe while you are waiting for feedback on your results chapter) you should revisit this chapter and turn all future tenses to past tense. You should also really review the sections about sample, data collection, and data analysis as they will change significantly - moving from the plan for the proposal phase - to what actually happened in the final dissertation manuscript phase.

Data Analysis

In this data analysis section you will provide information about descriptive analyses, inferential analyses and their assumptions tests (for a quantitative method study), OR information about your qualitative data analysis plan (general coding strategy and theme development). I have detailed information about dissertation data analysis in Chapter Nine of this book. You will actually need to decide on the analysis strategy here at the proposal stage (Chapter Three of your Disser). I didn't want this chapter to get too heady, so will you please flip to there when you are ready and then come back here. Thank you!

Some chairs prefer this section to be set up according to research question; some prefer a general discussion of the overall data analysis plan. You won't really know until you submit your draft and receive feedback, so don't be worried that you will get it wrong. In the worst case scenario (the chair provides feedback lol). I am lolling because that is not always so bad. It is really not bad at all - if we don't take it personally, but take it as a favor to us to help expand our skills. Yes, let's look at chair feedback that way! So back to the worst case scenario, through their feedback they will indicate what they want you to do, so it is not that bad at all!

Assumptions and Limitations

Most schools require a discussion of these two sections in the method chapter. Assumptions are things you assume relevant to your study. Some possible assumptions are assuming your respondents will answer honestly, that the instruments you selected will be valid and capture the perceptions of the sample, and your sample is representative of the intended population. You should state the assumption outright. Then note anything you will do to ensure the assumption is met. Example: It is assumed participants will provide honest responses to the study questionnaire. In order to encourage honest responding, participants will be assured of the anonymity and confidentiality of their questionnaire responses.

Limitations are a little different. A limitation is something that will limit the generalizability of your findings. Limitations can be about your selected design, sample, researcher bias, or instruments. All studies have limitations. Indeed, you will never be able to include all members of a population in your sample, so you just account for this by generalizing your findings to other appropriate groups. Similar to assumptions, you will state the limitation outright then note what will be done to account for the limitation. Example: A limitation of the current study is the inability to establish causality based on the use of a causal-comparative design instead of a true experiment. Still, the variable of gender cannot be manipulated, so a causal-comparative design is the highest level of constraint available to establish internal validity. Still, information about gender differences in stress has been called for (cite).

Ethical Considerations

In this ethics section you need to provide information the assure your readers you will conduct your study in accord with your school's IRB guidelines as well as the code of conduct put forth by the American Psychological Association. I ask students to develop information about each of the following important sections. You will likely have introduced your study invitation and informed consent form in the data collection section, so you don't need to note their appendix letter here in this section you can just refer to it (only introduce the appendix letter the first time you introduce an appendix and always use this format).... (see Appendix X), whereby the word see is not capitalized, but Appendix is and the appendix letter is.

Protecting participants from harm. Here provide information about how you will protect your participants from harm. Typically this is information about not identifying them in any way that all study information will be presented in aggregate form, and their association with the sample will not be divulged.

Informed consent. Here cover informed consent. Typically this is information noting you will seek their consent before they agree to participate and they can stop participating at any time.

Right to privacy. Here cover information how you will keep their information private. Note you will never use names to store the data, or report the findings. You may feel you are starting to repeat yourself. Try to keep the information organized, but there might be some overlap.

Honesty with professional colleagues. Here provide information about honesty, deception, and debriefing.

Summary of Method Chapter

Similar to other chapter summaries, clear and concise is the goal. Include a summary (about one or two sentences) of each section in the chapter. Present the sentences in order (don't discuss data collection before the population - go in order of the flush left headings in the chapter). Don't include any new information that didn't appear in the chapter. When in doubt - less is more for the summary. I have not ever received feedback to increase a summary; it has always been to remove text.

SECTION TWO: THE STUDY AND MANUSCRIPT

CHAPTER 8: Conduct your Study

Hi again! I am guessing you successfully defended your proposal if you are opening the book to this chapter. CONGRATULATIONS!! Can you believe it?!! I promise the hardest part is behind you now!! For ALL of my students (chairing and consulting) I guarantee them this fact is true. I know they don't believe me until we talk about it at graduation. Things will start to really pick up now (this is really the fun part!), so hang on to your mortar board and let's discuss the main points!

IRB Application

No matter how much work/preparation/blood/sweat/tears go into your first IRB application draft it will ALWAYS get returned. Each and every time I sign off on an IRB package (application and supplements), no matter how many times the student and I reviewed everything, and there will just be something wrong. Just go ahead and plan for it. If you end up having a different experience, please email me. I am sharing this observation with you to encourage a flexible attitude when it comes to the IRB application (okay to do your best on it, but not okay to avoid turning in the application because it is not "perfect"). Check with your school's IRB guidelines (FOR SURE your school with have that type of information!). Then follow it the best you can and then send it to your chair for feedback. Give yourself only a few days to mull it over and proof it before you send it on. There is no need to waste time at this phase. Your chair will tell you when it is ready for them to submit on your behalf and they will be the ones to share the news with you - that it didn't get approved on the first try. You will make some minor changes and submit again - and then it will be approved.

Students ask for sample study invitation letters and sample informed consent forms. Here they are! Other likely "supplements" for your IRB application are the actual questionnaire you will be using, so include that as an appendix to your proposal and in your IRB supplement packet (and refer to it in your IRB application file). You might also need to include site permission letters (a site typically agrees to send out your study invitation letter, or give you the email addresses of their people, so you can send out the study invitation). If you have a letter of permission to use an already published scale as an instrument in your study you will likely include that in the IRB supplement file as well.

_____

Sample Participant Invitation Letter

Hello,

My name is xx. I live in xx. As part of my Doctorate with xx University, I am performing research on xx. I will interview 15 participants. Each interview will take between 15 and 45 minutes. In order to be eligible you must:

1. Be between the age of 25 and 65;
2. Live in Eastern Canada;
3. Have at least one college level course in accounting;

If you are interested in being a participant in my research project, please contact me via the contact information below. I am attaching a letter of informed consent to this email. Thank you for your consideration.

My contact information:

xx@your school email address

Telephone xx

Dissertation Chair's contact information:

> **Comment [JB]:** Just give the title here, no need to give them too much info about the study, or purpose of it.

Sample Informed Consent Form

Introduction:
My name is xx. I live in xx. I am a doctoral student at xx University in xx. I am conducting research xx. I am completing this research as part of my doctoral degree. The data will be used for my Ph.D. dissertation and may result in additional presentations and publications. I invite you to participate.

Activities:
If you participate in this research, you will be asked to participate in an interview about xx. The interview should take 15 to 45 minutes.

Eligibility:
You are eligible to participate in this research if you:
1. Are between the ages of 18 and 65.
2. Live in Eastern Canada.
3. Took one accounting course.

If any one of these is not met, you are not eligible to participate in this research. I hope to include 15 participants in this research.

Risks:
There are minimum risks in this study. One possible risk is you may not want to answer questions. To decrease the impact of the risk, you can skip any question, stop at any time, and/ or refuse to answer a question.

Benefits:
If you decide to participate, there are no direct benefits to you.
The potential benefits to others are an increased understanding of views of financial statement note disclosures.

Confidentiality:
The information you provide will be kept confidential to the extent allowable by law. To keep your identity confidential I will use a code to identify you. No one will have access to your name and code to put them together.
The people who will have access to your information are: I, my transcriber, and my dissertation chair. The Institutional Review Board may also review my research and view your information.
I will secure your information with these steps:
1. I will file the signed letter of consent and interview data in separate locations.
2. I will lock information in a filing cabinet,
3. I will lock the computer file with a password.
4. I will transport information in a locked case.

I will keep your data for 7 years. Then, I will delete electronic data and destroy paper data.

Contact Information:
If you have questions you can contact me at xx@your school email or phone xx.
My dissertation chair's name xx. She works at xx University. You can contact her at xx.

> **Comment [JB]:** just the title again. Students are often giving way to much away about their study. This is simply not necessary and may impact the findings, so avoid.
>
> **Comment [JB]:** have this eligibility criteria exactly match the criteria noted in the invitation letter, and be sure both of these match the eligibility criteria you note in your IRB application.

If you have questions about your rights in the research, or if a problem has occurred, or if you are injured during your participation, please contact the Institutional Review Board at:xx.

Voluntary Participation:

Your participation is voluntary. If you decide not to participate, or if you stop participation after you start, there will be no penalty to you. You will not lose any benefit to which you are otherwise entitled.

Audiotaping:

I would like to use a voice recorder to record your responses. You can still participate if you do not wish to be recorded.

Please sign here if I can record you:_____

Signature:

A signature indicates your understanding of this consent form. You will be given a copy of the form for your information.

_____
Participant Signature   Printed Name   Date

_____
Researcher Signature   Printed Name   Date

How to Collect Qualitative Data

This comment applies for both this section and the next. Data collection is the fun part! If you look at it this way - things may go even better for you. Hopefully at this stage in your academic career you have had some experience collecting data. Maybe as a research assistant, a undergrad senior thesis, your Master's Thesis, or even a class. If not, that is okay, but may I please suggest you plan on collecting data on some practice people - that you won't include in your analysis. There is really no substitute for practice. Even if you are an expert data collector, you might still want to practice your set of materials for your dissertation data collection on a few people. That way you will feel more confident when you are collecting your actual data for analysis.

The qualitative interview will most likely be the manner in which you collect data for your dissertation. Even if you ran a field test on your interview guide questions, a few practice interviews can really make the difference in your confidence level and even accuracy with which you collect your important dissertation data. You can show up to your first interview with your reviewed interview guide in hand and hope for the best. It all could work out and that would be great. Still, if you have to consider the first few interviews as practice, please know that it was all in the name of research.

There are invaluable resources to assist in understanding about how to conduct your qualitative interviews and qualitative research overall. You should read at least one. Here is my favorite, the one I ask my students to read before they collect qualitative data.

- Kvale, S. & Brinkmann, S. (2015). InterViews: Learning the Craft of Qualitative Research Interviews 3nd ed. Sage Publications Inc.

How to Collect Quantitative Data

For quantitative data collection you want to have checked and rechecked your materials. If you are collecting quantitative data in person you want to show up with your study questionnaire copied and looking good. You should bring writing instruments and anything else you may need (that you wrote about in your instruments section of your method chapter). You will want to have a practiced and memorized script of how to deliver the instructions to your participants, so everyone receives the same level of interaction with you when you provide instructions to them. Be sure to have the plan for what you will do with their completed study questionnaire (and other materials) in place. Are you asking them to place the questionnaire in an envelope to ensure confidentiality (don't forget the envelop). What if you want them to feel anonymous, so you ask them to place their completed questionnaire in your envelope, but you need to indicate their gender or some other note (possibly their condition) on their questionnaire? In that case I suggest having a different envelope for each person and noting on the envelope any important information you needed to note. I have had the unfortunate experience of having five or more participants place their completed questionnaires in one envelope in front of me (to maintain their anonymity - I was so proud of myself), then after they left, kicking myself because I couldn't figure out how to figure out the important gender piece associated with each questionnaire. In almost every study I have experienced some glitch whereby I have to dismiss the first one to three articles of data collected in person. Each time I shake my head and say, oh, duh. Hopefully you can benefit from my experiences.

It may be the case you will administer your study questionnaire online via SurveyMonkey or Qualtrics. For those situations you will want to carry out a few practice runs with the application to make sure everything is running smoothly. Also make sure all the questions are showing up and any manipulations to a specific condition are taking place. You will want to send a friend the link to see if it is accessible and if they have any problems with any part of the process. Remember though, things may still go wrong and that is okay. It is always a learning experience and you don't have to include the data sets where something really went wrong. The bottom line for data collection is to enjoy the experience and do the best you can. Be organized when you show up to collect the data, be organized when your participants hand you their precious completed questionnaires, and have a plan for what you will do with the completed questionnaires once they are in your possession.

CHAPTER 9: Data Analysis and Reporting

Some students get a little nervous about data analysis and how to present results (typically Chapter Four of their dissertation). There is really no need for any stress about this. Based on your study method and design, and your research questions - you already know what analyses to run. Here are the strategies for quantitative method studies and qualitative method studies. There are very few other options, so just figure out which design you have, what kind of data you have, and declare you data analysis approach. Information is provided for the quantitative and qualitative dissertation.

Quantitative Method Studies (analyses and write up)

In a quantitative method study you will present your findings in a few main sections. You will likely open with a section about your participants (with descriptive stats). Then you will provide information about your study variables (again with descriptive stats). Next will be information about your inferential analyses assumption tests. Finally you will present your inferential analyses section.

Descriptive statistics to describe study sample. You can use SPSS (or a different data analysis software, but SPSS is the most common) to very easily conduct some summary descriptive analyses to characterize your sample (frequencies and percents) for characteristics such age gender, and other demographic questions you asked. These analyses will provide summary information about your sample. This will be one of your reader's favorite parts of the results section!

The one and only problem that almost always happens with first drafts of results sections is the presentation of the same exact (redundant) participant descriptive information in tables and in text. It is better to present your sample frequencies and percents in table format - isn't that how you prefer to read such information in an empirical article? Still, you need some text to present your table. Instead of just repeating what is in the table (There were 60% were male and 40% were female - which would be redundant with the table and inappropriate) make a surmise based on the frequency/percent analyses. You could write.... The sample was comprised of more males than females (see Table 1). OR.....The majority of the sample was men (see Table 1). OR...... There were fewer females in the current sample than men (see Table 1). See how that is different than the information reported in the table and it is even a little deeper, based on your assessment of the analyses. Oh, you only need to introduce the table in parentheses one time, I was just showing you different versions of the same sentence that always ended with the table introduction.

Descriptive analyses for study variables. After running the analyses and providing information about the demographic character of your sample, provide information about descriptive statistics (means, standard deviations, ranges) for your study independent and dependent variables. Similar to the note above, avoid redundancies between table and text as you will likely present your variable descriptive stats in table form, but still need to have some text about the analyses.

Parametric or non parametric data - it matters. Before we move on - we need to discuss the type of study variable data you have, as this will determine the type of inferential analyses you will conduct. The first thing to do is to consider the data you will be collecting from your measurement scale.

There are four types of quantitative scales yielding four types of data, nominal, ordinal, interval, or ratio. Nominal data examples are when your participants have categorical answer options (e.g., yes/no, agree/disagree brown eyes/blue eyes). Ordinal data is categorical, but also ordered (e.g., high, medium, low). Interval data has equal intervals between each data point, but no true zero (e.g., GRE scores). Ratio data has a true zero and all of the other data type characteristics (e.g., number correct on a memory test). I need to mention one questionable situation (unfortunately it is one of the most common data situations to be in, so too bad it is so questionable), the use of Likert-type scale data. Okay. No matter how you write up your first method section and identify your Likert-type data, which can be conceived of as either interval or ordinal, someone will say something to the contrary. If you describe your Likert-type data as ordinal, a committee member will comment that Likert-type data is in fact interval data. If you describe it as interval data, someone will note it is indeed ordinal. I have even seen two members from the same committee disagree about what type of data is yielded from a Likert-type scale!

Everybody stay calm, I have come up with a great fix for this problem. Theoretically and actually both camps are correct. But, whatever you say goes - as this is your dissertation - and you will be able to find a citation to support your desire to characterize your Likert-type data as EITHER ordinal OR interval. Once you have a citation or two to support your conceptualization of it as either ordinal or interval, the discussion/disagreement should be concluded. If not, you might have an ornery committee member on your hands.

One more comment about Likert-type scales. It never ceases to amaze me just how many published and frequently used scales include these Likert-type response items: 1-strongly disagree, 2-disagree, 3-neither disagree nor agree, 4-agree, 5-strongly agree. Hey, scale developers....what the heck do 2 and 4 mean (just the disagrees/agrees - with no qualifiers)? All the other response options have qualifiers, how are the respondents supposed to define these two? What am I supposed to do with this scale! I go off on this issue in the form of a 30 minute rant to each research methods class I teach. By the end of the course no student is using just the words disagree/agree (without qualifiers) on their scales (when presented with other disagree/agrees qualifiers). I just don't know why no one else is bothered by these inappropriate and confusing response options. I believe categories should be: 1-very strongly disagree, 2-strongly disagree, 3-slightly disagree, 4-slightly agree, 5-strongly agree, and 6-very strongly agree (right? doesn't that make so much more sense?). Oh and while we are at it, if you use an even number of response options you will get your participants to take a side instead of having an odd number of response options and them always just picking the middle option (number 3), which means ABSOLUTELY nothing (they don't agree or disagree - so, no opinion at all - what kind of data is that to include?).

There are consequences to conceptualizing Likert-type data as ordinal or interval. You can use **parametric** analyses for interval and ratio scale data, but you will use **non-parametric** analyses for ordinal and nominal data. Most students think parametric tests are better and that may be true (they are more powerful because they take more things into consideration), so there might be an advantage to conceptualizing your Likert-type data as interval. More information about this to follow.

Here is what I tell my students when I am their chair, "we really need a measurement scale with a decent range." Students most always begin with the idea they will add up the scores from each Likert-type question and then divide it by the number of questions to get an *average score* for the questionnaire. Why do you guys want to do that? It is so much better to have a *total scale score* with a range of 50, 100, even 25 for your dependent variable; than a range of 5 afforded by an *average score* for an instrument. I most always make my students use the total score and not the average score - of an already validated quantitative Likert-type instrument. If we use a total score with a large range (as opposed to an average score with a tiny range) I feel very confident advising the students they have interval data. If you are using an average score for your instrument (instead of a total score - which again is what I think to be a mistake) then you could argue your Likert-type data is ordinal and go for the non-parametric analysis, but I am not sure why you would want to do this.

When I was a dissertation consultant it was not my place to dispute anything or encourage my clients to get into arguments with their chairs, so we just made it work. If your chair feels strongly one way - I think that is fine. It will save you time and energy to just do it her way for the dissertation. One thing to remember is this is one research project and one where you have a boss. For your next project (after you have your PhD) you won't a boss and you can make all these decisions by yourself. ALSO, when it comes time to publish your dissertation study findings (not publishing the disser in ProQuest, but culling the manuscript to a publishable form and submitting it to peer reviewed journals you select) you can make any changes you want! You can even rerun an analysis your chair had you do (which you are sure was incorrect) and publish the information how YOU like. The goal for right now is to get your committee to accept your dissertation manuscript, so you can defend. Just do what they want - that is my best advice to you. I am sorry if you don't like it. The journey is almost over, so just hang in there!

Conducting inferential analyses. Now you know what type of data you have, the next step is to recall what our design and RQs were, so we can figure out what category of tests we will use. I like to think there are just two different categories of tests. Testing for differences and testing for associations. I tried to develop a chart to help students select the correct test, but they found it was confusing. Instead I use test names and test criteria and find this approach to be very helpful.

Try to figure out your test, but you can always your chair what is the correct analysis to run. They are actually supposed to tell you, as this is part of the training process (how to figure out what analysis to run). When I worked as a dissertation consultant only about 10% of the time was a chair wrong about their recommended analysis approach. I would note this to the student and leave it up to the student if they wanted to just do what the chair wanted, or tell them they though a different analysis would be better. For the students who just did what the chair asked, about 50% of that group had a committee member, or school approving body indicate the analysis was indeed incorrect and to rerun. Still, that means about half of the students in this boat did not have to do anything else. It is a gamble.

Testing for differences/parametric tests. If your design is a true experiment, or causal comparative then you are testing for differences between groups (or the levels of your independent variable), AND your dependent variable is continuous, AND you have normal a distribution here are the tests and use criteria.

Paired samples t-test:

- One continuous dependent variable
- One categorical independent variable with no more than two levels
- The independent variable is considered within subjects in nature (all participants received both levels of the independent variable)

Independent samples t-test:

- One continuous dependent variable
- One categorical independent variable with no more than two levels
- The independent variable is considered between subjects in nature (participants received different levels of the independent variable)

Repeated measures ANOVA:

- One continuous dependent variable
- One or more categorical independent variables
- There can be two or more independent variable levels
- All the independent variable(s) are considered within subjects in nature (all participants received both levels of the independent variable)

Between subjects ANOVA:

- One continuous dependent variable
- One or more categorical independent variables
- There can be two or more independent variable levels
- All the independent variable(s) are considered between subjects in nature (all participants received both levels of the independent variable)

Mixed ANOVA:

- One continuous dependent variable
- At least two categorical independent variables
- One of the independent variables is between subjects and one is within subjects in nature

ANCOVA (analysis of covariance):

- Certain variables that might impact the DV controlled for (most likely a demographic variable or a pretest score - when assessing posttest score differences)
- One continuous dependent variable
- One or more categorical independent variables
- There can be two or more independent variable levels
- The independent variable(s) can be both between subjects and within subjects in nature

MANOVA (multiple analysis of variance):

- More than one continuous dependent variable (the DVs are related and you control for that correlation with MANOVA)
- One or more categorical independent variables
- There can be two or more independent variable levels
- The independent variable(s) can be both between subjects and within subjects in nature
- Can have a controlled IV - in that case a MANCOVA

Testing for differences/non-parametric tests. If your design is a true experiment, or causal comparative then you are testing for differences between groups (or the levels of your independent variable), AND your dependent variable is categorical or ordinal, and you might have non-normal distribution here are the tests and use criteria.

Wilcoxon signed-rank test:

- One categorical/ordinal dependent variable
- One independent variable with no more than two levels
- The independent variable is considered within subjects in nature (all participants received both levels of the independent variable)
- Can be used for non-normal distributions

Wilcoxon rank-sum test:

- One categorical/ordinal dependent variable
- One independent variable with no more than two levels
- The independent variable is considered between subjects in nature (participants received different levels of the independent variable)
- Can be used for non-normal distributions

Kruskal-Wallis test:

- One categorical/ordinal dependent variable
- One or more independent variables with more than two levels
- The independent variable is considered between or within subjects in nature
- Can be used for non-normal distributions

Chi square:

- One categorical independent variable
- One categorical dependent variable

Testing for associations/parametric tests. If your design is correlational, or predictive correlational then you are testing for associations. If you have continuous variables and a normal distribution here are the tests and use criteria.

Pearson coefficient of correlation:

- Testing the strength/direction of two or more continuous dependent variables
- Normal distribution

Multiple Regression

- Testing predictive ability of several predictor variables on one criterion variable (tells which is most predictive)

Logistic Regression

- The one criterion variable is dichotomous
- Predictor variables can be categorical or continuous

Path Analysis (Structural equation modeling, GEE, etc.)

- Testing direct and indirect effects of predictor variables in a model (not only how A impacts B, but how A, B, and C impact each other)
- Can have more than one predictor and criterion variable

Testing for associations/non-parametric tests. If your design is correlational, or predictive correlational then you are testing for associations. If you have ordinal variables and a normal distribution, or continuous variables and a non-normal distribution here are the tests and use criteria.

Spearman's rank correlation:

- Testing the strength/direction of two or more categorical dependent variables
- Can be used for non-normal distributions with continuous variables

Assumption test analyses for your selected inferential analysis. Something I should have mentioned before the previous section - but the time wasn't right then, was - for your method section you will need to identify what inferential test you will conduct and in your results chapter you will need to provide a discussion of the assumption outcomes for your data before your inferential statistics section.

Each inferential test has associated data assumptions that must be met for the selected inferential analysis to be appropriate (based on your sample). You won't know if your identified inferential test is appropriate for your sample data until you run the assumption tests with your data to prove they are. At the proposal stage you write about what inferential test you will run. After you collection your data you will run these tests and determine if the inferential analysis plan you wrote about was appropriate. In your final dissertation manuscript you will write about the results of the assumption tests and note which inferential test you ended up using. If there was a change from the proposal, just go ahead and note that - and the reason (the assumptions of xx for the xx test was not met, so the xx inferential analysis was conducted).

You can consult your methods texts, or even Google to figure out each inferential test's assumptions. For example, the assumption tests for ANOVA are independence of cases, normality of distribution, and homogeneity of variance (homoscedasticity). For multiple regressions the assumptions are linearity, reliability of measure, normality, and homoscedasticity. After you have identified which inferential test to run, Google the assumptions for that test and note them in your proposal. Then Google what analysis to run to test for each assumption. For example, if you Google "what test to use for the assumption of normality" you would see you are to evaluate the skew and Kurtosis with SPSS. Google will also advise you are looking for both to be about 1.0 to indicate a normal distribution. You can also Google how to do this in SPSS and even Google what the results mean. See, there is no need to worry about data analysis!

I would estimate only about 5% of dissertation students have some kind of assumption violation, and of that small group only about half of them need to change the analysis plan (most can find a citation indicating the violation of a particular assumption is okay). In most cases where a change is needed it will be to move from a parametric statistical analysis (like ANOVA) to a non-parametric test (Kruskal-Wallis test) because your distribution (skew and Kurtosis) is not normal. Both analyses are similarly easy to run (i.e., you just tell SPSS to do it and it does it) and interpret. Even if you don't recall how to interpret a result from your stats class you can consult your stats text or Google it and figure out how to do it.

Reporting inferential analyses results. Once the analyses are run, breathe a sigh of relief, but don't sit down yet. You have to get the results on paper. I find this can be a point of great procrastination for students. But don't let it be that way for you! Just go for it and turn in a draft for your chair to review and assist you. They will need to point out problems and provide feedback anyway (and chairs can have different preferences about how to present results), so don't worry about this chapter draft being "perfect" and just get then a draft as soon as you finish the analyses. Suggestions for the chapter and samples by design follow.

Open your results chapter with an introduction paragraph. The introduction paragraph should have a sentence about the general problem, a sentence about the specific problem, and a restatement of the study purpose. Develop one sentence about your study sample, one sentence about data collection, one about the study variables, and one about the data analysis plan.

After the introduction to the results chapter have a section titled Results. Break up this section into the following subsections: demographic character of sample, descriptive statistics for study variables, assumption tests, and finally research questions. In the research questions section you will have further subsections for each individual research question - with a heading for that research question.

Open each research question subsection by restating the research question. Then note what test was used to get the information to answer the question. Provide the needed statistical information in words and refer readers to the table or figure that sums up the finding for that analysis.

A very important note to you is - Do not copy and paste SPSS output into your paper. You need to follow all rules for presenting data and in your tables and figures and SPSS output is never allowed. I never thought a student could make it through undergrad and grad school without that advice, but I often see SPSS output tables in dissertation student's drafts and only about 25% of the students are following APA style in table and figure reporting in their first drafts. If you do that you will really stand out in a good way!

Be sure to review the APA's guidelines for reporting statistics and table/figure presentation. Basically it means to italicize stats terms, get the stats statement correct (i.e., "$r(20) = .23, p = .02$"

instead of "the correlation was .02"), get the titles for your tables and figures correct, don't include vertical lines on tables. If you have one ANOVA table for all three of your research questions, don't repeat it three times under each research question. Just include the table under research question one and write (see Table 3), and then in research question two and three write (see Table 3). There is a giant temptation to use the words "above" and "below" in such a direction (see Table 3 below), but avoid this - as it is not scholarly and you never know where your tables will end up in published documents.

The way to end each individual research question section is a final sentence about the answer to the research question and mentioning the null hypothesis. Given the nature of the null hypothesis, there are only two ways this can go. You will either write... Based on the current findings the null hypothesis was rejected and women are indeed better than men (HA, this example is funny, so I am leaving it in, but you would really be more descript to demonstrate your design and dependent variable as well - "based on the current findings the null hypothesis was rejected and women report significantly higher happiness ratings than men"). OR if your results were not significant, "based on the current findings the null hypothesis was not rejected and there are no significant differences between men and women on happiness ratings." There is no need to get creative or to stress about how to develop this sentence - it is either the null hypothesis was rejected, or it was not rejected. Here are some samples:

Quantitative Samples:

Chapter 4: Findings (Ulmer, 2016)

> Comment [JB]: Here is a sample C4 for a Quantitative method and causal comparative design

The purpose of this quantitative causal-comparative (ex post facto) study was to investigate how teacher attitudes toward the school accreditation process and professional development, or an interaction between the two variables, effected their schools' accreditation outcome scores. The sample for the study was composed of teachers from across four schools accredited by AdvancED, the largest of the four regional accrediting agencies in the United States. The teachers were randomly identified from the AdvancED database according to specific criteria to ensure that schools from varied assurance rating levels and diverse geographical areas were represented. Sixty-one participants completed an online, two-part study questionnaire hosted by Survey

Monkey. The data collected included teacher attitudes toward the accreditation process (independent variable), teacher attitudes toward professional development (independent variable), and accreditation outcome scores (dependent variable).

To answer the three research questions, a between-subjects 2 X 2 factorial ANOVA was performed to determine if differences in teacher attitudes (positive or negative) toward the accreditation process existed on accreditation outcome scores, if differences in teacher attitudes (positive or negative) toward the professional development existed on accreditation outcome scores, and if there was an interaction between teacher attitudes (positive or negative) toward the accreditation process and differences in teacher attitudes (positive or negative) toward the professional development on accreditation outcome scores. This chapter provides information about the findings, including, descriptive and inferential analyses, as well as an evaluation of the study findings. The following research questions were addressed:

Q1. How do teacher attitudes (positive or negative) toward the accreditation process effect accreditation outcome scores?

Q2. How do teacher attitudes (positive or negative) toward professional development effect accreditation outcome scores?

Q3. What is the interaction between teacher attitudes (positive or negative) toward the accreditation process and professional development on accreditation outcome scores?

Results

Demographic characteristics of sample. The sample for this study consisted of 61 educators from four schools. The four schools were located in Georgia, Indiana, Nebraska, and Oregon and represented different levels of accreditation outcome scores and types of schools. The breakdown of school type with the number of participants and percentage of sample are presented in Table 1.

Table 1
School Breakdown

School	Type	Number of Participants	Percentage of Sample	Accreditation Outcome Scores M
A	PreK – 12	4	6.6%	364.10
B	PreK – 8	28	45.9%	323.08
C	9 – 12	18	29.5%	284.62
D	9 – 12	11	18%	264.10

Descriptive statistics for study variables. In total, 85 participants accessed the survey via Survey Monkey. Incomplete participant data sets were excluded from the sample and the final sample was 61, which exceeded the required sample size of 55 to demonstrate adequate power. Prior to analysis of the research question, participants were categorized by their independent level placement and descriptive and assumption analyses were conducted.

Independent variable of teacher attitude toward the accreditation process. For the independent variable of teacher attitudes toward the accreditation process, participant's responses to the 40 items on the Questionnaire on the School Accreditation Process (developed by Wood,

1999) were summed. Participants were asked to rate their level of agreement with 40 statements concerning accreditation (see Appendix B) using a 6-point Likert-type scale, where 6 - strongly agree, 5 - moderately agree, 4 - agree slightly more than disagree, 3 - disagree slightly more than agree, 2 - moderately disagree, and 1 - strongly disagree. To reduce the influence of response bias, items 26, 37, 38, 39, and 40 were worded for reverse scoring, such that a low level of agreement with the item indicated a favorable attitude toward the accreditation process. Because items 3, 15, 16, and 17 had multiple sub items, there were a total of 51 responses from each participant; consequently, there was a potential range of 51 – 306. The responses from the questionnaire were scored according to the instrument instructions. After ratings for statements 26, 37, 38, 39, and 40 were reversed, a total score for the 40 items, or 51 responses, were calculated; the actual range of scores for the 61 participants was 133 – 301 with a mean of 200.74.

Participants were categorized as manifesting either positive or negative attitudes toward the accreditation process based on their total score. Specifically, participants with a total score between 51 and 178 on the Questionnaire on the School Accreditation Process were categorized as possessing negative teacher attitudes toward the accreditation process. Participants with a total score between 179 and 306 were categorized as possessing positive teacher attitudes toward the accreditation process. Of the 61 participants, four were categorized as possessing negative attitudes toward the accreditation process, and 57 were categorized as possessing positive attitudes toward the accreditation process. Overall attitudes toward the accreditation process were 93.4% positive (see Table 2).

Independent variable of teacher attitude toward professional development. For the independent variable of teacher attitudes toward the professional development, participants' responses for the five items on the Teachers' Attitudes about Professional Development instrument (TAP) were summed. Participants were asked to rate their level of agreement with five statements concerning professional development (see Appendix D) using a 6-point Likert-type scale, where 6 - strongly agree, 5 - moderately agree, 4 - agree slightly more than disagree, 3 - disagree slightly more than agree, 2 - moderately disagree, and 1 - strongly disagree resulting in a potential range of 5 – 30. To reduce the influence of response bias, items two and five were worded for reverse scoring, such that a low level of agreement with the item indicated a favorable attitude toward professional development. After ratings for statements two and five were reversed, a total score for the five items was calculated; the actual range of scores for the 61 participants was 6 – 30 with a mean of 15.83.

Participants were categorized as manifesting either positive or negative attitudes toward professional development based on their total score. Specifically, participants with a total score between 5 and 17 on the TAP were categorized as possessing negative teacher attitudes toward professional development. Participants with a total score between 18 and 30 were categorized as possessing positive teacher attitudes toward professional development. Of the 61 participants, nine were categorized as possessing negative attitudes toward professional development, and 52 were categorized as possessing positive attitudes toward professional development. Overall, attitudes toward professional development were 85.2% positive (see Table 2).

Table 2

Frequencies for Teacher Attitudes Toward the Accreditation Process and Professional Development for the Sample

Attitude Type	Accreditation Process		Professional Development	
	N	%	N	%
Negative	4	6.6	9	14.8
Positive	57	93.4	52	85.2

Dependent variable of accreditation outcome scores. The dependent variable of accreditation outcome scores was determined by the Index of Education Quality (IEQ) ratings assigned to schools during AdvancED External Reviews. An External Review is "the hallmark of the accreditation process and energizes and equips the leadership and stakeholders of an institution or school system to maintain areas of high performance and tackle those areas that may be thwarting desired performance levels" (AdvancED Handbook, 2012, p. 4). The External Review Team utilizes Guttman Scaling rubrics to rate the school on the 33 AdvancED Indicators of Success, four student-performance evaluative criteria, and two stakeholder-feedback evaluative criteria (see Appendix A). Each of the 39 criteria has a range of 1 – 4. The mean of the 39 criteria multiplied by 100 produces the Index of Education Quality (IEQ) score, which was the accreditation outcome score. Consequently, the potential accreditation outcome scores ranged from 100 to 400. Since a school is accredited as a single entity and a single IEQ is assigned to a school, the IEQ of a school is representative of all stakeholders within that school; consequently, the school's IEQ is the same for each teacher within the school since teachers are an essential variable in the success of a school. The accreditation outcome scores from the schools from which the participants in this study came ranged from 264.1 to 364.1, with a mean of 308.96, and a standard deviation of 44.14 (see Table 1).

Assumption testing. Prior to conducting the hypothesis testing, analyses to ensure ANOVA was appropriate were performed. The six assumptions for ANOVA are (1) a continuous dependent variable, (2) two independent variables that are both categorical with two or more groups in each independent variable, (3) independent observations, (4) no outliers, (5) normality, and (6) homogeneity of variances.

The assumptions of a continuous dependent variable, two independent variables that are both categorical with two or more groups in each independent variable, and independent observations relate to the study design. The assumption of a continuous dependent variable was met by the dependent variable of accreditation outcome scores, which was determined by the IEQ, being able to take any value between the accreditation outcomes range of 100 – 400. The assumption of two independent variables that are both categorical with two or more groups in each independent variable was met by each of the independent variables of teacher attitudes toward the accreditation process and teacher attitudes toward professional development being categorized as positive or negative. The assumption of independent observations was met by the solicitation of volunteer participants from schools that fulfilled the study criteria.

The assumptions of no outliers, normality, and homogeneity of variances relate to the errors of the model. The assumption of outliers was met by the participants' scores being coded into the categories of positive or negative. In order to evaluate the assumption of normality, a Shapiro-Wilk test was performed on the dependent variable of accreditation outcome scores (see Table 3). The significant results of $W = .836$, $df = 48$, $p < .0001$ across both groups indicated that the normality assumption for accreditation outcome scores was violated. However, because factorial ANOVA is considered fairly robust to deviations from normality, the ANOVA was deemed appropriate for this study (Green & Salkind, 2008). In order to evaluate the assumption of homogeneity of variances for the 2 x 2 ANOVA, a Levene's test for equality of variances was performed with results of $F_{2, 58} = 3.067$ and $p = 054$.

Table 3

Results for Tests of Normality for the Dependent Variable Accreditation Outcome Scores

Shapiro-Wilk		
W	Df	P
.836	48	.001

Research question one. Research question one was, how do teacher attitudes (positive or negative) toward the accreditation process effect accreditation outcome scores. A 2x2 factorial ANOVA was used to evaluate whether or not there was a significant difference in accreditation outcome scores among teachers with positive versus negative attitudes toward the accreditation process, as it addressed the main effect of the independent variable of teacher attitudes toward the accreditation process. The ANOVA was significant, $F(1, 58) = 4.024$, $p = .050$, $\eta^2 = .065$ (see Table 5). That is, accreditation outcome scores were significantly higher for teachers with positive attitudes toward the accreditation process ($M = 305.43$; $SD = 28.68$) than teachers with negative attitudes toward the accreditation process ($M = 279.47$; $SD = 10.31$). The null hypothesis that school accreditation outcome scores for teachers with positive attitudes toward the accreditation process will be similar to school accreditation outcome scores for teachers with negative attitudes toward the accreditation process was rejected.

Table 5

Tests of Between-Subjects Effects for Accreditation Outcome Scores as a Function of Teacher Attitudes Toward the Accreditation Process and Professional Development

Source for IEQ	Type II SS	Df	MS	F	p	η^2
Attitudes Toward Accreditation Process	3054.224	1	3,054.224	4.024	.050	.065
Attitudes Toward Professional Development	2370.609	1	2,370.609	3.123	.082	.051
Attitudes Toward Accreditation Process by Attitudes Toward Professional Development [a]	.000	0	.	.	.	.000
Error	44,020.982	58	758.982			

Note [a]. Because the negative-by-negative combination for the two independent variables was not observed, the corresponding test yielded no results for the interaction.

Research question two. Research question two was, how do teacher attitudes (positive or negative) toward professional development effect accreditation outcome scores. A 2x2 factorial ANOVA was used to evaluate whether or not there was a significant difference in accreditation outcome scores among teachers with positive versus negative attitudes toward the professional development, as it addressed the main effect of the independent variable of teacher attitudes toward professional development., Although the ANOVA was not significant, $F(1, 58) = 3.123$, $p = .082$, $\eta^2 = .051$ (see Table 5), the results did suggest that the difference in means for both groups was larger than expected. That is, accreditation outcome scores for teachers with positive attitudes toward the professional development ($M = 306.01$; $SD = 28.59$) were higher than accreditation outcome scores for teachers with negative attitudes toward the accreditation process ($M = 290.54$; $SD = 25.93$). Still, the null hypothesis that school accreditation outcome scores of teachers with positive attitudes toward the professional development will be similar to school accreditation outcomes of teachers with negative attitudes toward the professional development was not rejected.

Research question three. Research question three was, what is the interaction between teacher attitudes (positive or negative) toward the accreditation process and professional development on accreditation outcome scores. A 2x2 factorial ANOVA was planned to evaluate whether or not there was a significant interaction among teachers with positive versus negative attitudes toward the accreditation process and among teachers with positive versus negative attitudes toward professional development on accreditation outcomes; however, this test was not possible as the negative-by-negative combination for the two independent variables was not observed; more specifically, no participant demonstrated a negative attitude toward both the independent variables of teacher attitudes toward the accreditation process and teacher attitudes toward professional development. Consequently, no test was conducted and it is not known whether the null hypothesis that there is no significant interaction between teacher attitudes (positive or negative) toward the accreditation process and professional development on accreditation outcome scores was rejected (Norusis, 2010).

Summary

The purpose of this quantitative causal-comparative study was to investigate how teacher attitudes toward the school accreditation process and professional development, or an interaction between the two variables, effected their schools' accreditation outcome scores. Sixty-one teachers from across four schools accredited by AdvancED completed an online, two-part, cross-sectional, single-stage-sampling survey instrument. To answer the three research questions, a between-subjects 2 X 2 factorial analysis of variance (ANOVA) was performed. The findings of the current study indicated that accreditation outcome scores were significantly higher for teachers with positive attitudes toward the accreditation process than teachers with negative attitudes toward the accreditation process. There was no significant difference in school accreditation outcome scores as a function of teacher attitudes toward professional development.

Chapter 4: Findings (Cerge, 2014)

The purpose of this quantitative, two-group experimental, pretest-posttest study was to determine the effects of a robotic teacher/instructor on science motivation and science achievement in ninth grade at-risk learners. Results from this study provided insight into robotic instruction and the effect on motivation and academic achievement in at-risk learners. An analysis of covariance (ANCOVA) was used to examine differences in the robotic manipulation grouping conditions on posttest motivation scores after controlling for pretest motivation scores before instruction. A second ANCOVA was performed to examine the differences in the robotic manipulation grouping on posttest academic achievement scores after controlling for pretest academic achievement scores before the instruction. Other researchers employed a similar approach, controlling for the pretest scores by including it as a covariate in the ANCOVA and comparing posttest scores as a function of the independent variable (Dugard & Todman, 1995; VanBreukelen, 2006). The following research questions were addressed:

Q1. Is there a significant difference in science motivation scores in at-risk ninth grade students who experienced the robot teacher science lesson as compared to a traditional teacher taught science lesson?

Q2. Is there a significant difference in science achievement scores in at-risk ninth grade students who experienced the robot teacher science lesson as compared to a traditional teacher taught science lesson?

In this chapter, the findings from the data analyses used to respond to these two questions are presented. The chapter begins with descriptive statistics summarizing the demographic characteristics of the sample population and the means and standard deviations of the study variables. Next, information about assumption testing and an explanation of these tests to assure the appropriateness of the ANCOVA is provided. The results of the inferential analyses for each research question are presented, and the findings are evaluated in relation to previous research on robotic instruction and at-risk learners. Finally, the chapter concludes with a summary of the findings.

> Comment [JB]: Here is a sample C4 for a Quantitative method and true experiment design

Results

Demographic characteristics of sample. The sample for the present study included 40 at-risk students, aged 11-17 from a high school in the United States Virgin Islands. The majority of participants were male (65%), 95% of the participants were black, and 5% were of mixed ethnicity (see Table 3). The majority of the participants (70%) were between the ages of 15-16, while only 20% were between 13-14 years, and the final 10% were aged 17 and up. The main language spoken in the home was primarily English (95%), and only 5% spoke another language, identified as Creole. The household size varied among the participants, with 20%-25% living in either three-member or five-member homes, 20% living in households of either two-members or four members, and 5% living in homes with six persons, seven members, or ten members.

Table 3
Demographic Information of Participants (N=40)

	Frequency	Percentage
Gender		
Male	26	65%
Female	14	35%
Age Groups		
11-12	0	0%
13-14	8	20%
15-16	28	70%
17 and up	4	10%
Ethnicity		
Black	38	95%
White	0	0%
Hispanic	0	0%
Asian	0	0%
American Indian	0	0%
Pacific Island	0	0%
Mixed	0	5%
Other	2	0%
Language		
English	38	95%
Spanish	0	0%
Chinese	0	0%
Arabic	0	0%
Farsi	0	0%
Polish	0	0%
Other	2	5%
Household Size		
1	0	0%
2	8	20%
3	10	25%
4	8	20%
5	10	25%
6	2	5%

7	1	2.5%
8	0	0%
9	0	0%
10+	1	2.5%

Descriptive statistics. Subjects were randomly assigned to one of two groups, the control group ($n = 20$) or the experimental group ($n = 20$), and administered a pretest for academic achievement (Introduction to Physical Science) and a pretest for motivation (SMTSL). Both sets of pretest scores served as the covariates for the ANCOVA analyses. A human teacher in the control group and a robot teacher in the experimental group presented instruction in physical science, the independent variable. After instruction, participants were given a posttest for academic achievement and a posttest for motivation. The posttest scores serve as the dependent variable in the study.

Motivation. Table 4 contains a summary of the means and standard deviations for pre and posttest motivation (SMTSL) scores. The experimental group motivation pretest score ($M = 119.30$; $SD = 14.74$) was the same as the control group motivation pretest score ($M = 119.55$; $SD = 14.15$), and both groups' motivation posttest scores improved, however, the experimental group had a higher motivation posttest score ($M = 123.75$; $SD = 12.64$) than the control group motivation posttest score ($M = 120.65$; $SD = 11.71$). Overall the experimental condition experienced a 4.45 gain in motivation, whereas the control group experienced a 1.10 gain in motivation.

Table 4
Descriptive Statistics for Study Dependent Variables Motivation (N = 40)

Variable	**Min.**	**Max.**	***M***	***SD***
Human Instructor Condition (control group)				
Pretest Motivation	88	141	119.55	14.15
Posttest Motivation	98	139	120.65	11.71
Robot Instructor Condition (experimental group)				
Pretest Motivation	91	148	119.30	14.74
Posttest Motivation	109	139	123.75	12.64

Academic achievement. Table 5 contains a summary of the means and standard deviations for pre and posttest academic achievement scores on the Introduction to Physical Science test The experimental groups' academic achievement pretest score was slightly higher ($M = 50.60$; $SD = 16.72$) than the control groups' academic achievement pretest score ($M = 45.45$; $SD = 12.04$). Both groups academic achievement posttest scores improved, however the experimental groups' academic achievement posttest score mean was slightly higher ($M = 71.65$; $SD = 8.95$) than the control group's academic achievement posttest score ($M = 67.55$; $SD = 13.57$). Overall the experimental condition experienced a 21.05 gain in academic achievement, whereas the control group experienced a 22.10 gain in academic achievement.

Table 5
Descriptive Statistics for Study Dependent Variables Academic Achievement (N = 40)

Variable	Min.	Max.	M	SD
Human Instructor Condition (control group)				
Pretest Academic Achievement	26	71	45.45	12.04
Posttest Academic Achievement	46	89	67.55	13.57
Robot Instructor Condition (experimental Group)				
Pretest Academic Achievement	20	83	50.60	16.72
Posttest Academic Achievement	57	86	71.65	8.95

Assumption testing. As the primary analytical technique used in this study consisted of one-way analysis of covariance (ANCOVA), assumption tests for homogeneity of variance, normality, linearity of regression, independence of error terms, and homogeneity of regression slopes were conducted. Equality of variances for both dependent variables as a function of treatment was assessed with Levene's test. For both variables homoscedasticy was demonstrated, posttest motivation, $F(1, 38) = 1.373$, $p = .249 > \alpha\ .05$, and posttest academic achievement, $F(1, 38) = 3.323$, $p = .076 > \alpha\ .05$. Shapiro-Wilk's test of normality was conducted to ascertain normal distribution of the dependent variables, posttest motivation, and posttest academic achievement (see Table 6). The posttest motivation test was significant, $p\ (.029) < \alpha\ (.05)$, and the null hypothesis was rejected suggesting a normal distribution. Moreover, the histograms and Q-Q plot for posttest motivation in Figures 2 and 3 appeared to demonstrate a normal distribution. In the case of posttest academic achievement, Shapiro-Wilk's test was not significant, $p\ (.176) > \alpha\ (.05)$, and the null hypothesis was not rejected suggestion a lack of normality. However, histograms and Q-Q plots demonstrated normality (see Figures 2 and 3), and no significant outliers were noted.

Table 6

Shapiro-Wilk Test of Normality

	Statistic	df	Sig.
Posttest Motivation	.938	40	.029
Posttest Academic Achievement	.961	40	.176

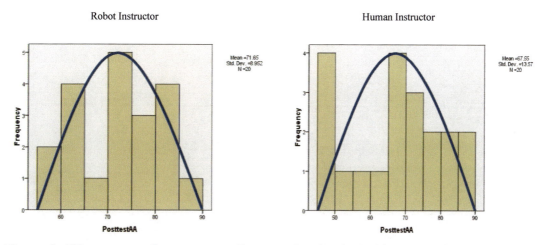

Figure 2. Histograms of responses to Posttest Academic Achievement for the Treatment Group and Posttest Academic Achievement for the Control Group

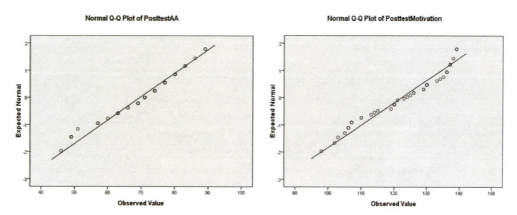

Figure 3. Q-Q Plot of Posttest Academic Achievement and Posttest Motivation

Histograms with fitted distributions were created (see Figure 4) for posttest motivation score for both the experimental and control groups. Review of the histograms suggested only a slight skew towards the negative, and the Q-Q plot demonstrated normality as well (see Figure 3).

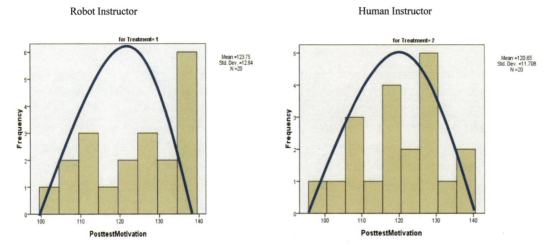

Figure 4. Histograms of responses to Posttest Motivation Treatment Group and Posttest Motivation Control Group

The covariate, pretest motivation, was linearly related to the dependent variable, offering further proof that ANCOVA was the appropriate test (see Figure 4). Similar results were demonstrated for posttest academic achievement. Results indicated a slight negative skew (see Table 7).

Table 7

Descriptive Statistics: Skewness on Linear Plots

	N	Skewness	
	Statistic	Statistic	Std. Error
Posttest Motivation	40	-.311	.374
Pretest Motivation	40	-.310	.374
Posttest Academic Achievement	40	-.386	.374
Pretest Academic Achievement	40	.106	.374
Valid N (list wise)	40		

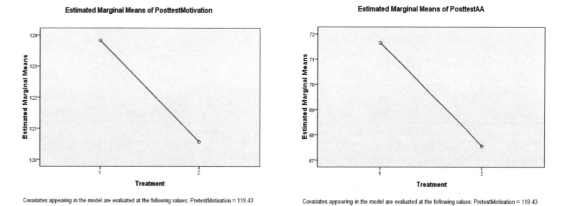

Figure 5. Linearity of Posttest Motivation vs. Pretest Motivation and Linearity of Posttest Academic Achievement vs. Pretest Academic Achievement

Research question one. Research question one was: Is there a significant difference in science motivation scores in at-risk ninth grade students who experienced the robot teacher science lesson as compared to a traditional teacher taught science lesson? The corresponding null hypothesis was:

H1$_0$. There will be no difference in science motivation scores of at-risk ninth grade students taught a lesson by a robot teacher or a human teacher.

An ANCOVA was conducted to test the main effect of a robot teacher manipulation on the dependent variable, while controlling for the covariate (pretest motivation score). The test showed that when controlling for pretest, the effect of treatment on motivation was not significant, $F(1, 37) = 1.56$, $p = .219$ (see Table 8). That is, posttest motivation scores in the human teacher condition ($M = 120.65$; $SD = 11.71$) were not significantly different than posttest motivation scores in the robot teacher condition ($M = 123.75$; $SD = 12.64$) when controlling for pretest motivation score and the null hypothesis was not rejected.

Table 8

Analysis of Co-Variance for Posttest Motivation

Source	SS	df	MS	F	Sig.
Pretest Motivation	3129.124	1	3129.124	46.105	.000
Treatment	106.073	1	106.073	1.563	.219
Error	2511.176	37	67.870		
Total	603050.000	40			
Corrected Total	5736.400	39			

Note. a. R Squared = .562 (Adjusted R Squared = .539)

The measure of association, 0.7% ($\omega^2 = .007$) proved to be insignificant, $F(1, 37) = 1.563$, $p > .05$, $\omega^2 = .007$. Only 0.7% of the total variance in posttest motivation scores was due to robot instruction / human instruction when controlling for the effect of the pretest motivation scores. The adjusted means took the covariate and pretest motivation into account. The unadjusted and the adjusted means are relatively the same (see Table 9). This verifies a non-significant main effect, and the null hypothesis was not rejected. That is, there were no differences in posttest motivation score as a function of the robot teacher manipulation.

Table 9

Adjusted Means: Posttest Motivation

Treatment	Mean	Std. Error	95% Confidence Interval	
			Lower Bound	Upper Bound
1	123.824[a]	1.864	120.044	127.604
2	120.567[a]	1.864	116.787	124.346

Note. a. Covariates appearing in the model are evaluated at the following values: Pretest Motivation = 119.43.

Research question two. Research question two was, is there a significant difference in science achievement scores in at-risk ninth grade students who experienced the robot teacher science lesson as compared to a traditional teacher taught science lesson? The corresponding null hypothesis was:

H2₀. There will be no difference in science achievement scores of at-risk ninth grade students taught a lesson by a robot teacher or a human teacher.

An ANCOVA was run to test the main effect a robot teacher manipulation on the dependent variable, posttest academic achievement, while controlling for the covariate pretest academic achievement score. The test showed that when controlling for pretest, the effect of treatment on academic achievement was not significant, $F(1, 37) = 0.449$, $p = 0.507$. That is, posttest academic achievement scores in the human teacher condition ($M = 67.55$ $SD = 13.57$) were not significantly different than posttest academic achievement scores in the robot teacher condition ($M = 71.65$; $SD = 8.95$), when controlling for pretest academic achievement score, and the null hypothesis was not rejected (see Table 10).

Table 10

Analysis of Co-Variance for Posttest Academic Achievement

Source	SS	df	MS	F	Sig.
Pretest Academic Achievement	1069.639	1	1069.639	10.015	.003
Treatment	47.911	1	47.911	.449	.507
Error	3951.861	37	106.807		
Total	198956.000	40			
Corrected Total	5189.600	39			

Note. a. R Squared = .239 (Adjusted R Squared = .197)

The measure of association, 0.6% ($\omega^2 = .006$) proved to be insignificant, $F(1, 37) = .449$ $p > .05$, $\omega^2 = .007$. Only 0.6% of the total variance in posttest motivation scores was due to robot instruction / human instruction controlling for the effect of the pretest academic achievement scores. The adjusted means took the covariate and pretest motivation into account. The unadjusted and the adjusted means are relatively the same (see Table 11). This verifies a non-significant main effect, and the null hypothesis is not rejected. That is, there were no differences in posttest motivation score as a function of the robot teacher manipulation.

Table 11

Adjusted Means: Posttest Academic Achievement

Treatment	Mean	Std. Error	95% Confidence Interval	
			Lower Bound	Upper Bound
1	70.705[a]	2.372	65.895	75.516
2	68.474[a]	2.399	63.610	73.339

Note. a. Covariates appearing in the model are evaluated at the following values: Pretest Academic Achievement = 48.03.

Additional findings. Further investigation revealed the within variant analysis for academic achievement was significant, suggesting that academic achievement for both treatment groups, human instructor and robotic instructor, increased significantly at $F(1, 38) = 98.094$, $p = .002$. That is, the posttest mean for academic achievement in both the experimental and control groups combined ($M = 69.60$, $SD = 1.81$) was significantly higher than the pretest academic achievement mean in both groups combined ($M = 45.03$, $SD = 2.30$).

Though not significant, the mean scores for pretest-posttest academic achievement increased in both the experimental and control groups. The mean scores in the control group academic achievement pretest ($M = 45.45$; $SD = 12.04$) and posttest ($M = 67.55$; $SD = 13.57$) increased by 22.1 points. The mean scores for the experimental group academic achievement pretest ($M = 50.60$, $SD = 16.72$) and posttest ($M = 71.65$, $SD = 8.95$) increased by 21.05 points. This may suggest that robotic instructors may still be a viable teaching instrument.

A similar non-significant increase was evidenced for motivation; however, the experimental group experienced a larger increase than the control group. The mean scores for the motivation in the experimental group increased from pretest ($M = 119.30$; $SD = 14.74$) to posttest ($M = 123.75$; $SD = 12.64$) at a rate of 4.45 points. The mean scores for motivation in the control group increased from pretest score ($M = 119.55$; $SD = 14.15$) to posttest score ($M = 120.65$; $SD = 11.71$) at a rate of 1.1 points. This may indicate that robotic instructors may still be feasible to assist students with practice.

Chapter 4: Findings (Ray, 2016)

Dissociation had been theorized to be a response to antecedent trauma (Dalenberg et al., 2012) and believed to increase the risk for PTSD development (Bryant, 2007). Although it had also been theorized individuals who dissociate following trauma are at greater risk for PTSD development (Bryant, 2007), empirical research was needed to evaluate this claim (Giesbrecht et al., 2008). Specifically information about internal mechanisms in development of PTSD was needed (Aumann et al., 2012). The purpose of this quantitative, predictive correlational study was to examine how psychological boundary permeability, type of dissociative experience (detachment and compartmentalization), and demographic variables (gender, ethnicity, combat experience status, and combat responder status) predict PTSD symptomology in combat and non-combat military veterans.

Using non-probability sampling, U.S. military veterans were recruited through online forums found on Facebook and were invited to participate in the study by completing a study questionnaire hosted by Qualtrics. Three already published instruments were used to assess the predictor variables: boundary permeability and type of dissociative experience, and the criterion variable of PTSD. The predictor variable, boundary permeability, was assessed with the Boundary Questionnaire-18 (BQ-18; Kunzendorf, Hartmann, Cohen, & Cutler, 1997). The predictor variable, type of dissociative experience, was evaluated with the Dissociative Experiences Scale-II (DES-II; Bernstein & Putnam, 1986). The criterion variable, PTSD, was measured with the PTSD Checklist-Military (PCL-M; Weathers, Litz, Herman, Huska, & Keane, 1993). Demographic variables included race, gender, combat exposure, and combat responder status (responding to/treating/caring for/witnessing someone killed or injured in a combat incident). A total of 104 participants completed the survey, which met the sample size requirement.

Descriptive analyses, including mean, variance, standard deviation, and range were calculated. Inferential analyses included multiple regression analysis to establish the predictive relationships of compartmentalization, detachment and boundary permeability status (predictor variables) on PTSD symptomology (criterion variable). The remainder of this chapter provides information about the findings of the study, followed by an evaluation, and a summary.

Results

Sample characteristics. A total of 104 U.S. military veterans participated in the study. Of the 104 participants, 77 were White (74%), 23 were non-White (22%), and 4 did not answer the question of ethnicity. Of the sample, 88 participants (84.6%) were male and 16 (15.4%) were female. In total, 53 of the participants (51.5%) answered yes to the question of combat exposure and 50 participants (48.5%) answered no. An equal number of participants were combat responders (see Table 1).

Table 1
Descriptive Statistics of Ethnicity, Gender, Marital Status, Education, and Rank

Variable		Frequency	%
Ethnicity	non-White	23	22.1
	White	77	74.0
	Total	100	96.2
	Missing	4	3.8
	Total	104	100.0
Gender	Male	88	84.6
	Female	16	15.4
	Total	104	100.0
Marital	Married	77	74.0
	Single	12	11.5
	Divorced	14	13.5
	Widowed	1	1.0
	Total	104	100.0

Edu	High School graduate	3	2.9
	Less than 2 years of coll	21	20.2
	Bachelor's Degree	35	33.7
	Master's Degree	33	31.7
	Doctorate	11	10.6
	Total	103	99.0
	Missing	1	1.0
	Total	104	100.0
Rank	Enlisted	72	69.2
	Officer	31	29.8
	Total	103	99.0
	Missing	1	1.0
	Total	104	100.0

Descriptive statistics for study variables. Descriptive analyses were conducted on the study variables (see Table 2). The predictor variable of boundary permeability was assessed with the Boundary Questionnaire-18 (BQ-18; Kunzendorf et al., 1997). BQ-18 answers were from 1-5 and were changed in the analysis to 0-4 and reverse coded and the range and mean scores were calculated for the sample. In the current sample, participants reported a minimum BQ-18 score of .22 and a maximum of 2.78 for boundary permeability ($M=1.58$; $SD=.56$). The predictor variable, type of dissociative experience, was evaluated with the Dissociative Experiences Scale-II (DES-II; Bernstein & Putnam, 1986). The factors of detachment and compartmentalization (as identified by the DES-II) were used in this research to evaluate type of dissociative experience. In the current sample, participants reported a minimum DES-II factor score for detachment of 1.00 and a maximum of 11.00 for type of dissociative experience ($M=1.79$; $SD=1.70$). For the DES-II factor score for compartmentalization participants reported a minimum score of 1.0 and a maximum of 11.00 for type of dissociative experience ($M=2.09$; $SD=1.85$).

The criterion variable, PTSD symptomology, was measured with the PTSD Checklist-Military (PCL-M; Weathers et al., 1993). PCL-M cutoff scores endorsing symptoms of PTSD were 36 and above. In the current sample, participants reported a minimum PCL-M score of 1.00 and a maximum of 4.94 for PTSD symptomology ($M=2.14$; $SD=1.06$).

Table 2
Descriptive Statistics of the Predictor and Criterion Variables

	Minimum	Maximum	M	SD
PTSD symptomology	1.00	4.94	2.14	1.06
Detachment	1.00	11.00	1.79	1.70
Compartmentalization	1.00	11.00	2.09	1.85
Boundary Permeability	.22	2.78	1.58	.56

Correlations between study variables. A correlation analysis was carried out to determine the relationship between PTSD and the three other study variables. Results of the Pearson correlation analysis demonstrated a significant positive correlation between boundary permeability and PTSD ($r = .43$, $p < .001$). There was also a significant and positive correlation between compartmentalization and PTSD symptomalogy ($r = .72$, $p < .001$), and between detachment and PTSD symptomology ($r = .69$, $p < .001$).

Assumption tests. Before the hypothesis tests were performed, several assumption tests for multiple regression were carried out and preliminary screening was performed for linearity, normality, homogeneity of variance, independence, presence of outliers, and multicollinearity. The Kolmogorov-Smirnov (K-S) analysis was used to evaluate the normality assumption. The K-S values demonstrated a p-value of .189, which was greater than .05, demonstrating they were normal. All of the assumptions of the regression model were determined to be satisfied. Descriptive statistics indicated the mean and the 5% trimmed mean of PTSD symptomology variable were slightly different (2.14 and 2.07) indicating that there were no extreme scores. The skewness and kurtosis values of PTSD symptomology variable were also within range from -1 to + 1 (Table 6) and therefore, the assumption of normality of the PTSD symptomology variable was not violated.

Table 6

Assumption of Normality of the Dependent Variable of PTSD Symptomology

PTSD	Statistic	Standard error
M	2.14	.10
5% Trimmed Mean	2.07	
SD	1.06	
Skewness	.96	.24
Kurtosis	-.18	.47

Histogram and box plot analyses were also performed to test the normality of the dependent variable PTSD. The histogram of PTSD shows a slight positive skew. However, the distribution of PTSD was normal (see Figure 1). The box plot of PTSD also indicated that there was no outlier (see Figure 2). Therefore, the assumption of normal distribution of PTSD variable

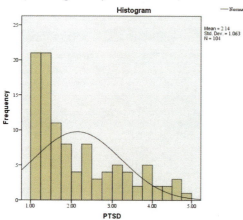

was met.

Figure 1. Histogram of PTSD development.

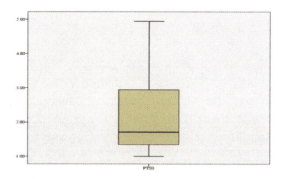

Figure 2. Box plot of PTSD development.

The assumptions of outliers, normality, linearity, homoscedasticity, and independence of the residuals were also checked by testing the normal probability plot (P-P) of the regression standardized residuals and the scatterplot. The histogram of regression standardized residual showed that the distribution of residuals was normal (Figure 3). The normal P-P plot (Figure 4) showed that the points were in a reasonably straight diagonal line, suggesting that there were no major deviations from normality. In the scatter plot of the standardized residuals presented in Figure 5, the residuals were roughly rectangularly distributed, with most of the scores concentrated in the center, which also supported the normality of residuals. The presence of outliers was checked from the scatter plot with standardized residual values of more than 3.3 or less than –3.3. No standardized residual was out of the range from -3.3 to +3.3, suggesting that there was no outlier.

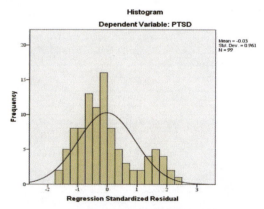

Figure 3. Histogram of the regression

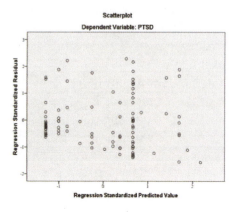

Figure 5. Scatterplot of the standardized residuals for PTSD symptomology.

The residual statistics for PTSD symptomology was also tested with two values, Mahalanobis distance and Cook's distance to assess for outliers. The critical value of Mahalanobis distance for four predictor variables is 18.47 (Pallant, 2011). The maximum value of Mahalanobis distance for PTSD symptomology was 11.67 that is less than the critical value of 18.47, suggesting there was no outlier. Further, the maximum Cook's distance was .17 that is less than 1, suggesting that there was no problem with the outlier (see Table 7).

Table 7
Residual Statistics for PTSD Symptomology

	Minimum	Maximum	M	SD
Mahal. Distance	1.52	11.67	3.96	2.77
Cook's distance	.000	.17	.01	.02

Collinearity diagnostics were used to test the assumption of multicollinearity of the independent variables with two values, tolerance and VIF. If tolerance value is less than .10 and VIF value is greater than 10, there is a possibility of multicollinearity (Pallant, 2011). Table 8 displays the collinearity statistics of the independent variables. As the tolerance values of all independent variables were greater than .10 and the VIF values were less than 10, the multicollinearity assumption was not violated.

Table 8
Collinearity Statistics of Independent Variables

Independent variable	Collinearity statistics	
	Tolerance	VIF
Gender	.91	1.10
Ethnicity	.95	1.05
Combat Exposure	.75	1.34
Combat Responder Status	.74	1.36

Research question one. Research question one was to what extent, if any, compartmentalization predicts PTSD symptomology in combat and non-combat military personnel as assessed by the DES-II and the PCL-M. The null hypothesis was compartmentalization would not predict PTSD symptomology in combat and non-combat military personnel as assessed by the DES-II and PCL-M. Results of the multiple regression analysis indicated compartmentalization significantly predicted PTSD symptomology and the null hypothesis was rejected.

A regression model for the predictive variable was created to examine whether compartmentalization would predict PTSD symptomology in combat and non-combat military personnel (see Table 6). That is, compartmentalization explained 52% of the variance of PTSD symptomology, $R^2 = .52$, $F(1, 102) = 109.99$, $p < .001$ (see Tables 6 and 7). The unstandardized coefficient used to build the regression model of compartmentalization and PTSD symptomology was: PTSD symptomology = 1.28 + 0.41* compartmentalization. This suggested compartmentalization significantly predicted PTSD symptomology, $B = .41$, $β = .72$, $t = 10.49$, $p < .001$ (see Table 8).

Table 6

Model Summary of the Linear Regression for Compartmentalization, Detachment, Boundary Permeability, Gender, Ethnicity, Combat Exposure, and Combat Responder Status and PTSD Symptomology

Predictor	R	R^2	Adjusted R^2	Std. error of the estimate
Compartmentalization	.72	.52	.51	.74
Detachment	.67	.45	.44	.79
Boundary permeability	.43	.18	.17	.97
Gender, ethnicity, combat exposure, and combat responder status	.37	.14	.10	1.01

Research question two. Research question two was to what extent, if any, does detachment predict PTSD symptomology in combat and non-combat military personnel as assessed by the DES-II and the PCL-M. The null hypothesis was detachment would not predict PTSD symptomology in combat and non-combat military personnel as assessed by the DES-II and PCL-M. Results of the multiple regression indicated that detachment significantly predicted PTSD symptomology and the null hypothesis was rejected.

A regression model for the predictive variable was created to examine whether detachment would predict PTSD symptomology in combat and non-combat military personnel (see Table 6). That is, detachment explained 45% of the variance of PTSD symptomology, $R^2 = .45$, $F(1, 102) = 82.18$, $p < .001$ (see Tables 6 and 7). The unstandardized coefficient used to build the regression model of detachment and PTSD symptomology was: PTSD symptomology = 1.39 + 0.42* detachment. This suggested that detachment significantly predicted PTSD symptomology, B = .42, β = .67, $t = 9.07$, $p < .001$ (see Table 8).

Research question three. Research question three was to what extent, if any, does boundary permeability predict PTSD symptomology in combat and non-combat military personnel as assessed by the BQ-18 and the PCL-M. The null hypothesis was boundary permeability would not predict PTSD symptomology in combat and non-combat military personnel as assessed by the BQ-18 and PCL-M. Results of the multiple regression indicated boundary permeability significantly predicted PTSD symptomology and the null hypothesis was rejected.

A regression model for the predictive variable was created to examine whether boundary permeability would predict PTSD symptomology in combat and non-combat military personnel (see Table 6). That is, boundary permeability explained 18% of the variance of PTSD symptomology, $R^2 = .18$, $F(1, 102) = 22.72$, $p < .001$ (see Tables 6 and 7). The unstandardized coefficient used to build the regression model of boundary permeability and PTSD symptomology was: PTSD symptomology = .86 + 0.81* boundary permeability. This suggested boundary permeability significantly predicted PTSD symptomology, B = .81, β = .43, $t = 4.77$, $p < .001$ (see Table 8).

Research question four. Research question four was to what extent, if any, gender, ethnicity, combat exposure status, and combat responder status predict PTSD symptomology in combat and non-combat military personnel as assessed by the PCL-M. It was hypothesized gender, ethnicity, combat exposure status, and combat responder status would predict PTSD symptomology in combat and non-combat military personnel as assessed by the PCL-M. Results of the multiple regression analysis indicated the combination of gender, ethnicity, combat exposure status, and combat responder status significantly predicted PTSD symptomology and the null hypothesis was rejected.

The unstandardized coefficient used to build the regression model of gender, ethnicity, combat exposure status, and combat responder status and PTSD symptomology was: PTSD symptomology = .86 + 0.81* gender, ethnicity, combat exposure status, and combat responder status. $B = .65$, $\beta = .31$, $t = 4.77$, $p < .001$ (see Table 9). The coefficients Table 9 showed only combat responder status significantly predicted PTSD symptomology, $t = -2.77$, $p = .007$. The current findings indicate combat responder status negatively correlated with PTSD symptomology, $B = -.65$, $\beta = -.31$. Gender, ethnicity and combat exposure did not predict PTSD symptomology, $p > .05$. That is, gender, ethnicity, combat exposure status, and combat responder status explained 18% of the variance of PTSD symptomology, $R^2 = .14$, $F(4, 94) = 3.7$, $p = .008$ (see Tables 6 and 7). This suggested the combination of gender, ethnicity, combat exposure status, and combat responder status significantly predicted PTSD symptomology. The t statistics was used to determine which variable significantly predicted PTSD symptomology.

Table 9

Coefficient Table for Gender, Ethnicity, Combat Exposure, and Combat Responder Status, and PTSD Symptomology

	Unstandardized coefficients		Standardized coefficients		
	B	Std. error	Beta	t	P
(Constant)	3.39	.52		6.55	.000
Gender	.19	.29	.06	.63	.53
Ethnicity	-.41	.25	-.16	-1.64	.10
Combat Exposure	-.11	.23	-.05	-.48	.63
Combat Responder Status	-.65	.24	-.31	-2.77	.007

Summary

This chapter provided information about study results, and an evaluation of the findings. A multiple regression model was used to assess how the predictor variables of compartmentalization, detachment, and boundary permeability status predicted PTSD. The findings indicated compartmentalization, detachment, boundary permeability status predicted PTSD symptomology. Another finding was of the four demographic variables of gender, ethnicity, combat experience status, and combat responder status, only combat responder status predicted PTSD symptomology.

Qualitative Method Studies (analyses and write up)

Your qualitative study results section will open exactly similarly to the quantitative study (see "Descriptive statistics to describe study sample" towards the beginning of this chapter). After you describe the sample with a table your results section will look different from the quantitative study sections. The best way for me to describe what you will need is to include a sample and point out (with margin comments) about special things to include/remember.

> **Comment [JB]:** Here is a results chapter sample for a Qualitative method/case study.

Qualitative results section sample:

Chapter 4: Findings (Prior, 2015)

The purpose of this qualitative holistic case study was to examine the needs that restaurant workers have at this time. The participants included 12 front-of-the-house employees, nine females and two males, from four different causal dine-in restaurants on the east coast of the United States. The study instrument included a semi-structured interview guide, which was field-tested and modified for clarity, usability, and succinctness. Following the field test, Northcentral University IRB approval was obtained to conduct the interviews for this study. Data were gathered between May 2015 and July 2015 and the data sources collected to answer the research questions were semi-structured interviewed transcripts, audio recording transcripts, and researcher reflective notes. A total of 12 semi-structured individual interviews were transcribed and assessed for this study. Eight of the interviews were audio recorded, which were transcribed and also used for assessment.

The sample included experienced front-of-the-house employees (i.e. servers, hosts, and bartenders). None of the participants had any supervisory or managerial roles, but two employees held dual jobs at their establishments, one worked as a bartender and server while the other worked as a bartender and trainer. Purposive sampling was used to identify potential participants because the interview questions only applied to experienced employees with a minimum of three years experience in this area of work. The predetermined parameter of three years work experience in this field helped ensure the sampling was not too narrow to provide rich, in-depth information about the needs and viewpoints under investigation (Frels & Onwuegbuzie, 2012).

Data collection consisted of one-on-one interviews with each restaurant worker. The individual interviews lasted for approximately 30 minutes each. The interview guide was followed for each participant interview, as was customizing some of the questions based on information revealed during the interviews (Jacob & Furgerson, 2012). Each participant was given time to speak as freely as possible, even if there was a pause or moment of silence. Participants were only interrupted if clarification was needed or if the researcher determined it was ideal to move on to the next question. Participant responses were written down and interviewer reflective notes were recorded during and after each interview. Audio recordings were made if the participant approved and eight of the 12 interviews were recorded. The recording began after dissemination and signing of the informed consent.

The research questions for this study were:

RQ1. What are the extrinsic needs of employees in the hospitality industry?

RQ2. What are the intrinsic needs of employees in the hospitality industry?
RQ3. What are the missing extrinsic factors associated with job dissatisfaction for employees in the hospitality industry?

This chapter is organized with three primary sections and presents the outcomes of this case study. The first section presents descriptive data and findings for each of the three research questions. The second section includes discussion of themes, codes, and evaluation of each question. The third section of this chapter includes a summary of the outcomes, assessment, and key points from study.

Results

The primary unit for this study was physical and psychological needs of restaurant workers employed in front-of-the-house positions. A holistic case study was chosen for this study because the single unit of analysis, employee needs, could be better understood by exploring in-depth information about workers' perceptions, feelings, and experiences with current reward strategies. Understanding workers' needs required thorough examination of the collected interview data, which included notes from all 12 interviews, audio recording transcripts from eight interviews, and post interview researcher reflective notes for each interview.

Participant demographic information. Participant demographic information was collected for gender, age, years of experience in the restaurant industry, level of education, and job roles in this industry (see Table 1). The sample was mostly female (83%) and mostly comprised of servers (58%). More than half of the participants, 67%, were between the ages of 20 and 29, 25% were between 30 and 39, and 8% were over the age of 40. Mostly all of the participants, 75%, had less than five years of experience and only one participant had more than ten years in the restaurant industry. More than half of the participants, 58%, were employed full-time and worked more than 35 hours per week at the same restaurant and almost half of the full-timers also had an additional second job at another restaurant. Mostly all of the participants, 83%, had a college degree or some college attendance.

Table 1
Participant Demographic Information (n = 12)

Demographic Information	Frequency	Percentage
Gender		
Male	2	17
Female	10	83
Age		
20-29	8	67
30-39	3	25
40 and up	1	8
Years in Restaurant Industry		
0-5	9	75
6-10	2	17
11 or more	1	8
Education		
Some college – no Bachelor's Degree	5	42
Bachelor's Degree or higher	5	42
No college	2	16

Job Roles		
Server-only	7	58
Host/Hostess	2	17
Bartender	1	8
Dual Jobs (server/trainer, server/bar)	2	17
Number of Jobs		
Employed at one restaurant	9	75
Employed at two restaurants	3	25

Participant interview data. The semi-structured interviews were conducted to explore workers' perceptions about workers needs, which were explored through topics like job satisfaction, rewards, and individual personal factors related to work. Data collection appeared to reach saturation during the 9th and 10th interviews because only one new theme emerged in interview nine and no new themes surfaced during interview ten; consequently, all 119 codes were identified and no novel information unfolded (Yin, 2009). However, the final two final interviews were still conducted to confirm saturation, and no additional themes or new data unfolded. It was determined that no further interviews were needed beyond the 12th because further analysis might just lead to redundancy (Yin, 2009).

Audio recording data. Audio recordings were collected for eight of the 12 interviews, which were then transcribed into Microsoft Word documents and imported into computer software, NVivo 10, to contribute to code construction. The researcher reviewed the audio recording transcriptions carefully to compare them with the original written notes during the interviews and synced the results with researcher reflective notes, which were also transferred into Microsoft Word documents and then into NVivo software. Notes from the audio recordings were compared with the interview written notes and written researcher reflective notes to check for accuracies and only one participant was contacted for follow-up clarification.

Participant 10 was contacted by phone in order to clarify work history details and to elucidate more about his current job role. As a result of the follow up and member checking process with this participant, edits were made to the transcribed notes and the theme for loss of extrinsic rewards was enhanced. There were no other unclear notes or discrepancies detected from any of the other recording transcriptions or written notes and so no other participants were contacted for additional member checking. The transcripts from audio recordings were synced with all of the hand written interview data, which allowed for two additional key phrases to be added to the codes and themes in the computer software.

Researcher reflective data. The interview guide (see Appendix A) included blank spaces for researcher reflective data to be recorded pertaining to themes, codes, and key points noted during and after the interview. The researcher wrote notes that were subjective and objective in order to identify a variety of direct and interpreted meanings from participant responses. The reflective notes were expanded during data analysis in order to identify codes and assess worker needs. In addition, the researcher notes helped with self-monitoring of the researcher's active role in the study, while the notes also contribute to maintaining an audit trail of study procedures.

The reflective notes were expanded as data were imported into the software and as themes emerged during analyses. Details from each interview setting were also considered in reflective notes and so were notes from crosschecking of notes and audio transcripts. As a result of the researcher reflective data, a third overarching question emerged about absent job rewards and the small factors that are associated with employee dissatisfaction. The three variables that emerged pertained to insufficient income, lack of fun at work, and not enough favorable work policies for employees.

Research question analyses. After data were collected and transcribed, a case study database was created using Microsoft Word and all data were imported securely into password-protected folders and then imported into qualitative computer software. Using a computer program to analyze data can help maintain consistency and organization (Yin, 2009). Atlas.ti software was initially explored for data assessment; however, the software was not the ideal fit for this study. Instead, NVivo 10 was chosen for data analysis as a better fit because the preset parameters allowed for hundreds of documents to be imported and assessed. NVivo 10 software is robust because it allows data to be examined by searching for specific words, phrases, or theme associations. NVivo 10 was used to classify and arrange information from written participant responses, transcribed audio files, and researcher reflective notes. Participant data were categorized to address the initial two research questions about extrinsic and intrinsic needs and themes and subthemes (see Table 2).

Table 2
Themes and Sub-themes from Research Questions

Research Question	Themes	Sub-themes
RQ1: What are the extrinsic needs of employees in the hospitality industry?	• Need for adequate income • Need for custom job perks	• Include gratuity • 10% to 20% tips • Tip sharing • Low hourly wage • Unfair rotation • Vendor goodies • Sales contests • Weekend night off • Apron and shirt fees • Meal/wine key fees • Nickel and dimed • Pressure for rent • Have debt • Job security • Need fast cash • Benefits • Shopping money
RQ2: What are the intrinsic needs of employees in the hospitality industry?	• Need for autonomy • Need for growth • Need for supportive supervisors	• Food trainings • Music during work • Learning • Relatedness • Colleague relations • Customer rapport • Advanced trainings • Team bonding games • Colleague stress • Thanked by boss • Seniority • Fair treatment • Difference in values

- Control over stations
- Flow during a shift
- Work-life balance

Data assessment during this holistic account of workers' experiences revealed shared commonalities among the majority of participants with extrinsic rewards that were not adequately received from work. A third research question unfolded from the data in order to address the missing extrinsic rewards associated with dissatisfaction, which were identified as inadequate income and lack of fun at work. Several themes and subthemes about absent extrinsic factors were identified (see Table 3).

Table 3

Themes and Sub-themes for Dissatisfiers.

Research Question	Themes	Sub-themes
RQ3: What are the missing extrinsic factors associated with job dissatisfaction for employees in the hospitality industry?	• Lack of sufficient income • Lack of fun at work	• Loss of rewards • Tips not added to large tables • Teambuilding games • Low hourly wage • Unreliability of pay • Extra fees • Feel nickel and dimed • More contests to earn money or prizes. • Not enough team building activities • Not enough time to bond with staff or customers • Bored when slow

Research question one. Research question one was, what are the extrinsic needs of employees in the hospitality industry? Analysis of the notes from the individual interviews, audio transcripts, and researcher reflective notes were used to answer this question. The search results for extrinsic needs revealed 405 common words and phrases associated with the general area of extrinsic needs. The words income, pay, tips, 20%, job perks, and individual differences were the most prevalent words as a result of the word frequency query for extrinsic needs. An additional refinement query was conducted to identify categories associated with tips, job perks, preferences, and other common reward words and phrases. As a result of the refinement, major categories produced two themes associated with extrinsic needs: (a) adequate income and (b) customized incentives.

Theme 1.1: A need to earn adequate income. The theme of adequate income emerged from a word frequency query and analysis of 525 common words and phrases such as sufficient salary, acceptable pay, and appropriate compensation. The interview guide (see Appendix A) used for each interview included a question that asked employees if they felt as if they received adequate pay for their work effort (Question 1G). This question led to a variety of responses from workers, but all participants implied that front-of-the-house restaurant employees do have the extrinsic need to earn sufficient money for living, as many are paying rent, car payments, student loans, etc.

Approximately one third of the participants in this study reported that they did not always make adequate income, and so they had roommates and second jobs in order to help make financial ends meets. Most of the workers reported earning between nine to 20 dollars per hour. More than half of the participants, 58%, responded with a reference to tip percentage when describing what they felt was adequate pay and noted that getting a tip that was 18% to 20% of the total bill was adequate pay and a compliment. P11 stated that earning one hundred dollars per shift was sufficient income for her. P10 shared that he was likely going to get a "real-job" later on, but added that he "usually makes more than twenty dollars an hour," and that is what keeps him at this current server job.

Some participants were unsure of what was considered adequate pay. For example, two participants, P5 and P9, answered that they were *not sure* what adequate pay should be, but felt they made enough to live on even during slow seasons. These two participants were also pursing college degrees and their restaurant positions were viewed as short-term work until they could eventually be employed in their main career. Three participants, P6, P8, and P9, stated that they thought a server's hourly wage should be adjusted during slow times to supplement times when tips are down. P1, an older employee, noted that her earnings were supplemental to her overall household income, so she had flexibility with how much income she brought home each week. P1 also shared that if she received less pay in a given week, it usually meant that "she did not shop" that week. Similarly, P6 did not communicate pressure to earn a certain amount of money each week. She had three roommates and reported that she earned more in four shifts of restaurant work than what some of her friends earned in five shifts in retail work.

A subtheme that unfolded from the theme of adequate income included the need to abolish tip sharing among servers, which P3 noted was a policy at one of her previous restaurant jobs. Tip sharing was described as pooling tips from multiple servers and then dividing the funds equally at the end of a shift, which usually was not perceived as fair by all employees. Another subtheme pertained to the need for tip inclusion on large parties. For example, P12 insisted that parties of six or more should have the tip included because servers were taxed on sales and "assumed" tips; consequently, if large parties did not tip enough, the server could end up paying taxes on money they did not earn, but were viewed as having earned.

Another subtheme under the income category related to station rotation. Two participants, P5 and P8, complained about not making as much as other workers because of unfair station rotation. P5 noted that certain stations were considered "cash cows" because they had large booths that customers preferred, and she noted that if she could have some of those stations, her income would be more sufficient. P5 shared that watching certain servers always get the "busier" stations was disheartening. Similarly, P8 noted that unfair station rotation was an issue for her when she was a server and it was one reason she quit serving and went back to work as a hostess. This employee perceived that stations were never assigned fairly and so in order to avoid being frustrated by the inequity, she said that she went back to a position that paid an hourly rate as opposed to being dependent on inconsistent incoming tips. This worker made less money at the host stand, but the consistent money earned was perceived as less stress. P8 also felt her hourly wage, which was under ten dollars per hour, was appropriate money for seating people and watching the front desk.

Theme 1.2: Extrinsic need for customized incentives. The theme of small job perks emerged from analysis of 583 words and phrases from data sources within the broad category of extrinsic rewards. Participants in the study were asked what are some things their employer could do to increase their level of satisfaction (Question 1F). The theme of small job perks emerged as a common topic. Participants reported a variety of differing incentives that motivated them at work, which included free meals, lockers, schedule flexibility, or a special parking space.

Participant responses indicated workers' preferences for small job perks varied for each employee. For example, three workers expressed personal preference for enjoying the energy and social interaction with customers in the restaurant industry. P11 reported that right now in her life, the "high energy and traffic of people" in her station was enjoyable for her and the atmosphere allowed her to have some social needs met through her job. P4, a host, also expressed a desire to interact with customers more. Similarly, P5 shared that working with customers is helping her develop people skills as she pursues her Master's degree. P5 noted that at this time in her career, she would appreciate having more time to interact with customers on slower shifts. However, most participants, 75%, did not mention desiring more time with customers and actually noted stress associated with the demands of working with customers in this line of work.

Another individual difference that unfolded from data analysis pertained to discounted shift meals. P6 reported that getting a discounted meal was a nice job perk for her right now because it saved her money on her weekly food costs. P6 also reported that receiving 50% off meals is a viewed as a bonus because her friends working in retail have to pay for 100% of their meals while working. In contrast, four participants, P7, P9, P10, and P11, reported during interviews that they did not like paying half price for meals. P9 expressed that meals should be free for employees during a shift and P11 noted that paying for a daily meal, even if discounted, was just one more expense that pulled from daily earnings.

Another job incentive that was not valued the same by all workers pertained to vendor perks. Vendor perks are promotional products that companies give to restaurants, which are often used as perks of prizes for workers. Vendor perks range in value from five to fifty dollars and includes items like bags and wine keys to consumables like food or wine. P1 reported that winning some of these promotional items supplemented her income. For example, if she won a bottle of wine or a set of coasters, she used them as birthday gifts for friends and family. While promotional items and freebies from work were perceived as an incentive for almost half of the employees, other workers did not either receive any vendor perks or did not care enough about them to mention them.

Prizes at work motivated participants who had a need to earn more money. P5 revealed she had a lot of personal debt and was highly motivated to earn extra cash or prizes. P5 shared that she also felt great pressure to earn more money this season, so she made arrangements with the lead manager to close the restaurant consistently on the best night to close. This customized arrangement was considered a job perk for this worker as it allowed her to earn extra money with some of the last incoming tables of the night. Similarly, P9 and P10 shared that they hustled or enjoyed participating in sales contests, and they also had pressure to earn money for bills.

For some workers, the daily cash was an important job perk from this industry. For example, two servers, P10 and P3, noted that they were motivated to work in this industry because they liked having cash on hand from making daily tips. In particular, P10 reported that he was motivated by comment cards for cash, which was a job contest where workers received money if they had the most comment cards turned in from customers. In contrast, P2 reported that she was highly motivated to win sales contests for free t-shirts and noted during the interview that she was wearing a t-shirt she had won from a contest earlier this year. For P2, small prizes were highly motivating as an incentive for her because she had many uses for prizes.

Participant responses also revealed that some workers had individual preferences for unique job perks. For example, P3 expressed a need for a better work environment with a "more comfortable" employee break room. P5 expressed a need for a break room with employee lockers because she often came to work from class and it would be nice to not have to leave things in her car. P11 expressed a need for more flexibility with getting a weekend night off. In addition, P4 noted that having the reward of a preferred parking space for a week would be a very nice thing for him right now because he arrives to work when all the close spots are gone. He said he never thought a parking spot would be such a good thing, but it helps. In sum, employee responses about unique job perks were varied, but all employees indicated having a need for tailored job perks.

The results for research question one, based on data analyzed from semi-structured individual interviews and researcher reflective notes, indicated that workers' need to earn sufficient income and were motivated by different incentives. Most participants viewed adequate pay as receiving tips that were 18 to 20% of the bill and more than half reported that they usually earned between nine and 20 dollars per hour. The responses for question one also indicated that not all employees favored the same job perks. While some workers appreciated incentives like prizes for sales contests, other workers perceived those rewards as an annoyance or distraction. Research question one addressed the intrinsic needs for workers and all participants in this study needed to earn enough money to live on, but not all workers favored the same job rewards.

Summary

This chapter provided information about the results of the study. The purpose of this qualitative, embedded single-case study was to explore the extrinsic and intrinsic needs of employees in the hospitality industry. The problem of ongoing low employee motivation could lead to negative job behaviors and unnecessary costs to organizations (DiPietro et al., 2014; & Lee & Ok, 2014). Researchers disagreed about the best strategies for enhancing motivation and more information was needed about hospitality workers' point of view regarding their needs. The results from this study unfolded from a purposeful sample of workers who have been employed in the restaurant industry for at least three years. A total of 12 front-of-the-house employees participated in this study. This chapter presented the findings from data gathered from 12 semi-structured interviews along with the transcriptions from eight audio recordings as well as researcher reflective notes.

The findings of this study revealed that front-of-the house restaurant workers had different needs and preferences for job incentives, but they also shared similarities when it came to their intrinsic needs. Themes were identified through data analysis of the initial two research questions, which pertained to extrinsic and intrinsic needs, respectively. The findings for extrinsic needs were: (a) sufficient income and (b) customized incentives. The themes for intrinsic needs were: (a) autonomy (b) growth and (c) supportive supervisors. A third research question emerged from the data, which identified two primary themes for absent extrinsic rewards, which were: (a) lack of sufficient income and (b) lack of fun at work.

CHAPTER 10: The Discussion Chapter

WOW! Can you believe you completed data collection, analysis, and reporting? There is a tendency to lose steam here at the discussion chapter. I completely understand where you are coming from, but this is the most important chapter of your entire dissertation. There was a reason for conducting the research (the whole project) and that was to tell readers what you learned and what has changed now as a result of YOUR study! This is a big deal. I can go back and forth with the students I chair several times before they seem to grasp the enormity of this responsibility (this discussion chapter).

I heard the student's passion in the beginning of the project. HERE is where to let that out, don't hold it in just because you are exhausted and maybe so sick of this project. For the dissertation consulting students I used to work with - helping with this chapter was challenging for me. I could guess at what a certain result could mean for an industry, or area, but I would need to make suggestions and the student, who was now the expert, would have to agree or disagree and then expand. Most of my consulting work at this phase was editing their expressed ideas, making logical suggestions about implications, or asking questions to get the student to start thinking/writing like an expert instead of a student.

One of my favorite things about working with students on their dissertations is the subtle shift from student to doctor. I call it subtle, but I can see it quite clearly each and every time. I have never not seen it. It is not a gradual transition. It is more of an abrupt shift. The shift happens almost always in the discussion chapter phase. I point it out to about 50% of the students and I have no idea how I make the distinction about who to share it with or not. I don't know if they can feel a change or not. The students I share my observation with don't seem to be too impressed by it, and/or I don't think they believe me. All students I worked with, in either capacity, don't seem to believe they are done until they walk out of the defense. Some don't even believe that is the end - and need to get a letter or their diploma from the school. Isn't that interesting - I think it suggests the trauma associated with this process!

Most discussion chapters will be comprised of three main sections, intro, implications, and recommendations. The intro section should open with a sentence or two about the general problem, one about the specific problem, and one restatement of the exact purpose sentence. The second paragraph of the discussion chapter introduction should be one general sentence about the study sample, data collection, variables, and findings in general.

Next is something new, you will develop a paragraph (or some schools call for a whole section) about the study limitations and how you addressed them. If you were not able to address them then note how the limitation will ultimately impact the findings. Most students get this section wrong the first time. What we are looking for is a restatement of the potential limitations you identified in the method section (of your dissertation proposal) and a determination if they were indeed problematic. You present one limitation at a time by noting it was a limitation. Then you note how you dealt with it. Then you note if it impacted your findings at all. Here is an example.

Sampling bias was a study limitation as participant recruitment was accomplished with only adult learners registered with either SurveyMonkey or Qualtrics. Although there is a likelihood adult learners from this sample differed from adult learners who are not registered with these online services, SurveyMonkey and Qualtrics panel base volunteers are proportional and reflective of the general population (Qualtrics, 2016; SurveyMonkey, 2016), allowing for generalization of the results.

After the discussion introduction section you will develop your implications section. I have a nice formula for this section that has been very well received by other chairs, committee members, and readers. It goes like this. Organize the implications section by research question - one at a time - and with a bold heading. Open by restating the research question. Then answer the question based on your finding. **You WILL NOT reiterate any statistics or numbers from the results chapter** just answer the research question and note the overall main finding for the research question with words. Then follow with comparison paragraphs and implication paragraphs.

Comparison to the Existing Literature

After you introduce your research question, note how your finding compares to the existing literature. I suggest one paragraph for the matches and one for the mismatches. In each sentence restate your finding and then say who it matches or doesn't match with. Develop one paragraph for each (matches and mismatches and keep it organized - don't go back and forth this one matches and this one doesn't in one paragraph - one paragraph for matches and one form mismatches. You can develop an idea about why they don't match as the ending sentence for the no match paragraph. You can also include either a concluding sentence, or a paragraph if you have more to say about how your findings **extend** the current literature. Extend is different than match or mismatch. An extension is saying there was no result about this to match or not match with, so here is what I did and what we know now - the extension! Here is a sample of evaluation paragraphs from a successfully defended dissertation.

Research question one evaluation (Sylver-Foust, 2015). The findings of the current study showed that separately and combined the CLS dimensions of collegiality, distributed power, and facilitative leadership have a statically significant positive relationship with and can predict employee satisfaction. Moreover, the contribution of each of the three dimensions of the CLS statistically contributed to the prediction of employee satisfaction. The findings suggest that leaders, who use the three CLS dimensions of collegiality, distributed power, and facilitative leadership, tend to have employees who affirm higher employee satisfaction. Also, the results indicated that leaders increased use of the CLS increases employee satisfaction.

The results of this study corroborate several researchers' findings. The current findings that the three dimensions of collegiality, distributed power, and facilitative leadership of the CLS predicted an increase in employee satisfaction corroborated the findings of, Locke (1995), Lorber and Skela (2012), Sakiru et al. (2013) and van den Pol-Grevelink et al. (2012). The current findings corroborated the findings of Locke (1995) and van den Pol-Grevelink et al. (2012) who demonstrated that employee satisfaction is influenced by employees' experiences and interactions with organizational leaders and colleagues, but extend that research to CLS concepts. The current findings also supported the findings of Lorber and Skela (2012) that assessed employee satisfaction and identified factors, which affected employee satisfaction with nurses at 4-hospitals in Slovenia. As in the current investigation, Lorber and Skela found leaders' behaviors had a large

> Comment [J]: Sum up what the findings mean - in paragraph one
>
> Comment [J]: Include a paragraph that covers the studies you discussed in C2 - that your findings corroborate (match with). Include a topic sentence just like this.

impact on employee satisfaction. The current findings also generally corroborate the findings of Loo (2006), who demonstrated that organizational leaders' behaviors can affects employee satisfaction, and organizational commitment, but extend the research to the CLS as a predictor of employee satisfaction, and organizational commitment. The current findings also support the findings of Singh (2013), who demonstrated the use of the CLS or dimensions of the CLS increased employee satisfaction. As in the current investigation, Singh (2013) found that employee satisfaction was significantly correlated with leaders' power distribution to employees, especially when the leaders were not viewed as authoritative figures who executed regulation without collaborating and considering the ideas and perspectives of employees. However, the findings of the current study extend the research of Lorber and Skela (2012) and Loo (2006) to the behaviors in the dimensions collegiality, distributed power, and facilitative leadership of the CLS as predictors of employee satisfaction.

In contrast, the current findings do not support the results of Jarvis (2010) who demonstrated that an excessive approach to distributed power negatively impacted employees. The present findings also do not corroborate findings of Heponiemi et al. (2014) who reported employee satisfaction would decrease when organizational leaders do not distribute power, which employees perceive as negative. One reason for the lack corroboration may be due to differences in the research approach.

Implication Paragraphs

Just when you thought you were done, you realize you are not. In my experience these implication paragraphs will be the most challenging for you to develop, but will be the most remembered, so take your time and let's break down the strategy. I end up saying this one main idea about five times and in about five different ways until a student connects with it. Here are some versions for you.... "What are the implications of your particular findings? What does it mean now that we know this? What does it tell us, change things, how does it add to the literature. The focus really needs to be about - how does this new information we have now (because of your study-findings!) change things. What does it all mean?" Here is another thing I say... "What is needed here is what are the IMPLICATIONS of YOUR findings. The purpose of this chapter/section is to now say what the implications are from YOUR findings. What does it mean now that we know what we do from YOUR study?" Here is my third way for you...."the implications of the findings (now that we know the answer to your research question - the question

150

has been answered by you), so how does that answered RQ inform us considering the stated problem with the literature, purpose, theory problem, and significance."

Do you see how many hoops I have to jump through to pull this important information out of the students? As an outsider (sometimes) to their topic area I can make suggestions about what I think is an implication. Most of the time they say, oh, yeah! that is one! I wonder if you can't always see the implications because you are too close, OR is it you don't have confidence in your findings to imply anything new? Well, good thing we don't have to figure that out now. Here are some sample implication paragraphs.

Implication paragraphs sample #1 (Bennett, 2016). There is an implication to this finding, as the development team has no set guidelines to follow procedurally as to which stakeholders to include input from on the development of the RRP. Although, most SROs concurred the majority of stakeholders are included, some development teams do not include the input of the utility companies. This can highly hinder a response to a critical incident if water, gas, or electric needs to be shut off to a school or the surrounding area. Oftentimes, these companies do not respond to incidents in a timely manner. If they are brought in during the development process utility companies may respond to a critical incident at a faster rate.

The current finding for this research question extend general systems theory by adding to the literature and demonstrating each agency's input (roles and responsibilities) must equal to insure balance in the response process, otherwise chaos will ensue at the school and responding agencies will not know how to respond (Bernard et al., 2005). The current findings established it was not always clear who was in command once all the stakeholders responded to the critical incident.

There are multiple implications to these findings. First, it is necessary to determine who is in charge of the critical incident crime scene. The majority of SROs stated it is a crime scene, thus law enforcement personnel is in charge; however, school officials oftentimes believe since it is a school, so school officials should be in charge. This creates chaos, which can be alleviated during the development process. Second, the development team must work in a collaborative way and stakeholders must learn to let their egos not play a role in the development of the RRP.

Implications paragraphs sample #2 (Puhlman, 2016). There are implications of these findings. Despite having the highest expenditures on health care, overall Quality of care/access to care in the U.S. is fair while quality of care/access to care for impoverished people and minorities is poor (Agency for Healthcare Research and Quality 2013). The Medicaid population, for which Health Insurer A provides health insurance coverage, consist primarily of low income members (TennCare Division of Health Care Finance & Administration, n.d.) where members' poverty level for most eligibility categories are less than or equal to 250% (TennCare Division of Health Care Finance & Administration, n.d.). Because LMASS principles focus efforts on quality improvement (Liker & Morgan, 2011), this study suggested the LMASS program implemented at Health Insurer A impacted quality improvement.

Hospitals, physicians, and other healthcare providers are primary suppliers for health insurance organizations (Sage, 2014). These suppliers are significant for health insurers as leaders of health insurers establish provider networks to direct customers toward the high-quality providers among other reasons (Howard, 2014). In addition, customers' interactions with these suppliers can influence the level of satisfaction from customers rating their overall satisfaction with their health plan question from CAHPS Health Plans Surveys (Health Insurer A, personal communication, December 2014). One major principle of LMASS application is to integrate suppliers into processes completely (Liker & Morgan, 2011); thus, this study suggested that the LMASS program impacted improvement of relationships with primary suppliers at Health Insurer A.

Another implication related to timing of realizable results. While LMASS is a long-term initiative (Liker & Morgan, 2011); Ferdow and Netland (2014) indicated that during the beginning stages of LMASS, senior management would not notice significant improvements. Findings in this study either suggested that contrary to Ferdow and Netland (2014), senior management could notice statistically significant improvement during the beginning stages of LMASS or the findings suggested business leaders could minimize the length of the beginning stages of LMASS.

> Comment [JB]: This is a great idea if you can develop it. it might speak to the theory extension for those working on a PhD study.

Implications paragraphs sample #3 (Rehman, 2016). The findings suggest the perception of social benefits is at least in part contingent upon the nature of one's relationship with AAPP programs. That is, non-participants, in general, scored high enough on social benefits to conclude AAPPP is beneficial to a certain degree, but did not perceive the benefits as strong as those who participated. It is likely, then, participation created an experience making the social costs more recognizable or impactful enough for participants to score them higher than non-participants.

Again, the implication of this finding is clearer when compared with the perceptions of economic costs. Program participants should perceive the economic and social benefits of AAPPP participation more positively because of their direct experience with the program. Such participation would privy them to insights non-participating minority business owners have not had. Yet, no significant difference on economic costs were found, but such a difference was found for social costs. A floor effect cannot fully explain this finding. These findings imply social costs are more salient because direct experience through AAPPP participation creates access to different information. That is, it is the target of the perception (the independent variable), which dictates this finding. For the economic costs, perceptions may be led by what information participants and non-participants receive through the media outside of the daily operations of their businesses. The current findings suggest social costs are also more easily observable by participants because they are more likely emerging in daily activities and in a more personal way. These are not only congruent with perspectives lending support for the benefits of AAPPP programs, but, paradoxically, they simultaneously make the case for the case against it.

General implications. One of the main contributions of this study to the existing literature is for its focus on perceptions. The literature is highly outcome-focused with little research conducted on the perspectives of affirmative action program participants and even less on minority business owners. This study ventured to explore the confluence of participant and non-participant perceptions of AAPPP in order to possibly identify meaningful information useful towards the case for or against sustaining these programs. This study, in turn, produced paradoxical findings challenging to interpret. In fact, the findings call into light concerns past researchers have had with perception-based data, affirmative action, and policy debate. Crosby, Iyer, Clayton, and Downing (2003) described perception research on this topic as muddling. They noted a phenomenon called *denial of personal discrimination*.

One final note about the implications section. Similar to how nervous you were to send your results chapter to your chair, you might be nervous to send this discussion chapter for feedback - especially this implication section - now that I have you all worked up about it. Still, please do not hesitate at this step. Your chair will have good ideas for you here. Basically you want to get what I am suggesting on the page and to your chair right away. Your chair will work with you to refine it - and still think you are a genius, so no worries about that. Once it is written and proofread - send it in! The last sections you need to develop for the discussion chapter are the recommendations and conclusions.

Recommendations Section

Begin this section with a brief intro then break up this section into two paragraphs, one about recommendations for practice, and then one about recommendations for future research. Your recommendations for practice are based on YOUR findings and their implications, and can be seen by a reader to logically follow from those outcomes. Each recommendation is clearly identified as such and to whom the recommendation is directed appears (avoiding the use of terms such as "should" and "must"). There is not much need for other citations in this section as the recommendations are based on your findings. Here are your samples.

Recommendations paragraphs sample #1 (Lawless, 2016). Based upon the results of the study, recommendations for practice and future research are offered. Two recommendations for practice include: (1) manufacturers improve existing leader efficacy as a means to influence Lean Six Sigma success rates; and (2) manufacturers hire and employ leaders with already established high self efficacy to lead Lean Six Sigma implementations. Two recommendations for future research include: (1) an experiment to explore aspects of leader efficacy that prove important in successful Lean Six Sigma implementations; and (2) to conduct a similar study in different geographic area(s) and/or other industries to evaluate the different aspects of leadership efficacy that have an influence on Lean Six Sigma success.

Recommendations for practice. Based on the results of this study indicating leaders with higher self efficacy have higher Lean Six Sigma success rates, two recommendations for practice are offered. It is recommended manufacturers improve leader efficacy as a means to influence Lean Six Sigma success rates. To improve leader efficacy, manufacturers must first determine the current level of leader efficacy within their organization. This can be accomplished by evaluating their leaders' self efficacy via self reported surveys, similar to the LEQ survey used in the current study. Once the manufacturer has identified low efficacy leaders, training and mentoring could be provided in order to cultivate these leaders to become high efficacy leaders. There are a variety of leadership training methods that could be utilized to accomplish increasing a leader's efficacy, such as mentoring by a senior manager or executive, web-based training modules, and classroom training. Proctor & Gamble, Microsoft, General Electric, and Toyota, are among the top rated companies for developing leadership through these formal leadership training programs.

Second, it is recommended manufacturing companies implementing Lean Six Sigma initiatives improve their leader efficacy by hiring leaders that possess already established high self efficacy. In order to influence the success of a Lean Six Sigma implementation, as implied by the current study, leaders with high efficacy would need to be in charge of the change initiative. When a manufacturer is planning a Lean Six Sigma implementation, a hiring process that includes determining a leader's efficacy would be beneficial. During the interview process the manufacturer would determine a prospective leader's efficacy by including strategic questions regarding the individual's self efficacy and previous success rates for Lean Six Sigma implementations they have lead. A questionnaire similar to the LEQ used in the current study would also help identify leaders with high efficacy as would a leadership skills assessment. Hiring only those with a high efficacy to lead the change project may positively influence the success rate. These strategies are important for ensuring the successful implementation of a Lean Six Sigma initiative.

Recommendations for future research. Based on the findings and limitations of this study, two suggestions are made for future research. One potential area for future research is to focus specifically on increasing leader efficacy via manipulation, rather than a selected variable of inherent leadership efficacy differences. This might be accomplished by assessing leadership efficacy and Lean Six Sigma success rates of an organization before and after a leadership classroom training and mentoring program has been implemented as the manipulation. Now that the effects of leadership differences have been established, future researchers can evaluate the impact of a leadership efficacy training program to determine such contributions to Lean Six Sigma implementation success. A second recommendation for future research is to carry out an investigation similar to the current study in a different geographic area(s) and/or other industries.

Recommendation section sample #2 (Prior, 2015). The findings of this study extend the work motivation literature regarding diverse employee needs and job incentives. The current findings supported Herzberg et al.'s (1959) motivation-hygiene theory and also added to the practical literature about the different needs workers have at this time and how it impacts their work effort (Gneezy et al., 2011; Moller & Deci, 2014; van Veen-Dirks, 2010). Based on the current findings the following recommendations for practice and further research are offered.

Recommendations for practice. Based on the findings of this case study, several recommendations for practice are proposed. The first recommendation pertains to the area of rewards management. Hospitality leaders should consider tailoring rewards based on the extrinsic needs and preferences of their employees. Managers should receive training on how to explore and identify worker's extrinsic needs continuously because workers' needs change regularly and so do their preferences for rewards. Workers need to be informed that their opinions are welcomed and managers will have to develop a work a climate that allows for worker feedback. One way to ascertain information about individual extrinsic needs and reward preferences may be to simply ask employees what they want. Managers can also use employee comment cards, staff discussions, and observation to identify what workers' want their work effort. The time and effort it takes to customize rewards for workers can pay off with a more motivated staff because rewards are more effective when they are perceived as meaningful to the worker.

It is also recommended managers in the hospitality industry be aware of the difference between hygiene and motivator variables in order to understand how these different factors interplay with motivation. Extrinsic rewards, or hygiene, are unrelated to inherent motivation because these incentives actually function to reduce dissatisfaction. Managers can use pay, benefits, and cash perks to prevent dissatisfaction and help employees meet basic needs, and then use training, interesting work, and autonomous opportunities to improve motivation. Job motivators are associated with job content and in the restaurant industry this refers to activities like running a station, building rapport with customers, and sharing a healthy relationship with colleagues and supervisors.

Another recommendation for practice pertains to the proper use of extrinsic incentives. Restaurant managers need to be trained to manage extrinsic rewards, or hygiene, effectively. The overuse of extrinsic rewards can actually pull from work motivation because the need for hygiene can escalate in an upward cycle that never becomes fully satiated for workers (Herzberg, 1968). Hygiene factors escalate because humans tend to need increasing amounts of money, status, and job perks if they are basing their performance on the reception of these factors. On the other hand, motivator factors do not escalate because they are additive and based on psychological growth (Herzberg et al, 1959). If managers place too much emphasis on pay and tangible rewards it can be costly for the organization while it also fails to satisfy workers' intrinsic needs. Offering enough appropriate extrinsic rewards could help alleviate stress for front-of-the-house restaurant workers, and possibly even provide short-term boosts to their work effort; however, managers will effectively improve motivation when they provide opportunities for workers to be motivated from within, which comes from experiencing psychological growth from different job tasks.

Based on the findings about demonstrated intrinsic needs, it is recommended leaders aim to come across as supportive to workers. Managers need to pay attention to the professional relationship they share with workers who labor under their authority because it influences worker affect and job motivation. All 12 participants in this study preferred supervisors that were perceived as helpful and considerate of workers' needs. Restaurant managers should look for small ways to assist workers during busy times while they also aim to build a healthy professional bond with each employee. The managerial effort invested in supporting workers can have positive impacts on employee motivation, procedural understanding, affect, and reward expectations (Tan & Waheed, 2011). Good communication and rapport between leaders and workers can also help to buffer unfavorable decisions or times when leaders have to put the organization's needs before the worker's needs.

It is also recommended managers in hospitality settings maintain a positive social work environment. Managers need to be informed about the ways that the social context of the workplace influences worker affect and overall job satisfaction. Worker motivation is shaped by the interaction between the workers' individual make-up and the social context in which they work (Judge & Kammeyer-Mueller, 2012). The atmosphere in the restaurant industry is sometimes hurried and chaotic while other times it can be slow and monotonous, so managers need to use different strategies for different work times. Team games can help prevent boredom during slow hours while sales contests can be used to help workers set goals during busy hours. Participants in this study intrinsically valued a work atmosphere that allowed workers a place to talk and process stress. Participants also highly valued independence and empowerment (intrinsic values), so restaurant managers need to ensure that workers have humanistic freedoms with a sense that the organization cares about their overall wellness. Managers also need to be trained about the layered social psychological factors that interplay with workers' perceptions, intrinsic needs, and experience with work environmental conditions.

Recommendations for future research. Based on the current study limitations and results the following recommendations for future research are offered. The first recommendation is based on the study limitation of generalizing to restaurant workers on the East Coast of the United States. Although the United States is one nation, workers from different regions could have dissimilar intrinsic and extrinsic needs and so sampling workers from other geographical locations could expand current findings. Future researchers could also focus on older workers in the restaurant industry because the majority of participants in this study were under the age of 30. Shierholz (2014) found that approximately half of all restaurant workers were between 25 and 54 years of age, so there are plenty of workers in this industry who are over the age of thirty and who could be interviewed to expand the outcomes of current findings. The data collected for this study was collected from front-of-the-house restaurant workers and it is recommended that additional qualitative studies be conducted investigating the intrinsic and extrinsic needs of workers from other restaurant jobs, like back-of-the-house positions, or from different work sectors, like retail or education, then compare and expand findings.

It is also recommended future researchers use quantitative inquiry to expand the findings from this qualitative study, which had a small sample of 12 participants. Researchers could collect self-report data from a larger sample of workers, which could provide insight about variable correlations or factor relationships in order to expand the literature about workers' intrinsic/extrinsic needs and reward preferences. In addition, future researchers could sample workers who have chosen restaurant work as their primary career choice, which was not the case for participants in this study. Only two participants in this study were interested in advancement opportunities at their current restaurant while the other ten participants were in this line of work only as a short-term career option. Future researchers could expand current findings by interviewing workers with the predetermined parameter of restaurant work as a long-term career.

Based on the current study findings the following recommendations for future research are also offered. Future researchers could focus on the managerial perspective of reward management because this study only examined the workers' perspective of their needs and experience with incentives. Understanding more about the leaders' experience could inform training tactics for managers while also adding insight to the literature about the managerial viewpoint of rewards management. Future research could also explore both the worker and managerial experience with reward efficacy and then assess any incongruities or consistencies between subordinates and supervisors' perspectives. Identified disparities between supervisor and subordinate perspectives could add to the organizational development literature or inform strategies that aim to improve the way human and social systems interact within organizational hierarchies.

Recommendation section sample #3 (Bourbina, 2016). The findings of the current study may be used to address educational institutions' accountability concerns for evidence of student learning (Armstrong & Fukami, 2010; Berdrow & Evers, 2010; Jackson, 2013) by providing evidence of gains in educational competencies and learning transfer with corresponding evidence of gains in job performance. Gains in educational competencies coupled with evidence of subsequent increases job performance may be satisfactory evidence of student learning and learning transfer. The findings also support developing educational competencies as a means of sustaining organizational productivity (Hanneman & Gardner, 2010), while accounting for changing undergraduate demographics (Cruce & Hillman, 2012), thus addressing the study problem.

Recommendations for practice. Based on the results of this study indicating educational competency predictive capacity on job performance, three recommendations for practice are offered. The first recommendation is for educational leaders and policy makers to include the growing undergraduate population of non-traditional learners. Adult learners are in an ideal position to bridge perspectives between higher education and the workplace (Schmitz and Hayholm, 2015). With their concurrent college and workforce experience, they can assess learning outcomes from both viewpoints. It is also suggested educational leaders include adult learners' ability to assess learning transfer from gains in educational competency to improvements in job performance in future learning outcome and accountability studies.

Based on the study findings, the second recommendation is for educational leaders to examine existing curricula and make revisions to improve acquisition of these competencies due to the ongoing concerns of gaps between educational outcomes and employer expectations in job performance. Although the findings from this study indicate a positive predictive capacity between educational competency and job performance, educational leaders' efforts in addressing outdated curricula and improper pedagogical techniques may help in raising the gain. Whereas Weaver and Kulesza (2013) encouraged faculty to incorporate soft skills such as analytical thinking, problem solving, and communication skills into curricula; revisions to all curriculum should include input from all stakeholders as means of providing valuable information regarding competencies required for learners (Brink & Costigan, 2015).

The final recommendation is for industry. Industry's concerns with educational institutions ineffectiveness in producing graduates with the required education competencies required by employers (Berdrow & Evers, 2010), could be mitigated by greater collaboration with educational leaders. Sharing evidence about the predictive relationships among four distinct educational competencies and job performance may foster greater understanding of the perceived gaps.

Recommendations for future research. Based on the findings, limitations, and delimitation of this study, four suggestions are made for future research. First, it is recommended future researchers use additional predictor variables to determine job performance. The four educational competency predictor variables included skill sets based on Evers et al. (1998) study. Researchers may consider updating the skill sets with what is currently recommended as evidence of student learning for accountability concerns in addition to what is being required for success in the workplace as outlined by employers.

It is also recommended future researchers conduct longitudinal research in this topic area. This study's design was cross-sectional; therefore, inferences were dependent on a single sample with conditions occurring in the timeframe. Researchers could validate the data using a longitudinal design with a select group of respondents following them from their freshmen years through senior year. This may provide evidence of competency attainment thru the educational hierarchy while assessing learning transfer to job performance.

Future researchers could replicate this study using a larger sample of career groups than was included in this study, which would address the fifth limitation. Due to the sample groups, it might be challenging to generalize these findings to the larger population of adult learners. Two groups (health care and education) made up 35% of the sample while 16% of the sample was unidentified. Researchers may want to seek a broader scope of respondents to improve the distribution for better generalization across the adult learner population.

Finally, future researchers could make use of a more general adult learner population. The current sample was comprised of adult learners registered with online survey service providers, which may have led to sampling bias. Although it has been established SurveyMonkey and Qualtrics panel base volunteers are proportional and reflective of the general population (Qualtrics, 2016; SurveyMonkey, 2016), the use of an unbiased sample with confirmation of the current findings will add to the validity of this study.

Conclusion Section

Are we really here now! The dissertation conclusion section!! This summary section of your discussion chapter is a bit more than the summary of each of the preceding chapters. In this chapter you provide the following information. Open with a sentence about the general problem, then the specific problem, then reiterate (by coping and pasting) the exact study purpose sentence. Note the sample and one small piece of information about data collection.

In the next paragraph report the answer to each of the research questions, then a summary of that research questions' evaluation and implication high points. Use this approach for each research question. Then provide one paragraph about a summary of your noted recommendations. Please see these samples.

Conclusion sample #1 (Lawless, 2016). Manufacturers demonstrate a high failure rate implementing Lean Six Sigma initiatives in US. Over 70% of the manufacturers in the US who have attempted implementing Lean Six Sigma admit they are not making good progress (Pay, 2008). More specifically, existence of leadership efficacy differences in Lean Six Sigma implementation success were unknown despite the suggestion in current literature that leadership efficacy differences influence implementation success (Bernett & Nentl, 2010). This study provided information on the impact of perceived leadership efficacy differences on Lean Six Sigma success rates in a manufacturing setting. The findings contribute to the literature by indicating that leaders with high self efficacy tend to have higher success rates implementing Lean Six Sigma in their organizations. The study results provide an important contribution to the success of Lean Six Sigma implementation in manufacturing by promulgating information about the impact of perceived leader efficacy on Lean Six Sigma implementation success rate in manufacturing, as measured by the OEE. An implication is manufacturers may be able to positively influence Lean Six Sigma implementation success rates by considering leader efficacy prior to implementation.

It was recommended manufacturers can improve Lean Six Sigma outcomes by thoughtful hiring and training initiatives, focused on leader efficacy. The current investigation revealed the importance of leadership differences on Lean Six Sigma implementation in the manufacturing industry, now future researchers can determine what components of leadership efficacy training are salient in Lean Six Sigma implementation success. The process improvements and the reductions in system breakdowns and errors in manufacturing resulting from successful Lean Six Sigma initiatives could have a significant impact on reducing the costs associated with manufacturing in the United States.

Conclusion sample #2 (Bourbina, 2016). Measuring the acquisition and application of educational competencies and subsequent application to job performance may provide important accountability evidence while also providing an alternate means of measuring investments in HC. Various educational stakeholders have made accountability a main concern of education both in the U.S. and internationally. In the U.S., educational institutions are failing to satisfy accountability concerns and both government and accrediting agencies are calling for evidence of student learning. In addition to inadequately addressing a growing adult learner population, educational institutions are facing challenges adjusting their curriculum to help develop the necessary educational competencies for meeting workforce needs. The purpose of this quantitative, cross sectional, predictive correlational study was to investigate the relationship between educational competencies (managing self, communicating, managing people and task, and mobilizing innovation and change) and job performance in adult learners.

The findings of this study indicated a predictive relationship exists among the four educational competencies and job performance. The current findings also suggested an alternative method of measuring investments in HC while addressing adult learners, learning outcomes, and suggest necessary evidence about the predictive relationships among four distinct educational competencies. The implications of these findings to educational leaders may be a means of addressing curriculum reform and accountability concerns. The current findings suggested an alternative method of measuring investments in HC while addressing adult learners, learning outcomes, and suggest necessary evidence about the predictive relationships among four distinct educational competencies. Educational institutions may also satisfy accountability concerns (AACU, 2008; Crawford et al., 2011; Hanneman & Gardner, 2010) by producing graduates with the educational competencies required by employers (Berdrow & Evers, 2010). The current research was needed to examine the predictive relationship between self-reported educational competencies and job performance in order to inform stakeholders charged with making curriculum decisions for a growing adult learner population. The findings supported and also extended the existing literature about students' perceptions of possessing the necessary educational competencies gained from undergraduate studies.

Three recommendations for practice were offered for educational leaders and policy makers and industry. First, include adult learner and other stakeholder viewpoints when revising curriculum as a means of reducing gaps between educational outcomes and employer expectations in job performance. Second, address outdated curricula and inappropriate pedagogical techniques and encourage faculty to incorporate soft skills such as analytical thinking, problem solving, and communication skills into curricula. All curriculum revisions include input from all stakeholders as means of providing valuable information regarding educational competencies and evidence of learning outcomes. The final recommendation for practice was directed to industry. Industry could mitigate their concerns of inadequate graduate preparation through greater collaboration with educational institutions. Sharing evidence about the predictive relationships among four distinct educational competencies and job performance may foster greater understanding of the perceived gaps.

Recommendations for future research were also provided. Future researchers could include using a population of adult learners in general, other predictor variables be included, alternative methods of measuring investments in HC, conducting a study using a longitudinal design, offering a more in-depth survey instrument designed to improve the accuracy of a respondent's estimate of educational competency and job performance, and replication of this study using a larger sample of career groups. In conclusion, gains in educational competencies and corresponding evidence of gains in job performance may address educational institutions' accountability concerns for evidence of student learning while also addressing concerns of learning transfer.

Conclusion sample #3 (Prior, 2015). The purpose of this qualitative holistic study was to explore the extrinsic and intrinsic needs of employees in the hospitality industry. The current study findings added to the existing literature regarding work motivation and extended it by providing information about workers' needs. Results of this study revealed workers have extrinsic needs for sufficient income and customized rewards while they also have the intrinsic needs for autonomy, growth, and supportive leadership. In addition, lack of adequate pay and lack of fun at work were found to be sources of dissatisfaction for most participants. Ongoing worker dissatisfaction could interfere with work effort while it could also impede a worker's ability to be motivated from intrinsic variables (Herzberg, 1968; Tilman et al., 2010).

The results of this study have implications for worker motivation. Overall, the study outcomes supported previous research findings, which demonstrated workers' extrinsic needs must be fulfilled in order for work effort to be improved (Hao & Zihanxin, 2011; Tews et al., 2014; Tudor, 2011). The current findings also extended the literature by exploring workers' intrinsic needs inductively, which helped offset the abundant deductive assessments in the area of work motivation (Degan, 2013). The outcomes for this study contributed to the theoretical framework for the motivation-hygiene theory by supporting previous researchers who found that job variables contributing to employee motivation are separate from the job variables that prevent job dissatisfaction (Herzberg, 1968; Tilman et al., 2010; Sachau, 2007). This implies that workers must have both tangible and intangible incentives for their work effort because different rewards fulfill different intrinsic and extrinsic needs. In addition, because workers' subjectively value different rewards at different stages in their careers, job incentives offered will be more effective when the rewards are perceived as meaningful to the worker at a given time. Managers can offer a variety of reward options for workers in order to help cater to the ongoing fluctuation in needs and preferences.

The problem that prompted this study was a need to know more about the intrinsic and extrinsic needs of workers' in the restaurant industry. The outcomes of this research extend the literature by highlighting that workers have many diverse needs, but have shared commonalties with intrinsic needs for job autonomy, personal growth from work, and to work with supportive leadership. An implication from this finding is that workers in this industry come to work for more than just a paycheck and the majority of participants were motivated from intrinsic job factors like advanced trainings, interesting work, and internal recognition. However, even though workers wanted more than a paycheck for their work effort, participants all shared the fundamental necessity to earn money in order to pay for basic living expenses. The implications for this finding are that while workers must fulfill intrinsic needs from work, their motivation will be impeded if they do not earn enough pay to satisfy extrinsic needs. Managers can help offset income shortfalls by offering cash prizes and other tangible perks at various times.

Based on the findings of this case study, several recommendations for practice were proposed. First, it was recommended that managers customize rewards because not all workers value the same incentives. Rewards are more effective when they are perceived as meaningful and so options for job incentives should be presented to workers. Managers should also be trained to understand that hygiene, or extrinsic rewards, function to prevent dissatisfaction where motivator variables, or intrinsic rewards, inherently inspire work effort. It was recommended that managers use pay and tangible job perks (extrinsic activities) to prevent employee job dissatisfaction, and then use trainings, interesting work, and autonomous opportunities (intrinsic activities) to improve motivation. A caution for managers is to not overuse monetary rewards in an attempt to improve work effort. The overuse of extrinsic rewards can actually pull from work motivation because the need for hygiene can escalate in an upward cycle that never becomes fully satiated for workers (Herzberg, 1968).

It was also recommended that hospitality managers put forth the effort to come across as supportive to employees. This does not mean that managers have to become friends or work pals with subordinates; instead, the implication is that managers need to build a healthy professional work relationship with employees because workers have an intrinsic need to be treated with dignity. Perceived supportive leadership can positively impact employee motivation, procedural understanding, affect, and reward expectations (Tan & Waheed, 2011; Wang & Hsieh, 2012). Finally, it is recommended managers create a positive social work environment for employees to address their intrinsic needs. This is not to say that workers need a happy or extremely cheery work atmosphere, because that would not be ideal; instead, a positive social work environment entails giving workers autonomy and humanistic freedoms. A positive work environment allows workers a place to talk, process stress, and builds relations with colleagues and customers. Managers should be trained with techniques for developing a healthy atmosphere that allows workers to satisfy psychological growth needs from work.

Based on the current study limitations and outcomes, there were several recommendations for future research presented in this chapter. It was recommended that similar inductive inquires be conducted by sampling workers who are over the age of 30, from different locations in the United States, from different positions in the hospitality industry or different job sectors. Future studies could also use deductive inquiry to collect self-report data from a larger sample of workers, which could expand the outcomes of this inductive study, which collected and assessed data from 12 participants. In addition, future researchers could sample workers who have chosen restaurant work as their primary career choice, which was not the case for most participants in this study who were in this line of work as a short-term job option. Lastly, future researchers could also focus on the managerial perspective of reward management or explore both the workers' and managers' experience with reward efficacy.

CHAPTER 11: The Defenses (proposal and dissertation defense)

Most schools will have you present or "defend" your dissertation work on two separate occasions in front of a small group (your committee) and quite possibly (but not likely) a few other students in your program. If you have not attended a defense you probably have all sorts of crazy images about just what goes on at a proposal and/or dissertation defense. I was preparing for some type of Spanish Inquisition, when what I experienced was a very small group of smiling people sitting around a table listening to me (while I was freaking the heck out!). If you would like to demystify these unknown phenomena for yourself, you can wait for your proposal defense, or you can attend a classmate's defense. Either way, I think you will be surprised by the proceedings.

The first time you will defend your dissertation is when you stand in front of your committee convincing them your proposal has merit and research is indeed needed, and the research that is needed - is your clever study. You will present the highlighted contents of your first three proposal chapters in a PowerPoint presentation. You will focus mainly on the justification for why additional research is needed and "defend" your method. The defense attendees will ask you questions to make sure you are capable of conducting the study (collecting data and analyzing it).

I know for a fact right now you are thinking you are not capable of such an endeavor and you are immediately feeling like this may be the deal breaker. It is not. For sure we (all of us who already have the PhD) felt exactly this same way. Some in the early stages of proposal development, some as they were walking in to their proposal defense. It is more the rule than the exception, so just hunker down and deal with those feeling by accepting them and then letting them float out of your mine (a meditative stance :). As you walk out of the proposal defense you will invariably note how, "gee that wasn't so bad" to yourself. Interestingly though, by the time your dissertation defense rolls around you will most certainly forget that main and important take away and be a nervous wreck all over again. Sorry about that. That is just how it goes.

That being said, you certainly don't want to slack and not be prepared. Here are the DOs and DON'Ts for your two defense presentations:

1. Do develop a PowerPoint presentation. For your proposal defense you will cover chapters one - three (introduction, lit review, and method). For your dissertation defense you will use the same three chapters for the PowerPoint (keep them in there, but don't even go over them in any amount of detail), and add chapters four and five of the dissertation to the PowerPoint. At the proposal defense you can spend time on the lit review and the justification for the study, but at the final dissertation defense you should just summarize the chapter one-three slides and focus on a refresher of the method, the results, the implications, and your recommendations.

Before you develop the PowerPoint presentation ask you chair for the slide number expectation and follow that guideline. Ask about how long she would like you to talk and then practice your presentation (with the PowerPoint) to exactly that amount of time. If your chair doesn't answer these questions and says it is up to you - then plan for about 25 minutes of your talking with the PowerPoint and the rest of the time for questions. Plan about 30 slides (see slide suggestions) Just in case there is a glitch with the technology on defense day, please bring printed out copies of the PowerPoint presentation. Don't make me tell you how many people have thanked me for that crucial piece of advice - I don't want to scare you.

2. Don't include too much information on each slide. This is not so easy to determine, but if the text is 16 point and running off the slide it is too much. Try to use 18 or even 20 font and have no more than three bullet points (with some text) in the text box. Always include a title for each slide. Think of it this way - the PowerPoint slides are there to guide the presentation, you should be augmenting that information with notes from your head (that you first had written out, but you practiced it so much it is now memorized).

If you read through the 30 PowerPoint slides with their information would be done in two minutes (that is how much information we are talking about for the slides) the real meat of this presentation will be you spending about a minute on each of the slides. For the proposal the information about the method should be in proposal language - a qualitative method is planned.... but for the final dissertation defense, the information on the slides should be in past tense - your study is already completed.

Make your first slide a title slide - presenting the manuscript title, your name, and your committee member's names. I find that defenses go better when the student thanks the members at the very beginning (briefly) by having the committee names here on this title slide - and when they just offer a few genuine words of appreciation before beginning (e.g., I just want to thank the committee members for their expert assistance and more than valuable feedback throughout the process, Dr X, the chair, I am not sure what words can describe my gratitude, but it is safe to say I wouldn't be here today without your and the committee's help). Nothing quite like softening up the crowd.

3. Do have notes written out about what you will say for each slide, but.....

4. Don't have your head down and read off the notes during the defenses! OR Don't start at the PowerPoint just reading off that either. Instead practice and practice, and then practice once again by reading the notes and trying to memorize what the heck you are trying to say.

5. Do pause and ask the group if they have any questions at certain stopping points.

6. Don't freak out if someone does ask you a question. You can answer it - don't worry. What if you can't answer it? Still, don't freak out. Look at them with wonder in your eye, crinkle your forehead like you are deep in thought, purse your lips, and utter, "Wow, that is a really great question." "May I please think about that and get back to you later today." The answer will always be yes AND your committee member will be glad she asked such a great question - she might even forget she needs an answer.

7. Do take any advice about the proposal or final dissertation manuscript and agree with it. Ask the committee member if they would like for you to update the proposal/manuscript based on that comment. If they say yes, always agree, and then ask them if they would like to see your changes before you submit your draft to the school. Make a note of their comment by jotting it down, even jot down notes about what their question was - because you will likely forget their question the minute you walk out the door - and you don't want to email the committee member to ask them to repeat themselves (although if this does happen it will be okay).

8. Don't get defensive during the defense. You are there to get feedback on the project, so it can be better. Remember, committees are your friends and they just want to make sure you are all set up for your research. Often times they may ask you to do less than what you were planning (for the proposal). Still, the entire committee had the opportunity to comment on your drafts - before the defenses are even set up - so it is okay to assume there are no significant problems, or significant changes needed. Your chair will step in if you faint, or cannot answer a question, so just hang in there.

9. DON'T try to break up a fight between your committee members. This happens more than I would like to be writing about, but always let your chair address the members to work out some compromise the chair comes up with.

10. Do - at your final dissertation defense accept feedback about your identified implications and recommendations and offer to make changes based on the feedback - even though you are really the expert now. It is important for your committee to feel they had input, but you can be a bit more confident in your responses (then you were at your proposal defense), but still not nearly as confident as they are. You know what I am saying :)

11. Right after the defense... Do try to tell your friends and family what a big deal this all is (even though they won't really understand, remember they have been asking you if you were finished with your dissertation for about five years now because they think it is just a paper, so we can just try and be patient about it). Share the news with a classmate! They will get it! Plan your own celebration and gifts for both defenses - gifts commensurate with the magnitude of the accomplishment - I think you know what I mean here (buy your own gift and don't let a family member who doesn't *get it* purchase the items - yes, I mean two different items/gifts for yourself)!!

12. Right after the defense...Do run to your bank and order checks with Dr. in front of your name. This is one of the more concrete and rewarding aspects of obtaining the PhD - I am just saying. If there are other concrete things you can identify to put a Dr. in front of do that too. I get people pens, mugs, and nameplates with Dr. and their name. These gifts (even if you buy them for yourself) are always a big hit. It was quite the journey - a little acknowledgement of your efforts will make you feel even better about being done!!!

Slide Suggestions (in order)

```
┌─────────────────────────────┐
│      Manuscript Title       │
│                             │
│         Your Name           │
│                             │
│         Chair Name          │
│                             │
│       Committee Names       │
│                             │
│            Date             │
└─────────────────────────────┘
```

```
┌─────────────────────────────┐
│    Introduction/Background  │
│                             │
│   •                         │
│   •                         │
│   •                         │
└─────────────────────────────┘
```

```
┌─────────────────────────────┐
│      Research Problem       │
│                             │
│   • General problem         │
│   • Specific problem        │
│   • Who called for the      │
│     research                │
└─────────────────────────────┘
```

```
┌─────────────────────────────┐
│      Purpose Statement      │
│                             │
│   • The main purpose        │
│     sentence                │
│   • Why the information was │
│     needed                  │
└─────────────────────────────┘
```

```
┌─────────────────────────────┐
│   Significance of the Study │
│                             │
│   • Practical significance  │
│   • Theoretical significance│
└─────────────────────────────┘
```

LITERATURE REVIEW

Lit Review Main Section #1

For your proposal defense you will spend time covering your lit review - to justify why your research is needed. You won't do this for your final defense. To change from the proposal to the final defense, mover from these four slides to just one that lists the four main sections and cover them for just about 2 minutes.

Lit Review Main Section #2
-
-

Lit Review Main Section #3
-
-

Lit Review Main Section #4
-
-

Research Method and Design

- Qual OR Quant
- Name the design
- Briefly state why this design/method was the most appropriate.

Participants

- Population
- Sample

Study Variables/Instruments

Variable #1 - how you measure(d) it

Variable #2 - how you measure(d) it

Data Collection Procedures

- for the proposal - your plan
- at the final defense - what exactly happened

Data Analysis Procedure

- for the proposal - your plan
- at the final defense - what exactly happened

Comment [JB]: Your proposal defense slides will stop here, but add one more slide in that says questions (like the one at the very end here).

Your final dissertation defense you will add these slides about the results.

You will also move the method slides to past tense and have them reflect more of what happened as opposed to the plan.

At this defense these next slides (and the method) will be the bulk of your presentation talking points.

Results

Descriptive Findings

Include table/chart (not SPSS output though-make it nice)

Results: Research Question One

- Restate hypothesis
- Answer it in words
- Include inferential result statement

Results: Research Question Two

- Restate hypothesis
- Answer it in words
- Include inferential result statement

Research Question One Implications

- Comparison to existing literature
- What do the new findings mean for the literature (another way to think about an implication)

Research Question Two Implications

- Comparison to existing literature
- What do the new findings mean for the literature (another way to think about an implication)

Recommendations for Practice

1.
2.
3.

Recommendations for Future Research

1.
2.
3.

Conclusions

1.
2.
3.

Questions?

Conclusion

You have likely heard, more than you liked.... "You know the dissertation journey is like a marathon and not a sprint." Still, it is a worthwhile journey and you will learn many things, but it doesn't have to be painful. As you gleaned, the whole point of the dissertation (study and manuscript) was to demonstrate to a small group of people you could conduct research and you could write in a scientific manner. It really boils down to these two things. It doesn't have to be more difficult than these two things.

After you coursework even if you do not feel confident about your scientific writing skills, or your ability to conduct a research project that is okay. You likely shouldn't. That is what this process (journey-lol) is - to develop the skills needed to conduct research and write technically like a scientist. It is likely your grad school coursework only brushed on these important topics. It will be up to you to make these two things happen after your coursework and before your defense. This is what will ultimately distinguish you between the Ds and the ABDs.

As I mentioned in the preface, I know you can do this. You bought this book - you want this to happen (end). You can do it. Even if you didn't learn exactly what you were supposed to do for the dissertation in your grad school coursework (and we know you DID NOT), even if your chair is sort of a jerk and is more of a picker than a helper, even if your writing skills (scientific or not) are not top notch yet, you can get to the finish line. By recognizing what needs to be done (the things in this book!) then applying yourself, seeking out resources/assistance (see Chapter 13 of this book for helpful resources) when you need it, and your belief in your ability to accomplish this task - you can do it! Of that - I have no doubt. Thank you for including this information in your journey toolkit! Congratulations for what you have accomplished thus far and for what you are about to accomplish in the near future! ONWARD!!

CHAPTER 12: Abstract Samples

Abstract (Lawless, 2016)

Manufacturers attempt to compete in the world economy and improve their business processes by implementing change management theory, often using Lean Six Sigma processes; however, these implementations are not always effective in manufacturing settings. Research was needed about leadership efficacy differences in Lean Six Sigma success to inform strategies aimed at augmenting success rates. The purpose of this causal comparative quantitative investigation was to determine the impact of perceived leadership efficacy differences on Lean Six Sigma success rates in a manufacturing setting. The sample was comprised of 128 leaders from the manufacturing industry in Illinois, Indiana, Iowa, and Wisconsin, who have conducted a Lean Six Sigma implementation. The independent variable was perceived leader efficacy and was gathered from McCormick's Leadership Efficacy Questionnaire (LEQ). The dependent variable was Lean Six Sigma implementation success rate and was gathered from a researcher-created checklist designed to measure overall equipment effectiveness of the respective leaders' operation. Analysis of variance was performed to assess the difference between high and low efficacy leaders on Lean Six Sigma success rates. The findings demonstrated individuals with high leader efficacy were significantly more successful in implementing Lean Six Sigma initiatives than those with low leader efficacy. Recommendations to increase leadership efficacy in manufacturing in order to positively impact the success rates of change initiatives were offered.

Abstract (Ray, 2016)

Posttraumatic stress disorder (PTSD) is a disturbing psychological problem which, prior to the revision of the Diagnostic and Statistical Manual of Mental Disorders was classified as an anxiety disorder. The general problem addressed in this study was the high rate of PTSD in combat veterans. The specific problem was the lack of understanding about how type of dissociative experience and psychological boundary permeability predicted PTSD in combat veterans. The purpose of this quantitative, predictive correlational study was to examine how psychological boundary permeability, type of dissociative experience (detachment and compartmentalization), and demographic variables (gender, ethnicity, combat experience status, and combat responder status) predict PTSD symptomology in combat and non-combat military veterans. The sample for the study included 104 current and former members of the United States military. Three already published instruments were used to assess the predictor variables. Boundary permeability was assessed with the Boundary Questionnaire-18 and type of dissociative experience was evaluated with the Dissociative Experiences Scale-II. The criterion variable, PTSD, was measured with the PTSD Checklist-Military. Demographic data (i.e., gender, ethnicity, combat exposure status, combat responder status) were included in the regression model as extraneous variables to examine their effect in the prediction to PTSD symptomology. Multiple regression analysis was used to determine boundary permeability and dissociative experience in the prediction of PTSD symptomology. Findings suggested compartmentalization, detachment, and boundary permeability significantly predicted PTSD. Holding combat responder status also significantly predicted PTSD. Recommendations for practice include the end of bifurcation of MTBI and PTSD treatments, consideration of treatment which do not rely on verbal processing of traumatic events, treatment designed for particular PTSD symptom differentials displayed, pre-deployment assessment testing using the predictive models offered, overhaul military training to include alternative methods of preparing for and managing the psychological stress and consideration of the impact of women serving in the military to determine differentials in PTSD symptomology. Recommendations for future research were also presented.

Abstract (Prior, 2015)

Maintaining employee motivation continues to be an important issue for most organizations, and improving motivation is especially important in the hospitality industry because more than half of the workers are unmotivated. The specific problem was ongoing low motivation can impair success for both the worker and organization, but before effective motivational strategies can be developed, more information is needed about workers' needs. Previous research findings have contradictory outcomes about reward efficacy and the purpose of this qualitative, holistic case study was to explore extrinsic and intrinsic needs of employees in the hospitality industry. The participants for this study included 12 employees from four different restaurant settings on the East Coast of the United States. Purposive criterion sampling was used to collect data from participants with at least three years of experience in this industry via face-to-face interviews. Data analysis was done with NVivo 10.0 software in order to identify themes from the transcribed employee interviews. The themes for extrinsic needs were: (a) sufficient income and (b) customized incentives. The themes for intrinsic needs were: (a) autonomy (b) growth and (c) supportive supervisors. A third research question emerged from the data and two additional themes for absent extrinsic rewards identified were: (a) lack of sufficient income and (b) lack of fun at work. Based on the study findings about intrinsic needs it was recommended that hospitality managers aim to come across as supportive while they help workers fulfill needs by providing a variety of reward options that cater to the changing needs of workers. Based on the study findings about extrinsic needs it was recommended that managers customize rewards because not all workers value the same incentives. It was also recommended that managers use pay and tangible job perks (extrinsic activities) to prevent employee job dissatisfaction, and then use trainings, interesting work, and autonomous opportunities (intrinsic activities) to improve motivation. Suggestions for future researcher included focusing on the managerial perspective of reward management, exploring the needs of workers from different job sectors, and the use of quantitative inquiry to expand the current findings. This research contributed to the literature on work motivation and findings can be utilized to develop and improve incentive plans for restaurant employees.

CHAPTER 13: Additional Resources if Needed

Scholarly Writing
- http://uncw.edu/son/documents/dexterphyllischolarlywriting.pdf
- http://writingcenter.waldenu.edu/312.htm
- https://owl.english.purdue.edu/owl/section/1/2/
- http://www.nextscientist.com/tips-improve-your-academic-writing/
- http://chronicle.com/article/10-Tips-on-How-to-Write-Less/124268/
- http://www.luizotaviobarros.com/2013/04/academic-writing-useful-expressions.html
- http://academicguides.waldenu.edu/writingcenter/writingprocess/revising

APA Style - American Psychological Association (2011). *Publication Manual of the American Psychological Association (6th Ed).* Washington, DC.

Quantitative Methods/Analysis

Field, A. (2013). *Discovering statistics using IBM SPSS Statistics (4th ed.).* Los Angeles, CA: Sage. (Andy Field has various entertaining video tutorials on YouTube)

Introduction to Power Analysis: http://www.ats.ucla.edu/stat/seminars/Intro_power/

Sample and Power Analysis Software: http://www.ncss.com/software/pass/

SPSS Tutorial: Mixed Design (Split Plot) ANOVA: http://youtu.be/u5JnILqlX9w **OR** http://youtu.be/APvlPjYSSaI

William D. Berry. (1985). *Multiple regression in practice.* Thousand Oaks, CA: SAGE Publications, Inc. doi: http://dx.doi.org.proxy1.ncu.edu/10.4135/9781412985208

Keith, T. (2006). *Multiple regression and beyond.* Boston: Pearson Education.

Choosing the right statistical test

Jaykaran. How to select appropriate statistical test?. J Pharm Negative Results [serial online] 2010 [cited 2014 Jan 28];1:61-3. Available from: http://www.pnrjournal.com/text.asp?2010/1/2/61/75708

Choosing a hypothesis test: http://www.diss-stat.com/files/choosing.pdf

A Painless Guide to Statistics: http://abacus.bates.edu/~ganderso/biology/resources/statistics.html

Variables

Types of Variables: http://www.indiana.edu/~educy520/sec5982/week_2/variable_types.pdf

Moderation & Mediation

Baron, R. M., & Kenny, D. A. (1986). The moderator–mediator variable distinction in social psychological research: Conceptual, strategic, and statistical considerations. *Journal of Personality and Social Psychology, 51*(6), 1173. Available online: https://umdrive.memphis.edu/grelyea/public/PUBH%207152-Stat%20Methods%20II/Chapter%2010/Mediation/Baron_%26_Kenny_1986.pdf

Field, Andy. YouTube video on Moderation & Mediation to accompany his text, "Discovering Statistics Using…." http://www.youtube.com/watch?v=RqkGMqDU20Q

> **Comment [JB]:** I didn't discuss this in the text. There is no need to do such an analysis for your dissertation. Do it for your next research project!!

Hayes, A. F. (2009). Beyond Baron and Kenny: Statistical mediation analysis in the new millennium. *Communication Monographs, 76*(4), 408-420. A pre-publication version available online: http://mres.gmu.edu/pmwiki/uploads/Main/Hayes2009.pdf

David Kenny's page on moderation: http://davidakenny.net/cm/moderation.htm

David Kenny's page on mediation: http://davidakenny.net/cm/mediate.htm

Quantitative Methods/Analysis

Yin, R. K. (2014). *Case study research: Design and methods, 5th edition*. Sage. Chapter 2 available: http://www.sagepub.com/upm-data/24736_Chapter2.pdf [Comment JB: This is the main resource you need to understand a case study :)]

Stake, R. E. (1995). The art of case study research. Thousand Oaks, CA: Sage Publications

Stake, R. E. (2013). Multiple case study analysis. Guilford Press. See excerpts: http://books.google.com/books?hl=en&lr=&id=rQWT5aDHiZYC&oi=fnd&pg=PT21&ots=IEmQByIsCj&sig=6Yj31dMXoYsWpLjGd9JybOCukkc#v=onepage&q&f=false

Qualitative Interviews

Brinkmann, S. (2013). *Qualitative Interviewing*. Oxford Univ. Press. (ISBN-13: 978-019 986 1392)

Kvale, S., & Brinkmann, S. (2009). *Interviews: Learning the craft of qualitative research interviewing*. Sage Publications, Incorporated.

Kvale, S. (2007). *Doing interviews*. Thousand Oaks, CA: Sage Publications. (e-book)

Rubin, H.J. & Rubin, I.S. *Qualitative interviewing: The art of hearing data*. Thousand Oaks, CA: Sage Publication. (e-book)

Turner, D. W., III (2010). Qualitative interview design: A practical guide for novice investigators. *The Qualitative Report, 15*(3), 754-760. Retrieved from http://www.nova.edu/ssss/QR/QR15-3/qid.pdf

Qualitative Analysis Software

Here is a link about popular qualitative analysis software: http://www.predictiveanalyticstoday.com/top-qualitative-data-analysis-software/ Maybe read up on all of them (user reviews) and then get a free trial to test it out before buying. Here is a link about a free one. http://www.umass.edu/qdap/

REFERENCES

Adhikari, H. (2010). Power dynamics in leadership: Decentralized power sharing leadership and its impact in business. *Globsyn Management Journal, 4*(1/2), 93-96. Retrieved from http://www.globsyn.edu.in/research/management_journal.php

AdvancED (2011). News Release: AdvancED accreditation commission drops accreditation of schools in Burke County, NC. Retrieved from http://www.advanc-ed.org/webfm_send/133

Akert, N., & Martin, B. N. (2012). The role of teacher leaders in school improvement through the perceptions of principals and teachers. *International Journal of Education, 4*(4), 284-299. doi:10.5296/ije.v4i4.2290

AlBattat, A. R. S., & Som, A. P. M. (2013). Employee dissatisfaction and turnover crises in the Malaysian hospitality industry. *International Journal of Business and Management, 8*(5), p 62.

Amabile, T.M., & Kramer, S.J. (2012). How leaders kill meaning at work. *The McKinsey Quarterly, 1*, 124-131.

Andersen, P. H., & Kragh, H. (2012). Managing creativity in business market relationships. *Industrial Marketing Management, 42*, 82-85.

Anderson, S. W., Dekker, H. C., & Sedatole, K. L. (2010). An empirical examination of goals and performance-to-goal following the introduction of an incentive bonus plan with participative goal setting. *Management Science, 56*(1), 90- 109.

Ankli, R. E., & Palliam, R. (2012). Enabling a motivated workforce: Exploring the sources of motivation. *Development and Learning in Organizations, 26*(2), 7-10. doi: 10.1108/14777281211201169

Armstrong, S. J., & Fukami, C. V. (2010). Self-Assessment of Knowledge: A cognitive learning or affective measure? Perspectives from the management learning and education community. *Academy of Management Learning & Education, 9*(2), 335–341.

Association of American Colleges and Universities (AACU). (2008). *College learning for the new global century: A report from the national leadership council for liberal education: America's promise*. Washington, DC: Association of American Colleges and Universities.

Astor, K. E. (2005). *A case study of instructional supervision, including teacher evaluation, and the impact on teacher practice* (Doctoral dissertation). Available from ProQuest Dissertations and Theses database. (AAT No. 3180459)

Aumann, C., Lahl, O., & Pietrowsky, R. (2012). Relationship between dream structure, boundary structure, and big five personality dimensions. *Dreaming, 22*(2), 124-135. doi: 10.1037/a0028977

Aydogdu, S., & Asikgil, B. (2011). An empirical study of the relationship among job satisfaction, organizational commitment and turnover intention. *International Review of Management and Marketing, 1*(3), 43-53. Retrieved from: http://www.econjournals.com/index.php/irmm/article/viewFile/30/24

Aziz-Ur-Rehman, Malik, M. A., Hussain, S., Iqbal, Z., & Rauf, M. (2012). Effectiveness of Brain-Based Learning Theory on Secondary Level Students of Urban Areas. *Journal of Managerial Sciences, 6*(1), 113-122.

Ballaro, J. M., & O'Neil, M. A. (2013). Transformational and transactional leadership behaviors: A phenomenological study of women executives in major league sports. *International Leadership Journal*, 45.

Balsmeyer, B., Haubrich, K., & Quinn, C. A. (1996). Defining collegiality within the academic setting. *Journal of Nursing Education, 35*(6), 264-267. Retrieved from http://www.healio.com/nursing/journals

Bandura, A. (1986). *Social foundation of thought and action: A social cognitive theory.* New Jersey: Prentice Hall.

Bandura, A. (1997). *Self-efficacy: The exercise of control.* New York, NY: W.H. Freeman.

Barth, R. S. (2006). Improving Relationships within the Schoolhouse. *Educational Leadership, 63*(6), 8-13. Retrieved from http://www.educationalleadership-digital.com

Bassett-Jones, N., & Lloyd, G. C. (2005). Does Herzberg's motivation theory have staying power? *Journal of Management Development, 24*(10), 929-43.

Batchelor, J. (2008, January 1). *Does standards-based teacher evaluation improve schools: An investigation of teacher perceptions of appraisal systems.* Available from ERIC Document Reproduction Service, No. ED502270.

Baxter, P., & Jack, S. (2008). Qualitative case study methodology: Study design and implementation for novice researchers. *The Qualitative Report, 13*(4), 544-559.

Beehner, C. (2015). *Examining the impact of workplace spirituality on worker turnover intention in the food service industry* (Doctoral Dissertation). Available from ProQuest Dissertation and Theses database. (No. 3705213)

Bell, R. L., & Martin, J. S. (2012). The relevance of scientific management and equity theory in everyday employee communication situations. *Journal of Management Policy and Practice, 13*(3), 106-115.

Bennett, J. (2016). *Combating school violence: School resource officers' perceptions of reactive response plans* (Doctoral Dissertation). Available from ProQuest Dissertation and Theses database.

Berdrow, I., & Evers, F. T. (2010). Bases of competence: An instrument for self and institutional assessment. *Assessment & Evaluation in Higher Education, 35*(4), 419-434.

Bernard, T., Paoline, E., & Pare, P. (2005). General systems theory and criminal justice. *Journal of Criminal Justice, 33,* 203-211. doi: 10.1016/j.jcrimjus.2005.02.001

Bernhardt, V. L. (2009). Data use: Data-driven decision making takes a big-picture view of the needs of teachers and students. *Journal of Staff Development, 30*(1), 24-29.

Bernstein, E., & Putnam, F. (1986). Development, reliability, and validity of a dissociation scale. *Journal of Nervous and Mental Disorders, 174,* 727-735. doi:10.1097/00005053-198612000-00004

Bess, K.D., Prilleltensky, I., Perkins, D.D. & Collins, L.V. (2009). Participatory organizational change in community-based health and human services: From tokenism to political engagement. *American Journal of Community Psychology, 43,* 134-148. doi: 10.1007/s10464-008-9222-8

Boachie-Mensah, F., & Dogbe, O. D. (2011). Performance-based pay as a motivational tool for achieving organisational performance: An exploratory case study. *International Journal of Business and Management, 6*(12), 270-285.

Boonen, T., Van Damme, J., & Onghena, P. (2013). Teacher effects on student achievement in first grade: Which aspects matter most? *School Effectiveness and School Improvement: An International Journal of Research, Policy and Practice,* 1-27. doi: 10.1080/09243453.2013.778297

Bourbina, A. M. (2016). *Adult learners' perceptions of their own educational competencies' effects on job performance* (Doctoral Dissertation). Available from ProQuest Dissertation and Theses database.

Brink, K. E., & Costigan, R. D. (2015). Oral communication skills: Are the priorities of the workplace and AACSB accredited business programs aligned? *Academy of Management Learning & Education, 14*(2), 205-221. Doi: 10.5465/amle.2013.0044

Brundrett, M. (1998). What lies behind collegiality, legitimation or control? An analysis of the purported benefits of collegial management in education. *Educational Management Administration and Leadership, 26*(3), 305-316. doi:10.1177/0263211X98263008

Bryant, R. (2007). Does dissociation further our understanding of PTSD? *Journal of Anxiety Disorders, 21*, 183-191. doi:10.1016/j.janxdis.2006.09.012

Bush, T. (2000). Administration and management in education: Theory and practice. In M. B.-P. Ben-Peretz, S. Brown, & B. Moon, *Routledge International Companion to Education* (pp. 272-282). Glasgow, UK: Taylor and Francis Ltd.

Caldwell, J. (2011). Disability identity of leaders in the self-advocacy movement. *Journal of Intellectual and Developmental Disabilities, 49*(5), 315-326. Retrieved from http://search.proquest.com/docview/856360587?accountid=28180

Cerge, D. (2014). *Using robots to motivate at-risk learners in science over the ninth grade hurdle* (Doctoral Dissertation). Available from ProQuest Dissertation and Theses database. (No. 3645233)

Chang, C., Lee, J., Chao, P., Wang, C., & Chen, G. (2010). Exploring the possibility of using humanoid robots as instructional tools for teaching a second language in primary school. *Journal of Educational Techonology & Society, 13*, 13-24. Retrieved from ERIC. (EJ895653).

Chen, G., & Chang, C. (2010). Using humanoid robots to develop a dialog-based interactive learning environment of elementary foreign language classrooms. *Journal of Interactive Learning Research, 21*(2), 215-235. Retrieved on March 30, 2013 from http://www.editlib.org/p/29417

Chenail, R. J. (2011). Interviewing the investigator: Strategies for addressing instrumentation and researcher bias concerns in qualitative research. *The Qualitative Report, 16*(1), 255-262.

Chileshe, N., & Haupt, T. C. (2010). The effect of age on the job satisfaction of Construction workers. *Journal of Engineering, Design and Technology, 8*(1), 107-118. doi:10.1108/17260531011034682

Ciulla, J. B. (2006). Ethics the heart of leadership. In T. Maak, & N. M. Pless, *Responsible leadership* (p. 251). Great Britain, London: Routledge.

Clark, L. A., Foote, D. A., Clark, W. R., & Lewis, J. L. (2010). Equity sensitivity: A triadic measure and outcome/input perspectives. *Journal of Employee Issues, 22*(3), 286-305

Clayton, T. W. (2008). *Perceptions of high school teachers and administrators concerning teacher evaluation* (Doctoral dissertation). Available from ProQuest Dissertations and Theses database. (AAT No. 0820400)

Cole, M. S., Walter, F., Bedeian, A. G., & O'Boyle, E. H. (2012). Job burnout and employee engagement a meta-analytic examination of construct proliferation. *Journal of management, 38*(5), 1550-1581.

Collins, C. (2007). Threat assessment in a post-columbine public school system: The use of crisis management plans in the public school sector as a means to address and mitigate school gun violence. *International Journal of Educational Advancement, 7*(1), 46-61. doi: 10.1057/palgrave.ijea.2150043

Cooper, R. (2012). The gender gap in union leadership in Australia: A qualitative study. *Journal of Industrial Relations, 54*(2), 131-146.

Corley, K. G., & Gioia, D. A. (2011). Building theory about theory building: What constitutes a theoretical contribution?. *Academy of Management Review, 36*(1), 12–32.

Cornell, D. (2011). A developmental perspective on the Virginia student threat assessment guidelines. *New Directions For Youth Development, 129,* 43-59. doi: 10.1002/yd386

Cox, J. (2013). Tenured teachers & technology integration in the classroom. *Contemporary Issues in Education Research (Online), 6*(2), 209

Crawford, A., Hubbard, S.S., Lonis-Shumate, S.R., & O'Neill, M. (2009). Workplace spirituality and employee attitudes within the lodging environment. *Journal of Human Resources in Hospitality & Tourism, 8,* 64-81. doi:10.1080/15332840802274445

Crawford, P., Lang, S., Fink, W., Dalton, R. & Fielitz, L. (2011). *Comparative analysis of soft skills: What is important for new graduates?* Washington, DC: Association of Public and Land-grant Universities.

Crosby, F., Iyer, A., Clayton, S., & Downing, R. (2003). Affirmative action: Psychological data and the policy debates. *American Psychologist, 58,* 93-115.

Cruce, T. M. & Hillman, N. W. (2012). Preparing for the silver tsunami: The demand for higher education among older adults. *Research in Higher Education, 53,* 593-613. doi: 10.1007/s11162-011-9249-9

Cubukcuoglu, B. (2013). Factors enabling the use of technology in subject teaching. *International Journal of Education and Development using Information and Communication Technology, 9*(3), 50-60.

Cummins, J., Azhar, M., & Sklar, E. (2008). Using Surveyor SRV-1 robots to motivate CS1 students. Association for the Advancement of Artificial Intelligence 2008 AI Education Colloquium, *WS0802,* 23-2

Cusumano, M. A. (2010). *Staying power: Six enduring principles for managing strategy and innovation in an uncertain world (lessons from Microsoft, Apple, Intel, Google, Toyota and more).* Oxford, UK: Oxford University Press.

Dalenberg, C., Brand, B., Gleaves, D., Dorahy, M., Loewenstein, R., Cardena, E.,...Spiegel, D. (2012). Evaluation of the evidence for the trauma and fantasy models of dissociation. *Psychological Bulletin, 138*(3), 550-588. doi:10.1037/a0027447

Daniels, J., Bilksy, K., Chamberlain, S., & Haist, J. (2011). School barricaded captive-takings: An exploratory investigation of school resource officer shootings. *Psychological Services, 8*(3), 178-188. doi: 10.1037/a0024738

Davis, K. (1968). Evolving models of organizational behavior. *Academy of Management Journal, 11*(1), 27-38. doi:10.2307/25519

Department of Education. (2013). *Guide for developing high-quality school emergency operations plans.* Office of Elementary and Secondary Education, Office of Safe and Healthy Students. Washington, D.C. Retrieved from http://www2.ed.gov/admins/lead/safety/emergencyplan/index.

Deci, E. L., & Ryan, R. M. (2014). The importance of universal psychological needs for understanding motivation in the workplace. *The Oxford Handbook of Work Engagement, Motivation, and Self-Determination Theory,* 13.

Degan, R. J. (2013). Wisdom, uncertainty, and ambiguity: A study of management decisions as based on theories and validated by research methods. *Center of Research in International Business & Strategy,* 94.

Delia, D., & Georgiana, P. (2013). Motivational dynamics in media organizations. *Procedia-Social and Behavioral Sciences, 76,* 312-316.

Despain, J., & Juarez-Torres, R. (2012). Evaluation as affecting teacher performance. *The John Ben Shepperd Journal of Practical Leadership, 6*(1), 87-120.

Developmental Disabilities Assistance and Bill of Rights Act of 2000, Public Law 106-402, 114 Stat. 1677.

DeWall, C. N., Anderson, C. A., & Bushman, B. J. (2011). The general aggression model: Theoretical extensions to violence. *Psychology of Violence, 11*(3), 245-258. doi:10.1037/a0023842

Dimitrov, D.M., & Rumrill, P.D. (2003). Pretest-posttest designs and measurement of change. *Work: A Journal of Prevention, Assessment and Rehabilitation, 20*(2), 159-165. Retrieved from: http://iospress.metapress.com/content/7X9HGPQ885T2YTTQ

DiPietro, R. B., Kline, S. F., & Nierop, T. (2014). Motivation and satisfaction of lodging employees: An exploratory study of Aruba. *Journal of Human Resources in Hospitality & Tourism, 13*(3), 253-276.

DuFour, R. & Eaker, R. (1998). *Professional Learning Communities at Work: Best Practices for Enhancing Student Achievement.* Bloomington, IN: Solution Tree Press.

Dugard, P., & Todman J. (1995). Analysis of Pre-test-Post-test Control Group Designs in Educational Research. *Educational Psychology: An International Journal of Experimental Educational Psychology, 15*(2), 181-189. doi:10.1080/0144341950150207

Evers, F. T., Rush, J. C., & Berdrow, I. (1998). *The bases of competence: Skills for lifelong learning and employability.* San Francisco: Jossey-Bass.

Ferdows, K., & Netland, T. (2014). What to expect from a corporate lean program. *MIT Sloan Management Review, 55*(4), 83-89. Retrieved from http://search.proquest.c om.proxy1.ncu.edu/abiglobal/docview/1543709930/D5F20314A9C24A26PQ/5?accountid =28180

Ferguson, C. J., & Dyck, D. (2012). Paradigm change in aggression research: The time has come to retire the general aggression model. *Aggression and Violent Behavior, 17*(3), 220-228. doi:10.1016/j.avb.2012.02.007

Fernet, C. (2013). The role of work motivation in psychological health. *Canadian Psychology/Psychologie canadienne, 54*(1), 72.

Fichter, C. (2011). Results: Role conflict, role ambiguity, job satisfaction, and burnout among financial advisors. *Journal of American Academy of Business, Cambridge, 16*(2), 54-59.

Frawley, P. & Bigby, C. (2011). Inclusion in political and public life: The experiences of people with intellectual disability on government disability advisory boards in Australia. *Journal of Intellectual & Developmental Disability, 36*(1), 27-38. doi: 10.3109/13668250.2010.54946

Freedman, S. (2012). Collegiality matters: Massachusetts public higher education librarians' perspective. *The Journal of Academic Librarianship, 38*(2), 108- 114. doi:10.1016/j.acalib.2012.02.003

Frels, R. K., & Onwuegbuzie, A. J. (2012). Interviewing the interpretive researcher: An impressionist tale. *The Qualitative Report, 17*(60), 1-27.

Fullan, M. (2008). *The six secrets of change: What the best leaders do to help their organizations survive and thrive.* San Francisco, CA: Jossey-Bass.

Furnham, A., Eracleous, A. & Chamorro-Premuzic, T. (2009). Personality, motivation and job satisfaction: Herzberg meets the big five. *Journal of Employee Psychology, 24*(8), 765-779.

Geh, E., & Tan, G. (2009). Spirituality at work in a changing world: Managerial and research implications. *Journal of Management, Spirituality & Religion, 6*(4), 287-300. doi:10.1080/14766080903290093

George, B., & Sims, P. (2007). *True north: discover your authentic leadership.* San Francisco, CA: Wiley.

Ghoshal, S. (2005). Bad management theories are destroying good management practices. Academy of Management Learning & Education, 4(1), 75–91.

Giacalone, R.A., & Jurkiewicz, C.J. (2010). The science of workplace spirituality. In R. A. Giacalone & C. J. Jurkiewicz (Eds.) *Handbook of workplace spirituality and organizational performance* (2nd ed., pp. 3-26). New York, NY: M. E. Sharpe.

Giesbrecht, T., Lynn, S., Lilienfeld, S., & Merckelbach, H. (2008). Cognitive processes in dissociation: An analysis of core theoretical assumptions. *Psychological Bulletin, 134,* 617-647. doi:10.1037/0033-2909.134.5.617

Giffords, E. D. (2009). An examination of organizational commitment and professional commitment and the relationship to work environment, demographic and organizational factors. *Journal of Social Work, 9*(4), 386-404. doi:10.1177/1468017309346232

Gilakjani, A. P., & Lai-Mei, L. (2012). EFL teacher's attitudes toward using computer technology in English language teaching. *Theory & Practice in Language Studies*, *2*(3), 630. doi:10.4304/tpls.2.3.630-636

Giliya, Z. (2006). A *study of teachers' perceptions of the evaluation process* (Doctoral dissertation). Available from ProQuest Dissertations and Theses database. (AAT No. 3239986)

Gneezy, U., Meier, S., & Rey-Biel, P. (2011). When and why incentives (don't) work to modify behavior. *The Journal of Economic Perspectives, 25*(4), 191-209.

Gray, A. T. (2009). *Co-teaching in inclusive classrooms: The impact of collaboration on attitudes, efficacy and student achievement.* Arizona State University. *ProQuest Dissertations and Theses,* http://search.proquest.com/docview/304828042?accountid=28180

Green, S. B., & Salkind, N. J. (2013). *Using SPSS for Windows and Macintosh* (7th ed.). New York, NY: Pearson.

HHS. (2011). *Most uninsured unable to pay hospital bills according to new HHS report.* Retrieved from http://www.hhs.gov/news/press/2011pres/05/20110510a.html

Halkos, G., & Bousinakis, D. (2010). The effect of stress and satisfaction on productivity. *International Journal of Productivity and Performance Management, 59*(5), 415 431.

Han, J., Kim, D., & Kim, J. (2009). Physical learning activities with a teaching assistant robot in elementary school music class. *Proceedings of the 2009 Fifth International Joint Conference on INC, IMS, and IDC,* 1406-1410. doi: 10.4156/jcit.vol5.issue5.3

Hannah, S., Avolio, B. J., Walumbwa, F., & Chan (2012). Leader self and means efficacy: A multi-component approach. *Organizational Behavior and Human Decision Processes*, 118, 143-161.

Hanneman, L., & Gardner, P. (2010). *CERI research brief 1-2010: Under the economic turmoil a skills gap simmers.* Collegiate Employment Research Institute, Michigan State University.

Hao, Y., & Zihanxin, L. (2011). Application of motivator-hygiene theory in modern human resource management. *Value Engineering, 14,* 83.

Harris, L. C., & Ogbonna, E. (2006). Service sabotage: A study of antecedents and consequences. *Journal of the Academy of Marketing Science, 34*(4), 543-558.

Harris, S.P., Owen, R., & DeRuiter, C. (2012). Civic engagement and people with disabilities: The role of advocacy and technology. *Journal of Community Engagement and Scholarship, 5*(1), 70-83. Retrieved from http://search.proquest.com.proxy1.ncu.edu/docview/1269698080/5F7AB5D52F99429CPQ/1?accountid=28180

Harunavamwe, M., & Kanengoni, H. (2013). The impact of monetary and non-monetary rewards on motivation among lower level employees in selected retail shops. *African Journal of Business Management, 7*(38), 3929-3935.

Hashimoto, T., Verner, M., & Kobayashi, H. (2013). Human-like robot as teacher's representative in a science lesson: An elementary school experiment. *Robot Intelligence Technology and Applications, 208*, 775-786. doi:10.1007/978-3-642-37374-9_74

Hassan, M., Hassan, S., Din Khan, K.U., & Naseem, M.A. (2011). Employee retention as a challenge in leather Industry. *Global Journal of Human-Social Science Research, 11*(2). Retrieved from: http://www.socialscienceresearch.org/index.php/GJHSS/article/viewFile/80/59

Hatfield, R. D. (2006). Collegiality in higher education: Toward an understanding of the factors involved in collegiality. *Journal of Organizational Culture, Communication and Conflict, 10*(1), 11-19. Retrieved from http://vlex.com

Hausknecht, J.P., & Trevor, C.O. (2011). Collective turnover at the group, unit, and organizational levels: Evidence, issues, and implications. *Journal of Management, 37*(1), 352-388. doi:10.1177/0149206310383910

Healthcare Effectiveness Data and Information Set. (2011). *HEDIS 2011 summary table of measures, product lines and changes.* Retrieved from http://www.ncqa.org/Portals/0/HEDISQM/HEDIS%202011/HEDIS%202011%20Measures.pdf

Hendricks, J.W., & Payne, S.C. (2007). Beyond the big 5: Leader goal orientation as a predictor of leadership effectiveness. *Human Performance, 20*, 317-343.

Herzberg, F. I. (1968). One more time: How do you motivate employees? *Harvard Business Review, 46*(1), 53–62.

Herzberg, F. I., Mausner, B., & Snyderman, B. B. (1959). *The motivation to work.* New York, NY: John Wiley & Sons.

Hirst, G., Mann, L., Bain, P., Pirola-Merlo, A., & Richver, A. (2004). Learning to lead: the development and testing of a model of leadership learning. *The Leadership Quarterly, 15*(1), 311 – 327. doi:10.1016/j.leaqua.2004.02.011

Holtom, B., Mitchell, T., Lee, T., & Eberly, M. (2008). Chapter 5: Turnover and retention research: A glance at the past, a closer review of the present, and a venture into the future. *The Academy of Management Annals, 2*(1), 231-274. doi:10.1080/19416520802211552

Hong, Y.J. (2012). Identifying spirituality in workers: A strategy for retention of community health professionals. *Journal of Social Service Research, 38*(20), 175-186. doi:10.1080/01488376.2011.615275

Howard, D. H. (2014). Adverse effects of prohibiting narrow provider networks. *The New England Journal of Medicine, 371*(7), 591-593. Retrieved from http://search.proquest.com.proxy1.ncu.edu/docview/1553747613/1F9ADF3345BF4960PQ/1?accountid=28180

Howell, D. C. (2010). *Statistical methods for psychology* (7th ed.). Belmont CA: Wadsworth Cengage Learning.

Howze, P. C. (2003). Perspectives on...collegiality, collegial management, and academic libraries. *Journal of Academic Librarianship, 29*(1), 40-44. Retrieved from http://www.elsevier.com

Hoy, W. K., Smith, P. A., & Sweetland, S. R. (2003). The development of the organizational climate index for high schools: Its measure and relationship to faculty trust. *The High School Journal, 86*(2), 38-49. Retrieved from http://muse.jhu.edu

Hu, Q., Schaufeli, W. B., & Taris, T. W. (2013). Does equity mediate the effects of job demands and job resources on work outcomes?: An extension of the job demands resources model. *Career Development International, 18*(4), 357-376.

Huck, S.W., & McLean, R.A. (1975). Using a repeated measures ANOVA to analyze the data from a pretest-posttest design: A potentially confusing task. *Psychological Bulletin, 82*(4), 511-518. doi:10.1037/h0076767

Huitema, B. E. (2011). *The analysis of covariance and alternatives: Statistical methods for experiments, quasi-experiments, and single-case studies* (2nd ed.) Retrieved from http://site.ebrary.com/lib/ncent/docDetail.action?docID=10510273&p00= nonequivalent%20group%20pretest-posttest%20design

Iqbal, A., Kokash, H. A., & Al-Oun, S. (2011). The impact assessment of demographic factors on faculty commitment in the Kingdom of Saudi Arabian universities. *Journal of College Teaching and Learning, 8*(2), 1-13. Retrieved from http://ehis.ebscohost.com/eds/pdfviewer/pdfviewer?sid=fcf67e12-7b4c-49b9-b5e3-7bf228c04a8f%40sessionmgr112&vid=3&hid=116

Ingvarson, L., & Rowe, K. (2008). Conceptualizing and evaluating teacher quality: Substantive and methodological issues. *Australian Journal of Education, 52*(1), 5-35. Retrieved from http://search.proquest.com/docview/205858285?accountid=28180

Jackson, B. (2012). Give your people a cause and inspiration will follow. *Human Resource Management International Digest, 20*(2), 32-34. doi:10.1108/09670731211208184

Jackson, D. (2013b) Business graduate employability – where are we going wrong? *Higher Education Research & Development, 32*(5), 776-790. doi: 10.1080/07294360.2012.709832

Jacobs, E. (2011). *Executive Brief: Differences in employee turnover across key industries.* Alexandria, VA: Society for Human Resource management. Retrieved from: http://www.shrm.org/Research/benchmarks/Documents/Assessing%20Employee%20Turnover_FINAL.pdf

Jakhar, K., Bhatia, T., Saha, R., & Deshpande, S. N. (2015). A cross sectional study of prevalence and correlates of current and past risks in schizophrenia. *Asian Journal of Psychiatry, 14*, 36-41.

Jarvis, A. (2012). The necessity for collegiality: Power, authority and influence in the middle. *Educational Management Administration & Leadership, 40*(4), 480-493. doi:10.1177/1741143212438223

Jeacle, I., & Parker, L. (2013). The 'problem' of the office: Scientific management, governmentality and the strategy of efficiency. *Business History, 55*(7), 1074-1099.

Jennings, W., Khey, D., Maskaly, J., & Donner, C. (2011). Evaluating the relationship between law enforcement and school security measures and violent crime in schools. *Journal of Police Crime Negotiations, 11*, 109-124. doi: 10.1080/15332586.2011.581511

Joaquín, M. E., & Park, S. M. (2013). Exploring the topography of performance and effectiveness of US federal agencies. *Public Personnel Management, 42*(1), 55-74. doi:10.177/0091026013484411

Jones, P., Rabbetts, J., & Holton, V. (2013). *Roles and challenges.* London, United Kingdom: Ashridge Business School.

Judge, T. A., & Kammeyer-Mueller, J. D. (2012). On the value of aiming high: The causes and consequences of ambition. *Journal of Applied Psychology, 97*(4), 758.

Kara, D., Uysal, M., Sirgy, M. J., & Lee, G. (2013). The effects of leadership style on employee well-being in hospitality. *International Journal of HospitalityManagement, 34*, 9-18.

Kelly, C. (2006). *Teacher evaluation and its relationship to teacher practice and student achievement in a successful urban middle school: A case study.* New York, NY: ProQuest.

Kim, N. (2012), Employee turnover intention among newcomers in travel industry. *International Journal of Tourism Research, 16*(1), 56-64. doi:10.1002/jtr.1898

Kim, S. (2012). The impact of human resource management on state government IT employee turnover intentions. *Public Personnel Management, 41*(2), 257-279. Retrieved from: http://ehis.ebscohost.com/eds/pdfviewer/pdfviewer?sid=3ce8b28a-79e0-46d5-a1dd-a5c7ff0a5cf1%40sessionmgr4&vid=8&hid=4

Komppula, R. (2014). The role of individual entrepreneurs in the development of competitiveness for a rural tourism destination–A case study. *TourismManagement, 40*, 361-371.

Krug, M. K., & Braver, T. S. (2014). Motivation and cognitive control: Going beyond monetary incentives. In *The Psychological Science of Money*, 137-162. New York, NY: Springer.

Kukanja, M. (2013). Influence of demographic characteristics on employee motivation in catering companies. *Tourism and Hospitality Management, 19*(1), 97-107.

Kumar, H., & Raghavendran, S. (2013). Not by money alone: The emotional wallet and talent management. *Journal of Business Strategy, 34*(3), 16-23.doi: 10.1108/JBS-11-2012-0073

Kunzendorf, R., Hartmann, E., Cohen, R., & Cutler, J. (1997). Bizarreness of the dreams and daydreams reported by individuals with thin and thick boundaries. Dreaming, 7(4). 265-271. doi:1053-0797/97/1200-0265S12.50/1

Kvale, S. & Brinkmann, S. (2015). InterViews: Learning the Craft of Qualitative Research Interviews 3nd ed. Sage Publications Inc.

Lamsma, J., & Harte, J. M. (2015). Violence in psychosis: Conceptualizing its causal relationship with risk factors. *Aggression and Violent Behavior, 24*, 75-82.

Lanfranchi, J., Narcy, M., & Larguem, M. (2010). Shedding new light on intrinsic motivation to work: Evidence from a discrete choice experiment. *Kyklos, 63*(1), 75-93.

Lansman, R. R. (2006). *A case study of teacher evaluation and supervision at a high-achieving urban elementary school* (Doctoral dissertation). Available from ProQuest Dissertations and Theses database. (AAT No. 3233791)

Laurie, N., & Cherry, C. (2013). Wanted. *Philosophy of Management, 1*(1), 3-12.

Lawless, T. (2016). *The impact of perceived leader efficacy differences on successful lean six sigma implementation in manufacturing* (Doctoral Dissertation). Available from ProQuest Dissertations and Theses database.

Lazega, E., & Wattebled, O. (2011). Two definitions of collegiality and their inter-relation: The case of a Roman Catholic diocese. *Sociologie du Travail, 53*(4), 57-77. doi:10.1016/j.soctra.2011.09.005

Lee, J. J., & Ok, C. M. (2014). Understanding hotel employees' service sabotage: Emotional labor perspective based on conservation of resources theory. *International Journal of Hospitality Management, 36*, 176-187.

Lee, L. (2012). *Voices less heard:Teachers' perspectives on the evaluation of teacher effectiveness through the use of value-added modeling.* Available from ProQuest Dissertations and Theses database. (AAT No. 3233791)

Levin, B. (2011). Mobilizing research knowledge in education. *London Review of Education*, 9(1), 15-26. doi: 10.1080/14748460.2011.550431

Liker, J. K., & Morgan, J. (2011). Lean product development as a system: A case study of body and stamping development at Ford. *Engineering Management Journal, 23*(1), 16-28. Retrieved from http://search.proquest.com.proxy1.ncu.edu/abiglobal/docview/862561306/13D6859B656509DB550/14?accountid=28180

Likert, R. (1977). Management styles and the human component. *Management Review, 66*(10), 23-45. Retrieved from http://www.amanet.org

Lin, Y., & Jou, M. (2013). Integrating popular web applications in classroom learning environments and its effects on teaching, student learning motivation and performance. *Turkish Online Journal of Educational Technology - TOJET, 12*(2), 157-165.

Linz, S. J., & Semykina, A. (2012). What makes workers happy? Anticipated rewards and job satisfaction. *Industrial Relations: A Journal of Economy and Society,51*(4), 811-844.

Ludi, S. (2011). Educational robotics and broadening participating in STEM for underrepresented student groups. *Robots in K-12 Education: A New Technology For Learning, * 343-361. doi:10.4018/978-1-4666-0182-6.ch017

Mackenzie, M., & Peters, M. (2014). Hospitality managers' perception of corporate social responsibility: An explorative study. *Asia Pacific Journal of Tourism Research, 19*(3), 257-272.

Malik, M. E., & Naeem, B. (2012). Towards understanding controversy on Herzberg's theory of motivation. *Journal of Basic Applied Sciences Research, 2*(11).

Malone, A., Carroll, A., & Murphy, B. P. (2012). Facial affect recognition deficits: A potential contributor to aggression in psychotic illness. *Aggression and Violent Behavior, 17,* 27-35. doi:10.1016/j.avb.2011.09.007

Marsden, P. V., Kalleberg, A. L., & Cook, C. R. (1993). Gender differences in organizational commitment. *Work & Occupations, 20*(3), 368-390. doi:10.1177/0730888493020003005

Marques, J. (2011). Turning inward to connect outward: Interbeing as motivational path in today's workplace. *Interbeing, 5*(1), 19-29.

Marshall, B., Cardon, P., Poddar, A., & Fontenot, R. (2013). Does sample size matter in qualitative research?: A review of qualitative interviews in is research. *Journal of Computer Information Systems, 54*(1).

Marshall, K. (2009). *Rethinking teacher supervision and evaluation: How to work smart, build collaboration, and close the achievement gap.* San Francisco, CA: John Wiley and Sons.

Maslow, A. H. (1943). A theory of human motivation. *Psychological Review, 50,* 370-396.

Matney, S. R. (2015). *Executive director perspectives about preparation to support the social inclusion of council members with developmental disabilities* (Doctoral Dissertation). Available from ProQuest Dissertation and Theses database. (No. 3706059)

Mayer, L. M. (2012). Social work practice with people with disabilities: Enhancing practice through catholic social teaching. *Social Work and Christianity, 39*(2), 172-188. Retrieved from http://search.proquest.com/docview/856360587?accountid=28180

McCormick, M.J., Tanguma, J., & Lopex-Forment, A.S., (2002). Extending self-efficacy theory to leadership: A review and empirical test. *Journal of Leadership Education, 1,* 34-49.

McGuinness, D., & Hutchinson, K. (2013). Utilising product knowledge: Competitive advantage for specialist independent grocery retailers. *International Journal of Retail & Distribution Management, 41*(6), 461-476.

Metzl, J. M., & MacLeish, K. T. (2015). Mental illness, mass shootings, and the politics of american firearms. *Framing Health Matters, 105*(2), 240-249.

Miah, D. M. K., Hossan, C. G., & Golam, C. (2012). Performance management system in UK retail industry: A case study. *Far East Journal of Psychology and Business, 7*(2), 13-25.

Miller, S. R., Drill, K., & Behrstock, E. (2010). Meeting teachers half way. *Phi Delta Kappan, 91*(7), 31-34.

Milliman, J., Czaplewski, A.J., & Ferguson, J. (2003). Workplace spirituality and employee work attitudes: An exploratory empirical assessment. *Journal of Organizational Change Management 16*(4), 426-447. doi:10.1108/09534810310484172

Moller, A. C., & Deci, E. L. (2014). The psychology of getting paid: An integrated perspective. In *The Psychological Science of Money* (pp. 189-211). New York, NY: Springer.

Morrison, I. (2007, February 2). Recruitment of foreign teachers helping V.I. fill classroom vaciencies. The Virgin Islands Daily News, pp. n/a.

Muchinsky, P.M., (2012). *Psychology applied to work, 10th ed.* Summerfield, NC: Hypergraphic Press.

Mustata, R. V., Fekete, S., & Matis, D. (2011). Motivating accounting professionals in Romania: Analysis after five decades of communist ideology and two decades of accounting harmonization. *Accounting and Management Information Systems, 10*(2), 169-201.

National Council on Disability. (2011). *Rising expectations: the developmental disabilities act revisited.* Washington DC: Author.

Navarro, W. (2009) A review of Maslow, Herzberg and Vroom in the construction industry over the last 25 years. *In:* Dainty, A.R.J. (Ed) *Procs 25th Annual ARCOM Conference,* 7-9, 2009, Nottingham, UK: *Association of Researchers in Construction Management,* 63-73.

Nederlof, A. F., Muris, P., & Hovens, J. E. (2013). The epidemiology of violent behavior in patients with a psychotic disorder: A systematic review of studies since 1980.*Aggression and Violent Behavior, 18*, 183-189.

Negron, R., DeRaad, C., Huggins, M., & Sciabica, J. (2011). Air force research laboratories investments in science, technology ,engineering, and math education. *Astropolitics*, 193-212. doi:10.1080/1477622.2011.626717

Neild, R., Stoner-Eby, S., & Furstenberg, F. (2008). Connecting entrance and departure: The transition to ninth grade and high school dropout. *Education and Urban Society*, July 2009, 40, 543-569. doi:10.1177/0013124508316438

Norusis, M. J. (2010). *PASW statistics 18 guide to data analysis.* Chicago, IL: Prentice Hall Press.

Oren, L., & Littman-Ovadia, H. (2012). Does equity sensitivity moderate the relationship between effort–reward imbalance and burnout. *Anxiety, Stress & Coping*, (ahead of-print), 1-16. doi:10.1080/10615806.2012.753060

Padgett, S. M. (2013). Professional collegiality and peer monitoring among nursing staff: An ethnographic study. *International Journal of Nursing Studies, 50*, 1407-1415. doi:10.1016/j.ijnurstu.2012.12.022

Pagano, R. R. (2009). *Understanding statistics in the behavioral sciences* (9th ed.). Belmont CA: Wadsworth Cengage Learning.

Pallant, J. (2010). *SPSS survival manual* (4th ed.). New York, New York: McGraw-Hill.

Park, E., Kim, K. & Del Pobil, A. (2011). The effects of robot instructor's positive and negative feedback on attraction and acceptance towards the robot in the classroom. *Social Robotics*, 135-141. doi:10.1007/978-3-642-25504-5_14

Park, T-Y., & Shaw, J.D. (2013). Turnover rates and organizational performance: A meta-analysis. *Journal of Applied Psychology, 98*(2), 268-309. doi:10.1037/a0030723

Partnership for Public Change. (2012). *Best place to work in the Federal Government Analysis: The federal leadership challenge.* Washington, DC: Office of Personal Managment. Retrieved from http://www.fedview.opm.gov/

Pater, R. (2011). Two types of leaders - Which are you?. *Professional Safety, 56*(1), 25-26.

Patnaik, J. B. (2011). Organizational culture: The key to effective leadership and work motivation. *Social Science International, 27*(1), 79-94.

Pay, R. (2008). Being taken for a lean ride. Lean Manufacturing. *Industry Week, 257*(5), 62.

Pechlaner, H., & Volgger, M. (2012). How to promote cooperation in the hospitality industry: Generating practitioner-relevant knowledge using the GABEK qualitative research strategy. *International Journal of Contemporary Hospitality Management, 24*(6), 925-945.

Peterson, J. K., Skeem, J., Kennealy, P., Bray, B., & Zvonkovic, A. (2014). How often and how consistently do symptoms directly precede criminal behavior among offenders with mental illness. *Law and Human Behavior, 38*(5), 439-449.

Pettigrew, A. M. (2012). The conduct of qualitative research in organizational settings. *Corporate Governance: An International Review, 21*(2), 123-126. doi: 10.1111/j.14678683.2012.00925.x

Pinto, E. P. (2011). The influence of wage on motivation and satisfaction. *International Business & Economics Research Journal (IBER), 10*(9), 81-92.

Pratt, M. G. (2009). For the lack of a boilerplate: Tips on writing up (and reviewing) qualitative research. Academy of Management Journal, 52(6), 856–862.

Preskill, H., & Catsambas, T. T. (2006). Reframing evaluation through appreciative inquiry. Thousand Oaks, CA: Sage Publications.

Prior, Y. (2015). *Investigating extrinsic and intrinsic employee needs in hospitality workers* (Doctoral Dissertation). Available from ProQuest Dissertation and Theses database. (No. 3733853)

Puhlman, M. E. (2016). *Lean management and six sigma potential on customer satisfaction in health insurance* (Doctoral Dissertation). Available from ProQuest Dissertation and Theses database.

Qualtrics. (2016). Retrieved from http://www.qualtrics.com

Quick Service Restaurant. (2012). *Three trends hitting food service.* Retrieved from: http://www.qsrweb.com/blog/7163/3-trends-hitting-foodservice

Radermacher, H., Sonn, C., Keys, C., & Duckett, P. (2010). Disability and participation: It's about us but not without us! *Journal of Community & Applied Social Psychology, 20,* 333-346. doi: 10.1002/casp1039

Radzi, S.M., Alan Ramley, S.Z., Sallehudin, M., Othman, Z., & Jalis, M.H. (2009). An empirical assessment of hotel managers turnover intentions: The impact of organizational justice. *International Journal of Business and Management, (4)*8, 173-183. doi:10.5539/ijbm.v4n8P52

Rasch, R., Shen, W., Davies, S. E., & Bono, J. (2008). The development of a taxonomy of ineffective leadership behaviors. In *23rd Annual Conference of the Society for Industrial and Organizational Psychology, San Francisco, CA.*

Ray, J. (2016). *Factors involved in the potentiation of posttraumatic stress disorder in military veterans* (Doctoral Dissertation). Available from ProQuest Dissertation and Theses database.

Raymond, B. (2010). Assigning police officers to schools. *Problem-Oriented Guides for Police Response Guides Series No. 10.* Retrieved from http://cops.usdoj.gov/RIC/ResourceDetail.aspx?RID=567

Redmond, B. F. (2010). Reinforcement theory: What are the rewards for my work? *Work Attitudes and motivation.* The Pennsylvania State University World Campus.

Rehman, S. (2016). *The perceptions of costs and benefits of affirmative action public procurement programs by racial minority business owners* (Doctoral Dissertation). Available from ProQuest Dissertation and Theses database.

Robers, S., Zhang, J., & Truman, J. (2012). *Indicators of school crime and safety: 2011*. National Center for Education Statistics, U.S. Department of Education, and Bureau of Justice Statistics, Office of Justice Programs, U.S. Department of Justice. Washington, D.C. Retrieved from http://nces.ed.gov

Robles, F. (2007). *Veteran teachers' perspectives on teacher evaluation and how they want to be evaluated* (Doctoral dissertation). Available from ProQuest Dissertations and Theses database. (AAT No. 3299730)

Rooke, D., & Torbert, W. R. (2005). 7-Transformations ofl leadership. *Harvard Business Review, 83*(4), 66-76. Retrieved from https://hbr.org

Rose, T. M., & Manley, K. (2012). Motivating construction organisations through incentives: A case study for client employees. *The Project as a Social System:Asia Pacific Perspectives on Project Management.* Melbourne, Victoria: Monash University.

Sabir, M. S., Sohail, A., & Khan, A. M. (2011). Impact of leadership style on organization commitment: In a mediatiing role of employee values. *Journal of Economics and Behavioral Studies, 3*(2), 145-152. Retrieved from http://www.econbiz.de

Sachau, D. (2007). Resurrecting the motivation-hygiene theory: Herzberg and the positive psychology movement. *Human Resource Development Review,6*, 377-393.

Sage, W. M. (2014). Getting the product right: How competition policy can improve health care markets. *Health Affairs, 33*(6), 1076-1082. Retrieved from http://searc h.proquest.com.proxy1.ncu.edu/docview/1534525085/288D7EB3246E45B4PQ/18?account id=28180

Salman, S., & Khan, A. (2014). Career management and employee motivation in low skilled, low margin environments. In *IOP Conference Series: Materials Science and Engineering, 65*(1), IOP Publishing.

Schmitz, H. J., & Havholm, K. (2015, Spring). Undergraduate research and alumni: perspectives on learning gains and post-graduation benefits. *Council on Undergraduate Research Quarterly, 35*(3), 15-22.

Schuman, R. (2014). ABD Company. What's worse than getting a PhD in today's job market? Not finishing one. Slate.com. http://www.slate.com/articles/life/education/2014/08/abds_all_but_dissertation_ph_d_cand idates_who_can_t_quite_finish.html

Secretan, L. H. (2005). Inspiring people to their greatness. *Leader to Leader, 36*, 11-14. Retrieved from http://www.wiley.com

Shah, M., & Abualrob, M. M. (2012). Teacher collegiality and teacher professional commitment in public secondary schools in Islamabad, Pakistan. *Procedia-Social and Behavioral Sciences, 46*(1), 950-954. doi:10.1016/j.sbspro.2012.05.229

Shaw, J.D. (2011). Turnover rates and organizational performance: Review, critique, and research agenda. *Organizational Psychology Review, 1*(3), 187-213. doi:10.1177/2041386610382152

Shierholz, H. (2014). Low wages and few benefits mean many restaurant workers can't make ends meet. *EPI Briefing Paper.*Washington, DC: Economic Policy Institute.

Shrifian, L. (2011). Collegial management to improve the effectiveness of managers, organizational behavior in educational institutions. *Procedia-Social and Behavioral Sciences, 29*, 1169 – 1178. doi:10.1016/j.sbspro.2011.11.351

Shin, T. (2013). Fair pay or power play? Pay equity, managerial power, and compensation adjustments for CEOs. *Journal of Management*. doi:0149206313478186.

Singh, P. (2013). A collegials approach in understanding leadership as a social skill. *International Business & Economics Research Journal, 12*(5), 489-502. Retrieved from http://journals.cluteonline.com

Simintiras, A. C., Ifie, K., Watkins, A., & Georgakas, K. (2013). Antecedents of adaptive selling among retail salespeople: A multilevel analysis. *Journal of Retailing and Consumer Services, 20*(4), 419-428.

Simpson, A. I., Grimbos, T., Chan, C., & Penney, S. R. (2015). Developmental typologies of serious mental illness and violence: Evidence from a forensic psychiatric setting.*Australian & New Zealand Journal of Psychiatry*, *49*(11), 1049-1059. doi:10.1177/0004867415587745

Singh, D. K., & Stoloff, D. L. (2008). Assessment of teacher dispositions. *College Student Journal, 42*(4), 1169-1180. Retrieved from http://search.proquest.com/docview/236589003?accountid=28180

Sinkovics, R., & Alfoldi, A. (2012). Progressive focusing and trustworthiness in qualitative research. *Management International Review, 52*(6), 817– 845.doi: 10.1007/s11575-012-0140-5

Slattery, S. M., & Goodman, L. A. (2009). Secondary traumatic stress among domestic violence advocates: Workplace risk and protective factors. *Violence Against Women, 15*(11), 1358-1379. doi:10.1177/1077801209347469

Smerek, R. & Peterson, M. (2006). Examining Herzberg's theory: Improving job satisfaction among non-academic employees at a university. *Research on Higher Education, 48*(2),229-250.

Stake, R. E. (2010). *Qualitative research: Studying how things work.* New York, NY: Guilford Publications, Inc.

Statler, S. (1961). Recent growth patterns of accreditation of secondary schools by the regional accrediting association. *NASSP Bulletin,* 45(16), 16-22. Advance online publication. doi:10.1177/019263656104526703

Stone, W., & Spencer, D. (2010). Enhancing an active shooter school emergency plan using ambient materials and school resource officers. *The Southwest Journal of Criminal Justice, 7*(3), 295-306. Retrieved from http://www.swacj.org/swjcj/Masthead.htm

Supovitz, J. (2009). Can high stakes testing leverage educational improvement? Prospects from the last decade of testing and accountability reform. *Journal of Educational Change,* 10, 211-227. doi: 10.1007/s10833-009-9105-2

SurveyMonkey. (2016). Retrieved from http://www.surveymonkey.com

Swanson, D. P., & Spencer, M. B. (2011). Resilience in Educational Contexts. *Urban Education: A Model for Leadership and Policy*, 283.

Sylver-Foust, D.E. (2015). *Exploring how the collegial leadership style predicts employee satisfaction and organizational commitment within federal agencies* (Doctoral Dissertation). Available from ProQuest Dissertation and Theses database. (No. 3704257)

Tadajewski, M., & Jones, D. B. (2012). Scientific marketing management and the emergence of the ethical marketing concept. *Journal of Marketing Management, 28*(1-2), 37-61.

Tan, T. H., & Waheed, A. (2011). Herzberg's motivation-hygiene theory and job satisfaction in the Malaysian retail sector: The mediating effect of love of money. *Asian Academy of Management Journal, 16*(1), 73–94.

TennCare Division of Health Care Finance & Administration. (n.d.). *TennCare overview*. Retrieved from http://www.tn.gov/tenncare/article/tenncare-overview

Teti, E., & Andriotto, M. (2013). Effectiveness of employee welfare schemes: Differences of specific professional profiles. *The International Journal of Human Resource Management*, (ahead-of-print), 1-15.

Tevichapong, P., Davis, A., & Guillaume, Y. (2010*). Individual Spirit at Work and Its Outcomes.* Paper presented at the 70th Annual Conference of Academy of Management, Montréal, Canada (August 6-10, 2010).

Tews, M. J., Stafford, K., & Michel, J. W. (2014). Life happens and people matter: Critical events, constituent attachment, and turnover among part-time hospitality employees. *International Journal of Hospitality Management, 38,* 99-105.

Thibodeau, J. (2011). *Appreciative accreditation: A mixed methods explanatory study of appreciative inquiry-based institutional effectiveness results in higher education.* (Doctoral dissertation). Retrieved from ProQuest Dissertations and Theses. (858158726).

Tilman, J. T., Smith, F., & Tilman, W. (2010). Work locus of control and the multi-dimensionality of job satisfaction. *Journal of Organizational Culture, Communication and Conflict, 14*(2), 107-125.

Torff, B., Sessions, D., & Byrnes, K. (2005). Assessment of teachers' attitudes about professional development. *Educational and Psychological Measurement, 65*(5), 820-830. doi: 10.1177/0013164405275664

Tracey, J. B. (2014). A review of human resources management research: The past 10 years and implications for moving forward. *International Journal of Contemporary Hospitality Management, 26*(5).

Tudor, T. R. (2011). Motivating employees with limited pay incentives using equity theory and the fast food industry as a model. *International Journal of Business and Social Science, 2*(23), 95-101.

Tuggle, F. D. (2010). Building and maintaining soulful organizations. *Interbeing, 4*(1), 1-9.

Ulmer, P. G. (2015). *Accreditation outcome scores: Teacher attitudes toward the accreditation process and professional development* (Doctoral Dissertation). Available from ProQuest Dissertation and Theses database. (No. 10017012)

U.S. Department of Commerce/Bureau of Economic Analysis. (2014). *Orlando-Kissimmee-Sanford (MSA)*. Washington, D.C.: Author. Retrieved from: http://www.bea.gov/regional/bearfacts/pdf.cfm?fips=36740&areatype=MSA&geotype=4

U.S. Department of Labor/Bureau of Labor Statistics. (2013). *Food and beverage serving and related workers.* Washington, D.C.: Author. Retrieved from: http://www.bls.gov/ooh/Food-Preparation-and-Serving/Food-and-beverage-serving-and-related-workers.htm

VanBreukelen. (2006). ANCOVA versus change from baseline: More power in randomized studies, more bias in nonrandomized studies. *Journal of Clinical Epidemiology, 59*(9), 920-925. doi:10.1016/j.jclinepi.2006.02.007

van Veen-Dirks, P. (2010). Different uses of performance measures: The evaluation versus reward of production employees. *Accounting, Organizations and Society, 35*(2), 141-164.

Vardaman, J.M. (2012). Turnover intentions and voluntary turnover: The moderating role of network centrality. *Academy of Management Proceedings* (Meeting abstract supplement). doi:10.5465/AMBPP.2012.90

Vasquez, D. (2014). Employee retention for economic stabilization: A qualitative phenomenological study in the hospitality sector. *International Journal of Management, Economics and Social Sciences (IJMESS), 3*(1), 1-17.

Vasillopulos, C. (2011). Barnard's surprise: Competence as a moral quality. *International Journal of Business and Social Science, 2*(12).

Vogt, W. P. (2007). *Quantitative research methods for professionals*. Boston, MA: Pearson Education.

Wang, Y., & Hsieh, H. (2012). Toward a better understanding of the link between ethical climate and job satisfaction: A multilevel analysis. *Journal of Business Ethics, 105*(4), 535-545. doi:10.1007/s10551-011-0984-9

Walters, G. D., & Crawford, G. (2014). Major mental illness and violence history as predictors of institutional misconduct and recidivism: Main and interaction effects. *Law and Human Behavior, 38*(3), 238-247. doi:0147-7307/14/S12.00

Walsh, A., & Yun, I. (2013). Schizophrenia: Causes, crime, and implications for criminology and criminal justice. *International Journal of Law, Crime, and Justice, 41*, 188-202.

Waters, L. (2012). Predicting job satisfaction: Contributions of individual gratitude and institutionalized gratitude. *Psychology, 3*(12A), 1174-1176.

Weathers, F., Litz, B., Herman, D., Huska, J., & Keane, T. (1993). *The PTSD Checklist (PCL): Reliability, validity, and diagnostic utility*. Paper presented at the annual meeting of the International Society for Traumatic Stress Studies, San Antonio, TX.

Weaver, P, & Kulesza, M. (2014). Critical skills for new accounting hires: What's missing from traditional college education? *Academy of Business Research Journal, 4*, 34-49.

Weiler, S., & Cray, M. (2011). Police at school: A brief history and current status of school resource officers. *Clearing House, 84*(4), 160-163. doi: 10.1080/00098655.2011.564986

Welsh, J. F., & Metcalf, J. (2003). Cultivating faculty support for institutional effectiveness activities: Benchmarking best practices. *Assessment & Evaluation in Higher Education, 28*(1), 33-45. doi: 10.1080/0260293032000033044

White, K., Carvalho, T., & Riordanc, S. (2011). Gender, power and managerialism in universities. *Journal of Higher Education Policy and Management, 33*(2), 179-188. doi:10.1080/1360080X.2011.559631

Wilkerson, J. R., & Lang, W. S. (2007). *Assessing teacher dispositions: Five standards-based steps to valid measurement using the DAATS model*. Thousand Oaks, CA: Corwin Press.

Williams, F. I., Campbell, C., McCartney, W., & Gooding, C. (2013). Leader derailment: the impact of self-defeating behaviors. *Leadership & Organization Development Journal, 34*(1), 85-97.

Wood, R. M. (1999). *An analysis of administrators' and teachers' perceptions of the accreditation process and its impact on school improvement in a selected group of public schools in east Alabama*. (Doctoral dissertation). Retrieved from ProQuest Dissertations and Theses. (9920223).

Yeski, J. (2014). An Alternative to ABD. Inside Higher Ed. https://www.insidehighered.com/advice/2014/07/25/higher-ed-should-create-alternative-abd-status-essayInside Higher Ed.

Yin, R. K. (2009). *Case study research: Design and methods*. (Applied social research methods series) (4th ed.). Thousand Oaks, CA: Sage Publications.

Yin, R. K. (2011). *Applications of case study research*. Thousand Oaks, CA: Sage Publications.

Zhang, M., & Qi, Y. (2014). Incentives and its role in modern human resource management. In *2014 International Conference on Management Science and Management Innovation (MSMI 2014)*. Amsterdam, Netherlands: Atlantis Press.

Zeffane, R. (2010). Towards a two-factor theory of interpersonal trust: A focus on trust in leadership. *International Journal of Commerce & Management, 20*(3), 246-257

Made in the USA
Lexington, KY
29 July 2016